WORLD FILM LOCATIONS
MOSCOW

Edited by Birgit Beumers

First Published in the UK in 2014 by Intellect Books, The Mill, Parnall Road, Fishponds, Bristol, BS16 3JG, UK

First Published in the USA in 2014 by Intellect Books, The University of Chicago Press, 1427 E. 60th Street, Chicago, IL 60637, USA

Cover photo: *Night Watch* (2004) Bazelevs Production / Channel One Russia / The Kobal Collection

Copy Editor: Emma Rhys

Typesetting: Jo Amner

A Catalogue record for this book is available from the British Library

World Film Locations Series
ISSN: 2045-9009
eISSN: 2045-9017

World Film Locations
ISBN: 978-1-78320-196-9
ePDF ISBN: 978-1-78320-267-6
ePub ISBN: 978-1-78320-268-3

WORLD FILM LOCATIONS
MOSCOW

EDITOR
Birgit Beumers

SERIES EDITOR & DESIGN
Gabriel Solomons

CONTRIBUTORS
Jose Alaniz
Erin Alpert
Nadja Berkovich
Vincent Bohlinger
Rad Borislavov
Vitaly Chernetsky
Frederick Corney
Chip Crane
Sergey Dobrynin
Greg Dolgopolov
Joshua First
Rimma Garn
Ian Garner
Tim Harte
Jamie Miller
Jeremy Morris
Stephen M. Norris
Sasha Razor
John A. Riley
Sasha Rindisbacher
Tom Roberts
Peter Rollberg
Larissa Rudova
Emily Schuckman Matthews
Sasha Senderovich
Giuliano Vivaldi

LOCATION PHOTOGRAPHY
Birgit Beumers (unless otherwise credited)

LOCATION MAPS
Greg Orrom Swan

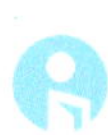

PUBLISHED BY
Intellect
The Mill, Parnall Road,
Fishponds, Bristol, BS16 3JG, UK
T: +44 (0) 117 9589910
F: +44 (0) 117 9589911
E: info@intellectbooks.com

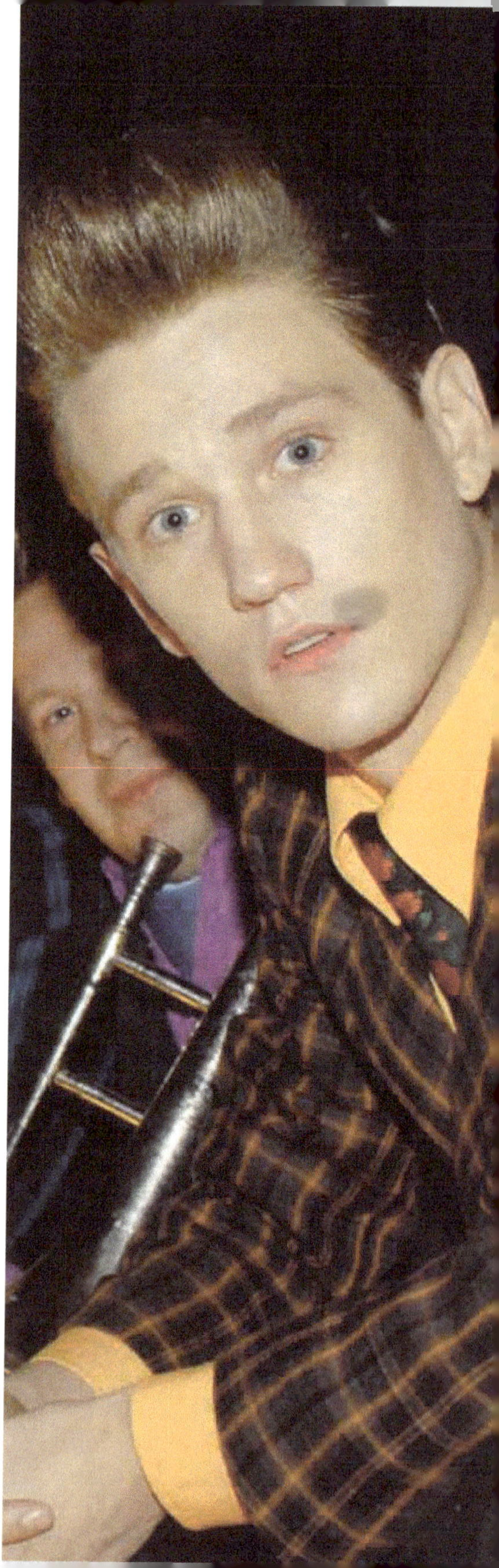

CONTENTS

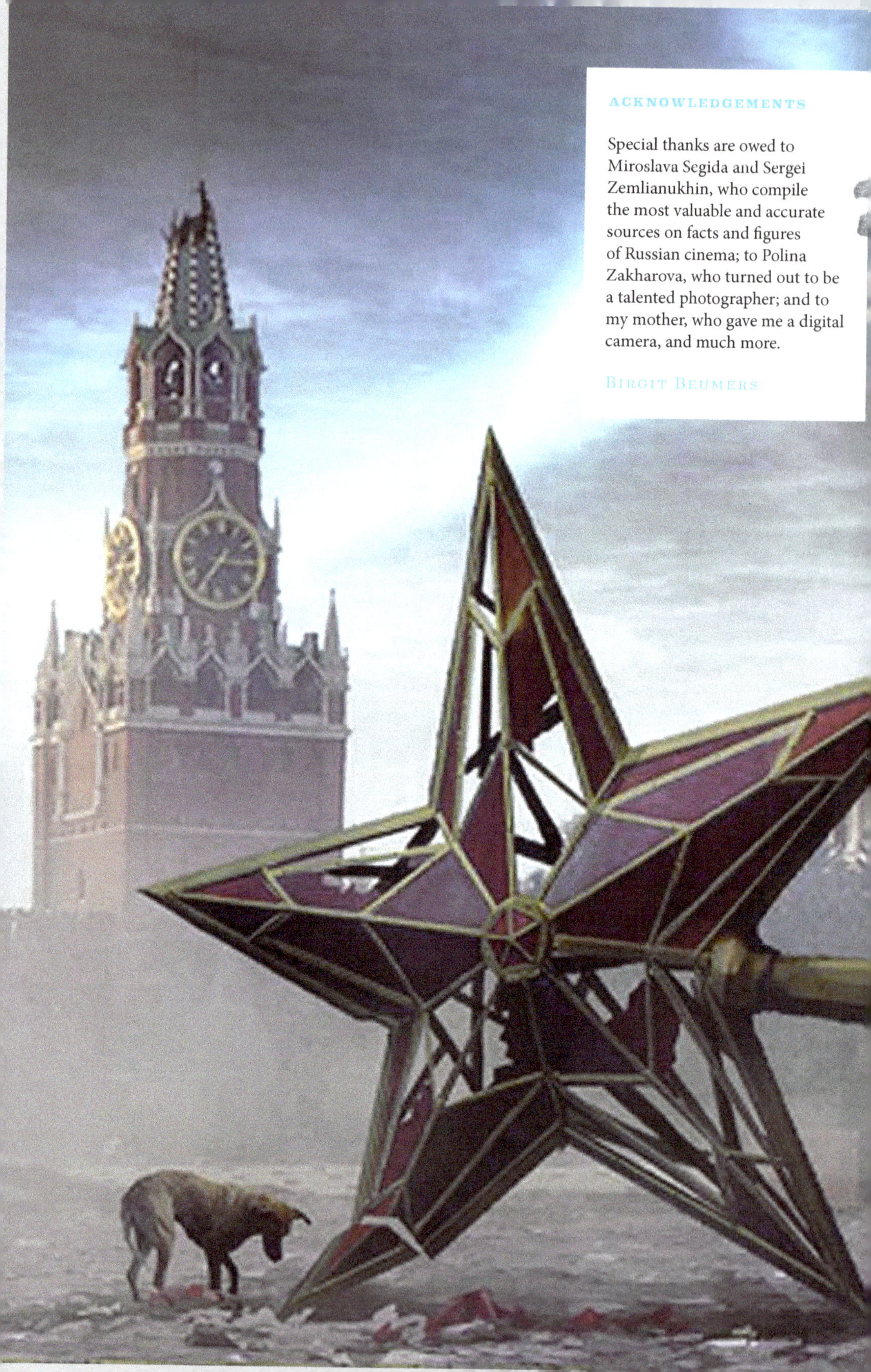
ACKNOWLEDGEMENTS

Special thanks are owed to Miroslava Segida and Sergei Zemlianukhin, who compile the most valuable and accurate sources on facts and figures of Russian cinema; to Polina Zakharova, who turned out to be a talented photographer; and to my mother, who gave me a digital camera, and much more.

BIRGIT BEUMERS

INTRODUCTION

World Film Locations Moscow

THE WORLD FILM LOCATIONS SERIES strives to combine short texts on film scenes with images, embossing in our memory the most famous filmic representations of a city. As such, the series attaches a cinematic story to a specific location, underlining the importance of urban space in the creation of a filmic narrative. The volume contributes to the exploration of architecture and urban planning, as well as filmic and other visual representations of the world's sixteenth largest city.

This volume explores the location Moscow, a megapolis with over 12 million inhabitants and a city with a rich and varied history that has not always been the country's capital. First mentioned in 1147, the town was one of the principal cities of the ancient Rus and had come under frequent attack from the Mongols since the thirteenth century. Under Ivan III Moscow became the capital city, which it remained until 1712 when St Petersburg was founded, only to dominate for the following 200 years the cultural life of eighteenth- and nineteenth-century literature and the arts. In 1918, following the Revolution, Moscow became the capital of the Soviet Union and remained capital of the Russian Federation after 1991. Moscow's status as capital, from 1918 to the present, thus more or less coincides with the life of the silver screen, since there are only a few preserved filmic depictions of the city from pre-Revolutionary years. In the Soviet era, film often served propaganda purposes; therefore, the image of Moscow on celluloid echoes the political ambitions of the country, and film locations and settings reflect the cultural agenda of the times.

This volume therefore follows the historical and political developments of twentieth-century history, and with it the classical division into periods: the Revolutionary period of the 1920s (scenes 1-6); the Stalin era (scenes 7-13); the Thaw (scenes 14-19); the Stagnation (scenes 20-26); the perestroika period (scenes 27-32); the post-Soviet era under Yeltsin from (scenes 33-39); and Putin's Russia (scenes 40-46). The films have been not chosen for their own merit in terms of cinematic history, but for the image of Moscow they create.

Contemporary images of the locations highlight the massive changes that have taken place in Moscow's architecture over the last century, but particularly over the last two decades, echoing the political developments from Stalin's grand capital over Khrushchev's leisure and housing spaces to the post-Soviet craze for high-rises that now demonstrate economic rather than political power.

The selection of essays covers subjects associated with different periods of the city's development: the representation of the metro on screen, both as a place of pride and a place of subversion; the image of the prostitute both in the years after the Revolution and after the collapse of the Soviet Union – first to promote proper employment for women, then to reverse that prospect and show the harsh reality of capitalism; the home, turning from public to private space in the post-war period; and the urban planning and the uniformity of Soviet housing. Moreover, there is a brief survey of the locations of film production and demonstration – studios and cinemas. ' ✠

Birgit Beumers, Editor

MOSCOW

Text by
BIRGIT
BEUMERS

City of the Imagination

IRINA: To go back to Moscow. To sell the
house, to make an end of everything here,
and off to Moscow. …
IRINA: From Moscow? You have come
from Moscow?
IRINA: … My God, every night I dream
of Moscow …
(ANTON CHEKHOV, *THREE SISTERS*)

MOSCOW HAS ALWAYS BEEN a city of desire,
a place of longing: to get there has been a wish of
Chekhov's Irina as much as Soviet citizens from
the provinces and today's migrant workers from
Tajikistan and Uzbekistan. Once a dream, Moscow
has turned into a nightmare – at least according to
recent, post-apocalyptic visions of Moscow created
by Chris Gorak in *The Darkest Hour* (2011) and
produced by Timur Bekmambetov.

As opposed to the beautiful St Petersburg,
which has hardly featured in Soviet cinema,
Moscow has been a favourite location for various
visual media throughout the twentieth century.
By looking at its filmic images, we can trace
the projection and construction, as well as the
representation of Moscow. Moscow has always

been the centre of Soviet culture, the centre from
which the Soviet Union was ruled and controlled.
Political leaders have used Moscow to imprint their
largely centre-based ideology onto the city, and
these traces can be found in Moscow's topography
and architecture. Thus, Stalin's General Plan for the
reconstruction of Moscow has left traces on the
silver screen of the plans for the Palace of Soviets;
of a Hotel Moskva under construction; or of not
yet functional metro stations. The General Plan
also encompassed the All-Union Agricultural
Exhibition (VDNKh), leisure parks (notably the
Gorky Park) and the metro as public spaces that
echoed the achievements of the Soviet state. The
reconstruction of Moscow's former glory under
Moscow Mayor Yuri Luzhkov (1992–2010) after
the collapse of the Soviet empire involved elaborate
construction plans for Moscow as a business centre
– the Manège underground mall, the Moscow-City
business district, and the Third Ring Road – as
well as a number of high-rises that replicate Stalin's
neoclassicist style and the reconstruction of the
Cathedral of Christ the Saviour.

On screen, the Moscow of the 1920s is a city
created through montage, a city in motion: the
chase scene in *Neobychainye prikliucheniia Mistera
Vesta v strane bol'shevikov/The Extraordinary
Adventures of Mister West in the Land of the
Bolsheviks* (Lev Kuleshov, 1924) is indicative.
The themes of 1920s films often confirm the
correctness of the socialist system, as the
American entrepreneur Mr West finds the USSR
rather different than portrayed in American
anti-Bolshevik propaganda. While *Aelita* (Yakov
Protazanov, 1924) asserts that the Revolution
had already happened on other planets, the films
also highlight the problem of the NEP (New
Economic Policy) temporarily introducing private
enterprise to remedy the economic effects of the
Civil War. Such enterprise is shown as subversively
bourgeois and the housing shortage is also

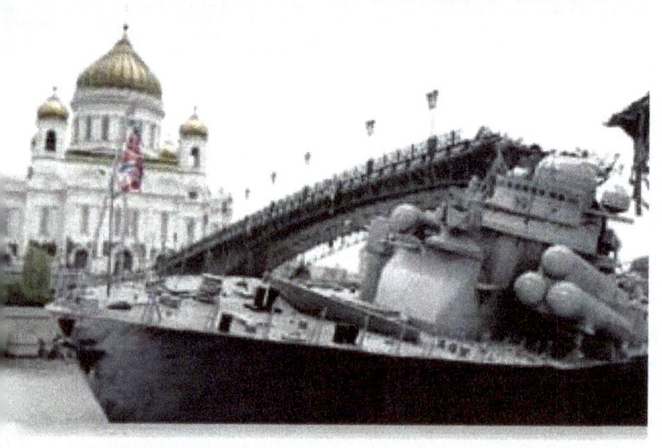

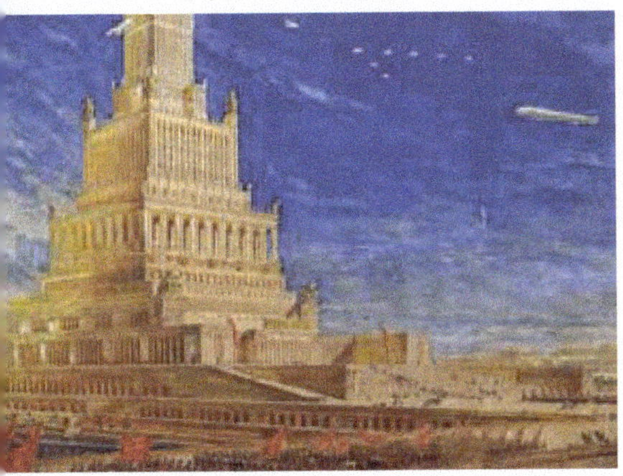

mansion in Gorki Leninskiye. *Novaia Moskva/New Moscow* (Alexander Medvedkin, 1938) subverts this teleological narrative by reversing the animated model of the city and taking it back to medieval times, before showing the Grand Plan: the Palace of Soviets, projected on the site of the Cathedral of Christ the Saviour and never built, animated only in the final film of this volume that used CGI to bring this location to life: *Shpion/The Spy* (Alexei Andrianov, 2012).

The sites of post-war and post-Stalinist cinema differ significantly from the previous locations: instead of showing monumental architecture, the films focus on private housing, embankments, leisure parks, department stores, squares and the metro as a (radial) connection to suburbs rather than showcasing the palace-like stations (on the circle line). Attention shifts from exterior to interior spaces: even if the location is an eminent building (Rostovskaya Embankment), the action is set in the yard. Similar spaces continue to appear during the Stagnation era, such as hospitals, houses and office buildings. The Moscow locations of perestroika films are even less recognizable, including obscure halls of residence, boulevards, factories, streets.

The cinema of the 1990s chose well-known film locations and subverted them. In a postmodernist engagement with the historical past of the 1930s, the sites of Stalinist cinema are replicated: VDNKh, the House on Embankment, the Stalinist high-rises. Similarly, films set in contemporary Moscow subvert the historical significance of buildings: the Historical Museum becomes a site for criminal action, where yesterday's weapons are wielded against today's Mafia. *Moskva/Moscow* (Alexander Zeldovich, 2000) ultimately subverts all prime locations and turns them into empty, meaningless spaces.

The Moscow of the twenty-first century is an unsettled and unsettling space: Timur Bekmambetov's *Nochnoi dozor/Night Watch* (2004) and *Dnevnoi dozor/Day Watch* (2006) subvert classical spaces (metro, hotels, television towers), turning them into places of horror; crime locations and places of prostitution move from the periphery into the centre, while new crime locations appear notably in the new business complexes of Moscow-City.

If most films set in Moscow have been shot on actual location rather than in pavilions, then the recent CGI manipulation of the city in such blockbusters as *The Spy* and *The Darkest Hour* would appear to suggest a change in Moscow's image to a virtual one. ✠

prominently in evidence- problems that would have to disappear from the screen under Socialist Realism, which would become the only method of artistic expression in 1932. The central roles are played by women (Alexandra Khokhlova, Yulia Solntseva, Anna Sten and Vera Maretskaya), whose characters come to Moscow from the provinces and are trapped by the vicissitudes of urban life and corruption, even if at the end there is a way out thanks to Soviet government plans. Railway stations are therefore a frequent site of action: they form the connection between the centre and the periphery, and facilitate mobility to and away from the centre.

Stalin's Moscow was being built in the 1930s, marking a peak for the film location Moscow: houses were moved, architectural projects were made, the metro was built and the Hotel Moskva was being completed. The lead actress of the era was Lyubov Orlova, the wife of Grigori Alexandrov and star of all his films. The Bolshoi Theatre remains a prime location, as a place where high art meets low art, where the centre meets the periphery. Characters come from the provinces to conquer the capital: they arrive by boat (river station) and by train (railway station); they conquer the new sights of the capital: the Hotel Moskva and the VDNKh, projects of Stalin's plans for the reconstruction of Moscow, but also old monuments, such as Red Square or Lenin's

Moscow has always been the centre of Soviet culture, the centre from which the Soviet Union was ruled and controlled.

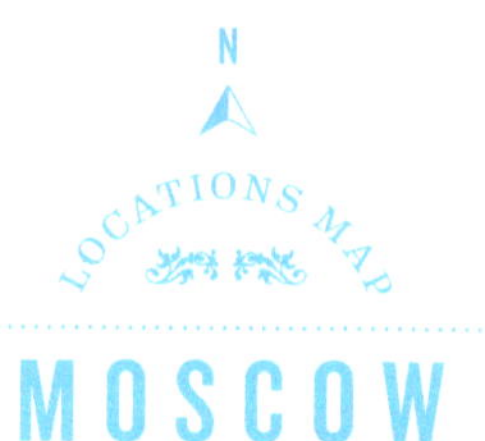

N
LOCATIONS MAP
MOSCOW

maps are only to be taken as approximates

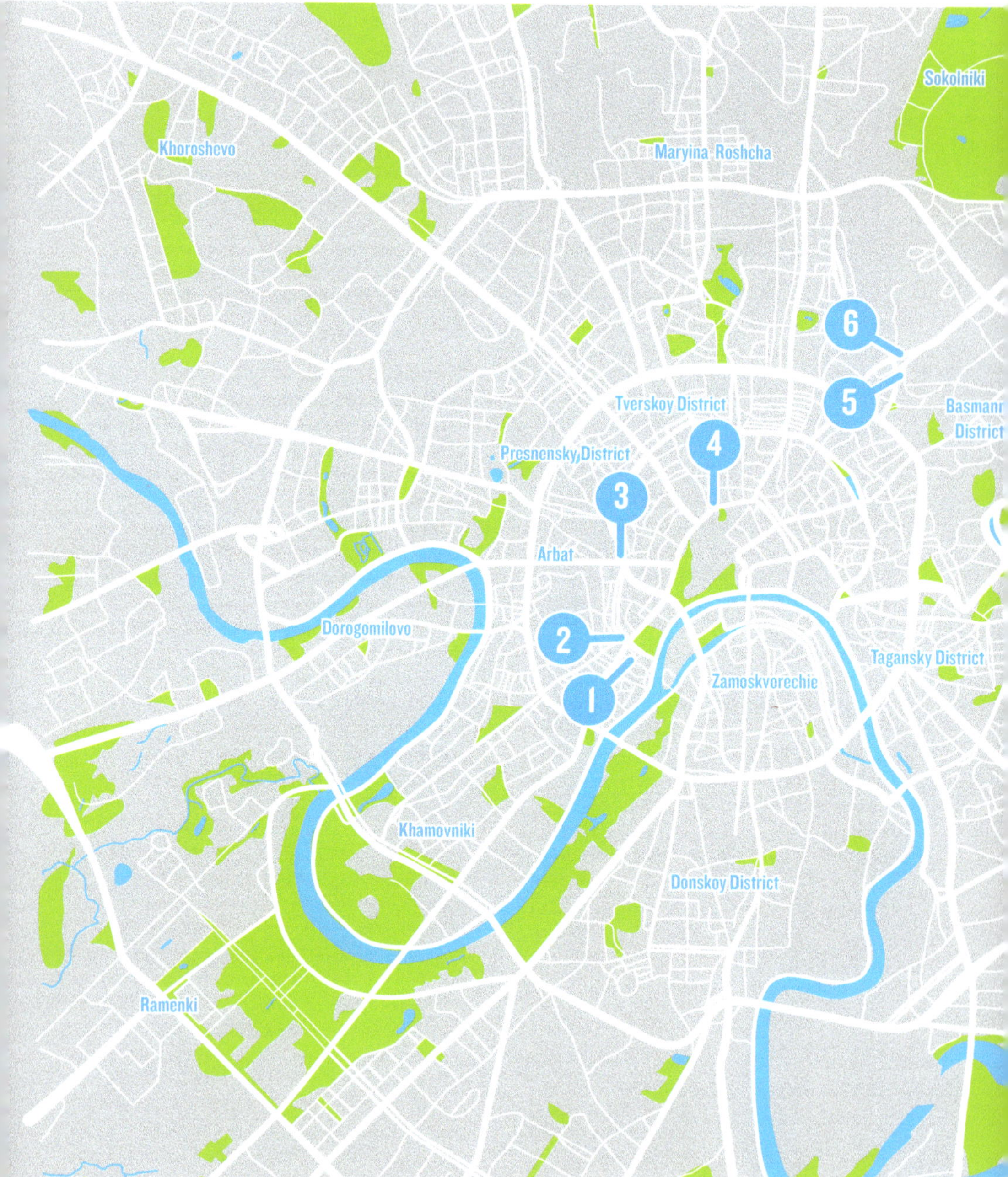

Sokolniki
Khoroshevo
Maryina Roshcha
6
Tverskoy District
5
Basmann District
Presnensky District
4
3
Arbat
2
Dorogomilovo
1
Zamoskvorechie
Tagansky District
Khamovniki
Donskoy District
Ramenki

MOSCOW LOCATIONS
SCENES 1-6

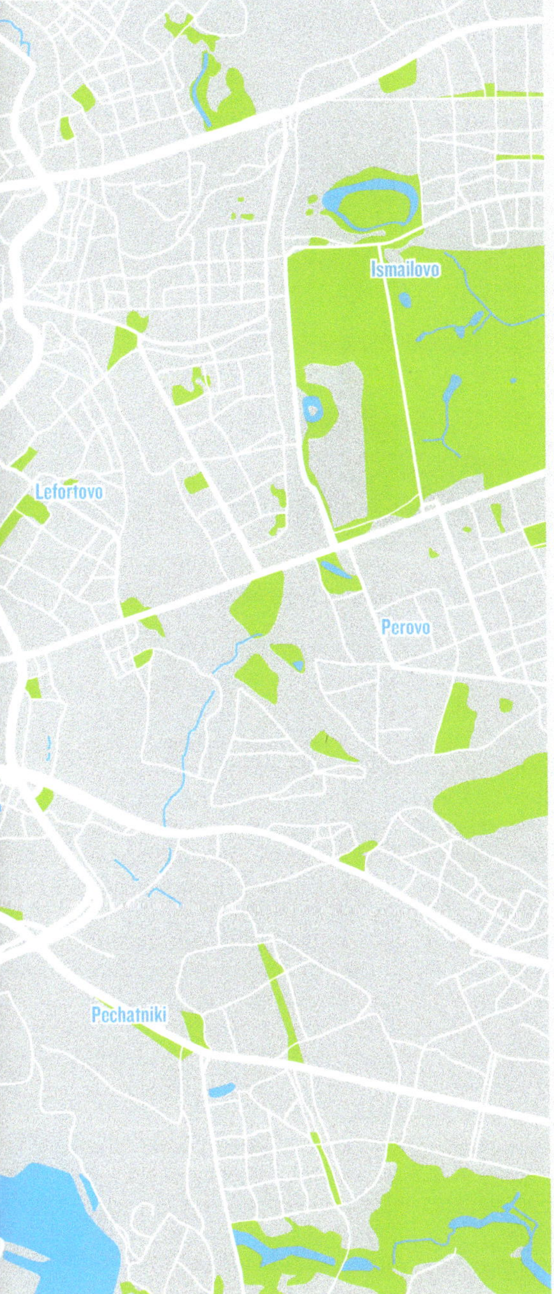

LOCATION | *The vicinity of the Cathedral of Christ the Saviour*

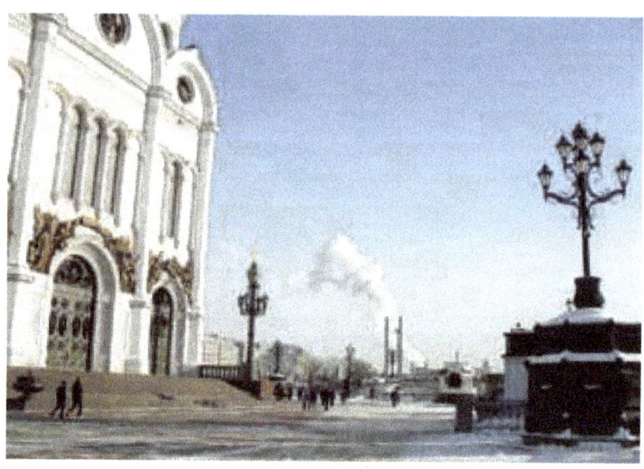

MADE IN 1924, *The Extraordinary Adventures of Mister West in the Land of the Bolsheviks* boasts a remarkable cast of collaborators from Lev Kuleshov's cinema workshop at the State Film School, including Alexandra Khokhlova and Porfiri Podobed, as well as future Soviet directors Boris Barnet and Vsevolod Pudovkin. Misled by anti-Bolshevik media propaganda, the titular Mister West (Podobed) travels to Moscow to observe the Soviet project with his bodyguard Cowboy Jeddy (Barnet). Accidentally separated from Jeddy, West falls into the hands of criminals (led by Khokhlova and Pudovkin), who attempt to extort money from the American by exploiting his fears of Bolshevik savagery, before he is rescued by the actual Bolsheviks. In this scene, Jeddy has hijacked a horse-drawn sledge in search of West, leading to a police chase across the streets and rooftops of Moscow. The Cathedral of Christ the Saviour appears repeatedly in the chase, from several perspectives. The nineteenth-century building has a rich history: it was demolished in 1931 to clear space for the monumental Palace of Soviets; construction stalled in the 1930s, however, and the site remained vacant until the Khrushchev era, when the foundation pit was converted into an enormous outdoor swimming pool. Kuleshov's film thematizes the deliberate misidentification of public space: Pudovkin's Zhban takes West on a 'tour' of Moscow, substituting dilapidated structures for famous landmarks as falsified evidence of the Bolshevik attack on culture. Ironically, the prominent, recognizable cathedral would be destroyed only a few years after the film's production, only to be resurrected as an icon of post-Soviet authority in the 1990s. **•❖ Tom Roberts**

Photo © Birgit Beumers

Directed by Lev Kuleshov

Scene description: Police pursue Cowboy Jeddy through Moscow
Timecode for scene: 0:15:30 – 0:20:46

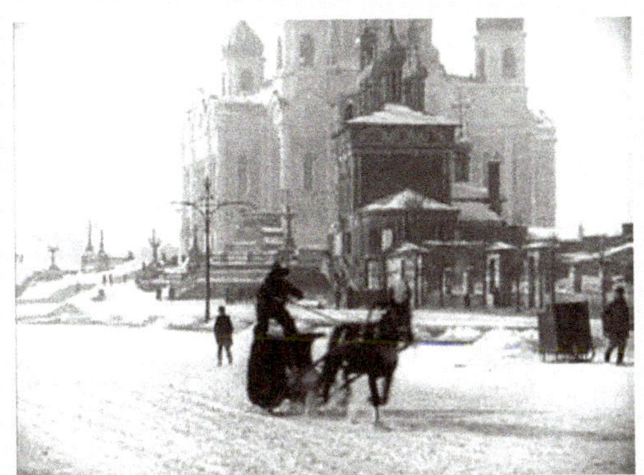

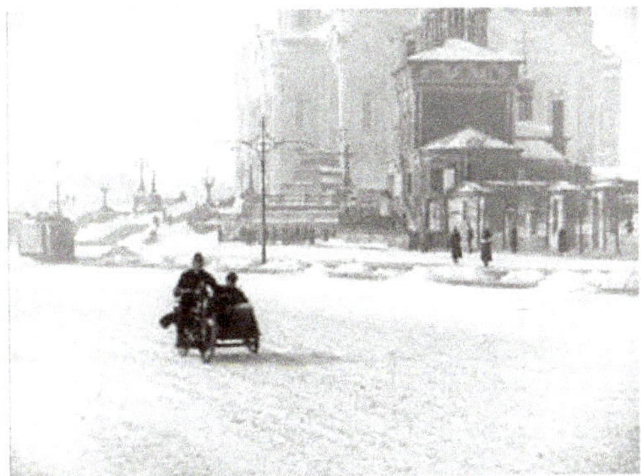

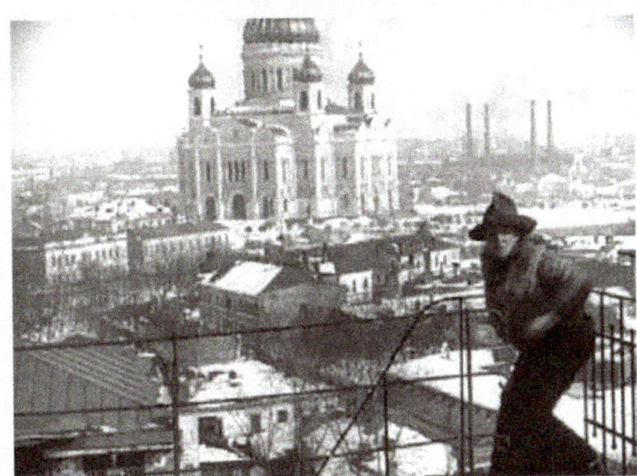

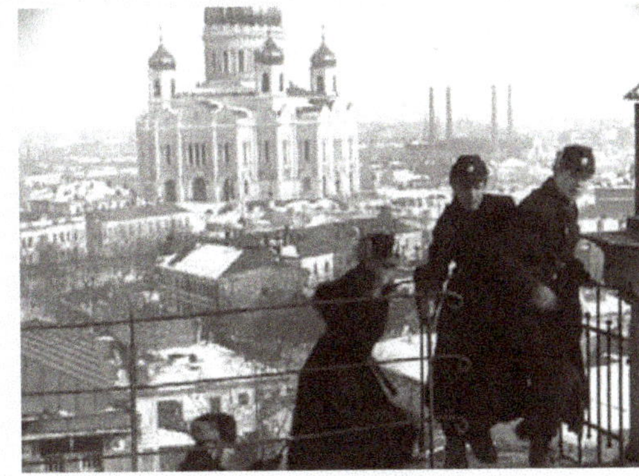

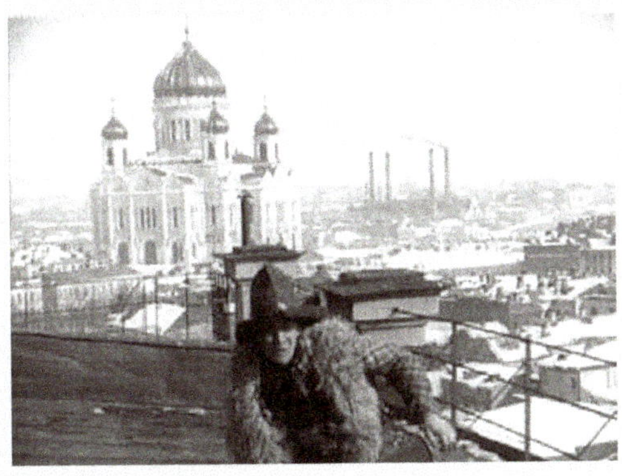

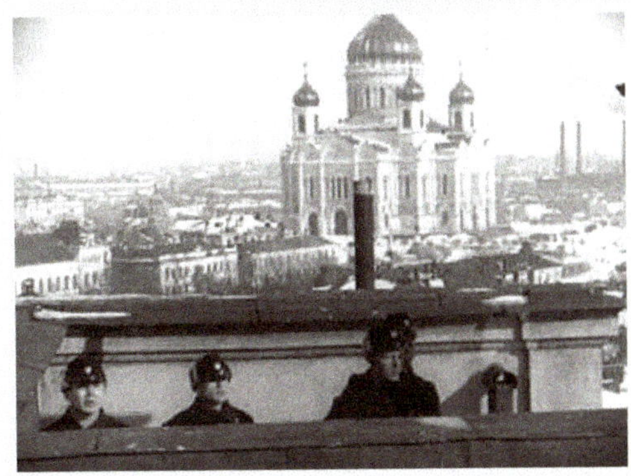

AELITA (1924)

Top of the Cathedral of Christ the Saviour

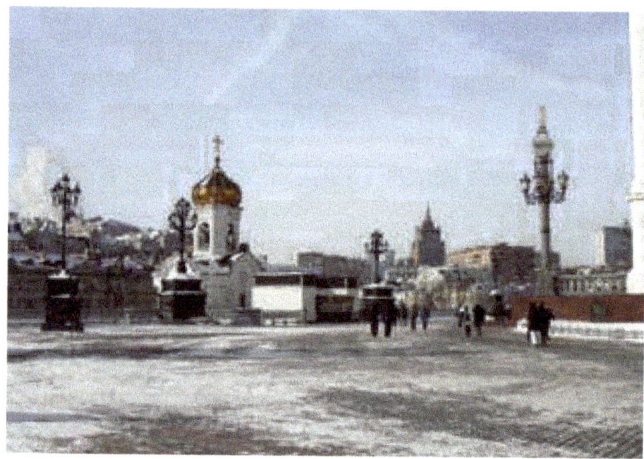

THE FIRST SOVIET science fiction film about space travel is best known for its scenes set on Mars and for the costumes designed by Alexandra Ekster, although most of the action takes place in contemporary Moscow. In one scene Aelita, Queen of Mars (Yulia Solntseva), uses a new telescope to look at life on earth, while the Soviet engineer Los dreams of life on Mars. Eventually Aelita's gaze falls upon Los, who is waiting on the observation deck at the top of the Cathedral of Christ the Saviour for a rendezvous with his beloved. The snow-covered Moskva River sits frozen below him and the great towers of the south-western wall of the Kremlin dominate the background. When his wife Natasha comes into view, he playfully kisses her hands and wraps her up in a passionate embrace. Natasha coquettishly hides beneath her fur collar before Los artfully coaxes her out. Aelita is mesmerized by this curious ritual and stands frozen, staring in amazement at the adoring earthlings. She sees Los and Natasha in a close-up now, framed as if by a saintly halo. Los ardently kisses Natasha on the lips. While Gor, the guardian of Mars's energy, stands oddly shocked, Aelita is spellbound and implores Gor to kiss her. This is a rare shot from the top of the world's largest Orthodox cathedral before its destruction in 1931. The scene contrasts the tenderness on earth to an angular eroticism on Mars, set against a playful and unusual angle of an ever-changing Moscow monument. **➻Greg Dolgopolov**

Directed by Yakov Protazanov

Scene description: Aelita, Queen of Mars, looks down on earth through a telescope and sees engineer Los kissing his wife Natasha as they stand on the Cathedral of Christ the Saviour

Timecode for scene: 0:10:31 – 0:12:45

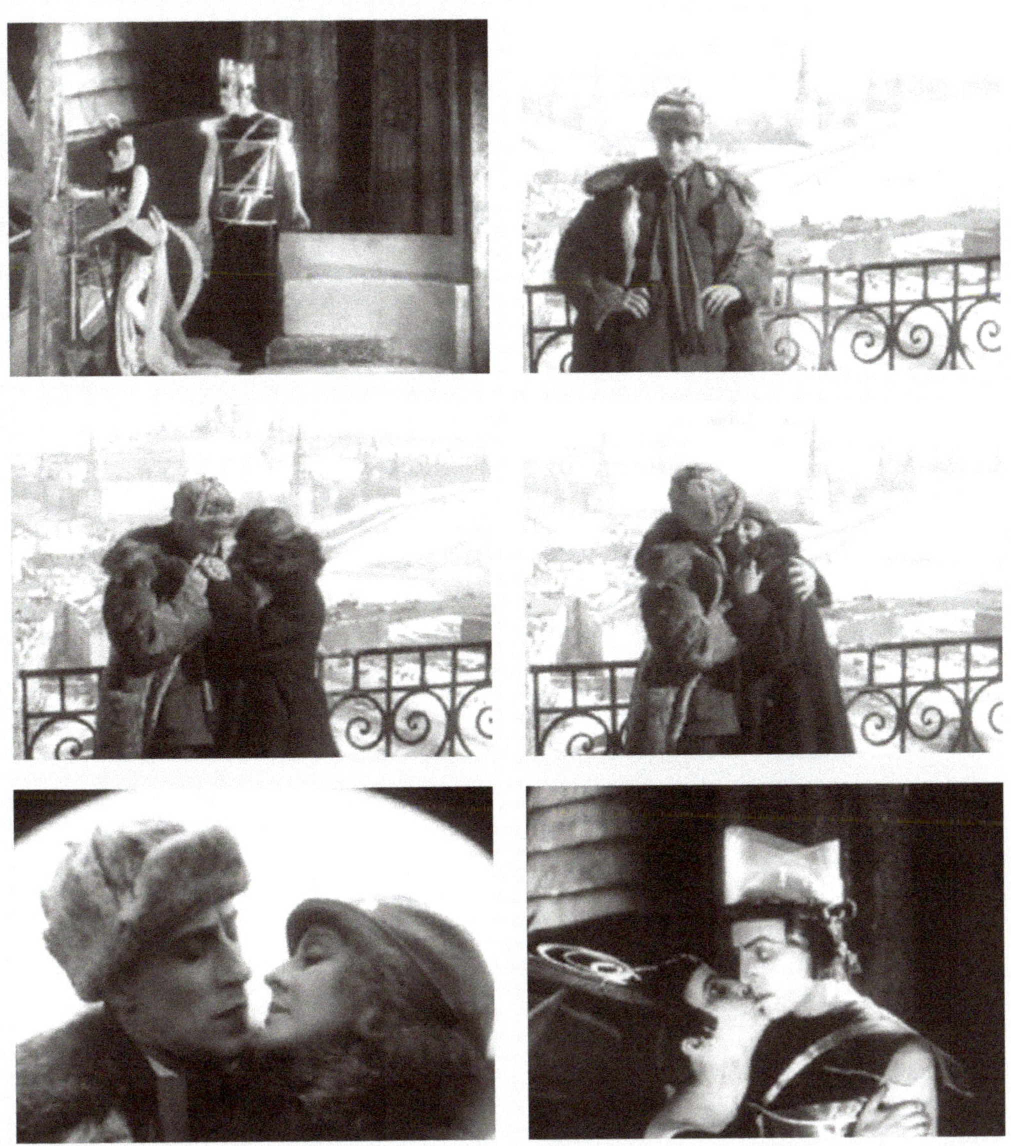

THE CIGARETTE GIRL FROM MOSSELPROM/ PAPIROSNITSA OT MOSSEL'PROMA (1924)

Mosselprom Building

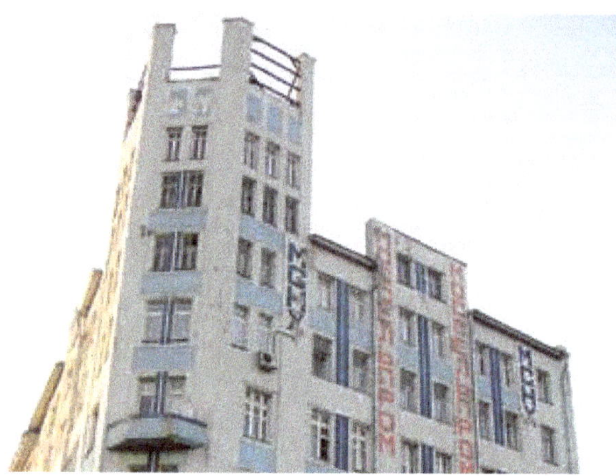

ZINA VESENINA (Yulia Solntseva) works as a cigarette girl, peddling a wide variety of cigarettes on the streets of Moscow. Zina's appeal is such that the love-struck accountant's assistant Nikodim Mitiushin (Igor Ilyinsky) buys a pack from her every day, even though he does not smoke. When a film crew shoots a scene on location, the cameraman Latugin (Nikolai Tsereteli) spots Zina and is instantly smitten. So begins Zina's acting career, and she temporarily quits her job at Mosselprom. Mosselprom, an acronym for 'Moskovskoe upravlenie sel'skoi promyslovoi kooperatsii', was the Moscow Rural Cooperative Administration, a purveyor of delightful consumerist decadence: flour and yeast, candy, cookies, beer, and, of course, cigarettes. Today's viewer likely cannot help but think of the impressive Mosselprom Building, which was restored to its former glory in 1997 and still stands at the corner of Kalashny and Nizhny Kislovsky streets. A constructivist wonder by David Kogan, the building was among the first skyscrapers in Moscow. Mosselprom is also well known for having employed artists Alexander Rodchenko and Varvara Stepanova and poet Vladimir Mayakovsky to create colourful, bold advertising with catchy rhyming jingles. The Mosselprom Building itself, however, was only finished in 1925, so it is absent from its seemingly own promotional film. The film opens with aerial views of Moscow, and many major landmarks can be spotted throughout, including Triumphal Gate (back when it was still on Tverskaya Street), the Kremlin, Resurrection Gate, St Basil's, the Cathedral of Christ the Saviour, the Bolshoi Theatre, Kievsky Railway Station, and the Moskva River. •→ *Vincent Bohlinger*

Photo © Vincent Bohlinger

Scene description: Zina quits her job to become an actress
Timecode for scene: 0:24:02 – 0:24:38

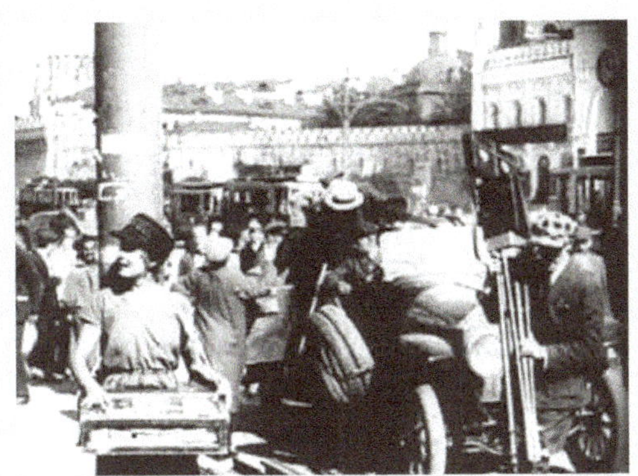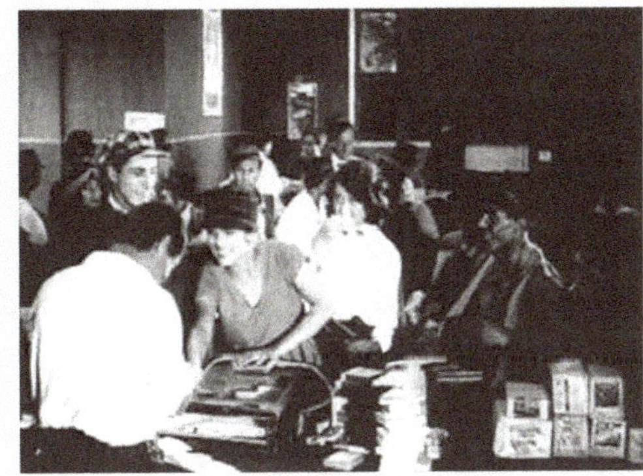

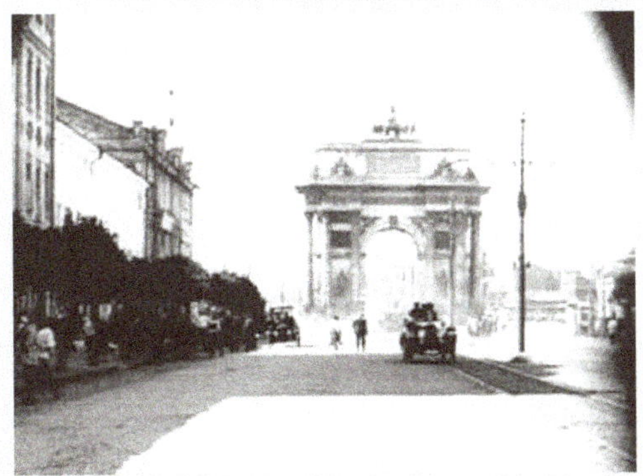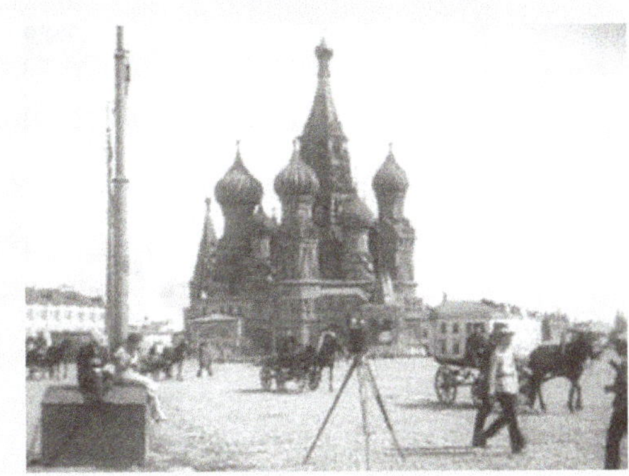

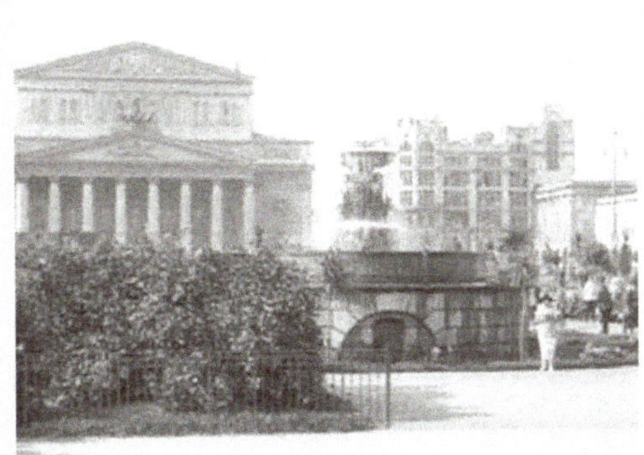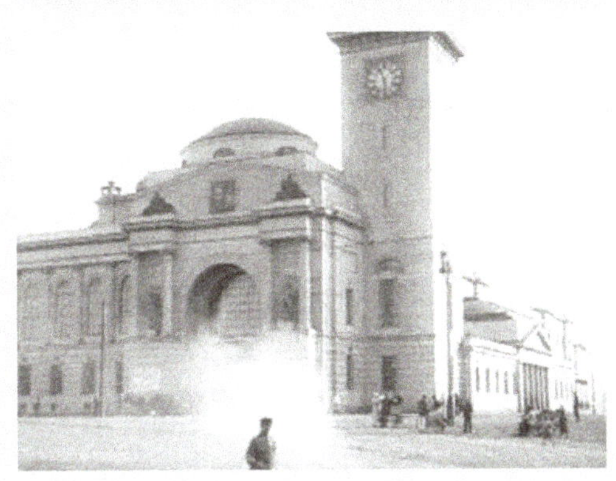

Images © 1924 Mezhrabpom-Rus

BED AND SOFA/TRET'IA MESHCHANSKAIA (1927)

Atop the Bolshoi Theatre

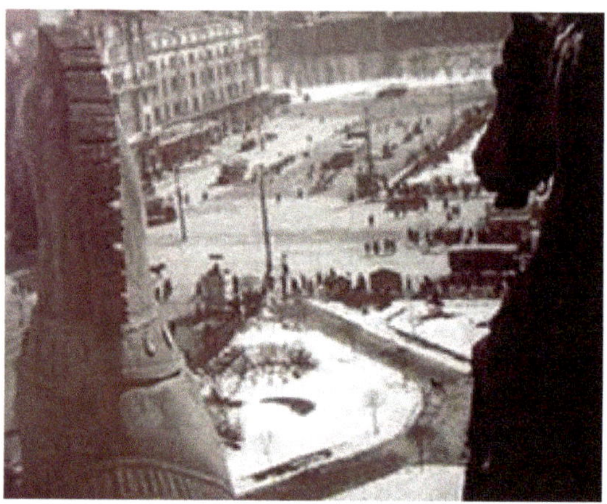

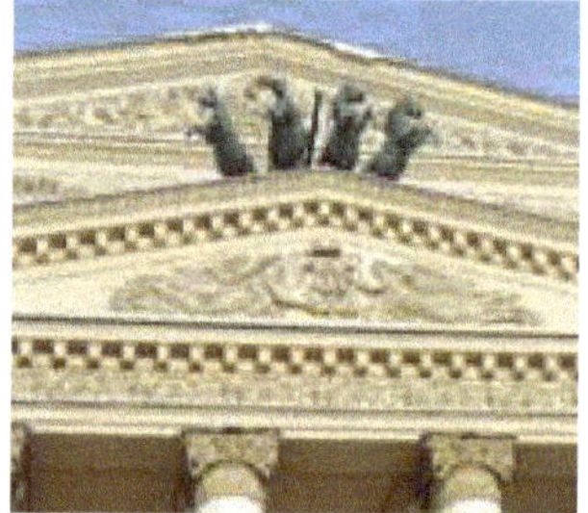

NEAR THE BEGINNING of the film, Kolya (Nikolai Batalov), the foreman of a construction crew renovating the facade of the Bolshoi Theatre, takes a lunch break at the Apollo statue on the theatre's pediment. The film's cameraman Grigori Giber gives us a stunning vista from atop the Bolshoi, and it is as if we are in Apollo's Quadriga (a four-horse chariot), below us Theatre Square, then called Sverdlov Square. The viewpoint almost matches a photograph taken a couple years later by Alexander Rodchenko for his 1929 series on the Bolshoi (above). We may see the theatre in a dynamic new way, as Rodchenko would wish, but it is still the Bolshoi, among the most well-known and venerated cultural institutions of the Tsarist era. The staging of action in such a locale points to the interest of screenwriter Viktor Shklovsky and director Abram Room in exploring the problematic circumstances of contemporary Soviet life. Can monuments of the past – the grand nineteenth-century neoclassicism of sculptor Peter Clodt von Jürgensburg and architects Andrei Mikhailov, Joseph Bové and Alberto Cavos – truly be repurposed for Soviet ends? Can Kolya, his wife Lyuda (Lyudmila Semënova), and his friend Volodya (Vladimir Fogel) free themselves from the behaviours and aspirations of the not-yet-bygone petite bourgeoisie (the 'meshchanstvo' suggested in the original Russian title)? The scene ends with Kolya enjoying a smoke beside the phallus of Apollo, an unsettling juxtaposition and perhaps wry foreshadowing of the additional member ('chlen') soon to join his household and possibly even impregnate his wife. ◆ *Vincent Bohlinger*

Photo © Alexander Rodchenko/Birgit Beumers

Scene description: Nikolai at work and at lunch
Timecode for scene: 0:09:39 – 0:10:50; 0:11:33 – 0:13:03

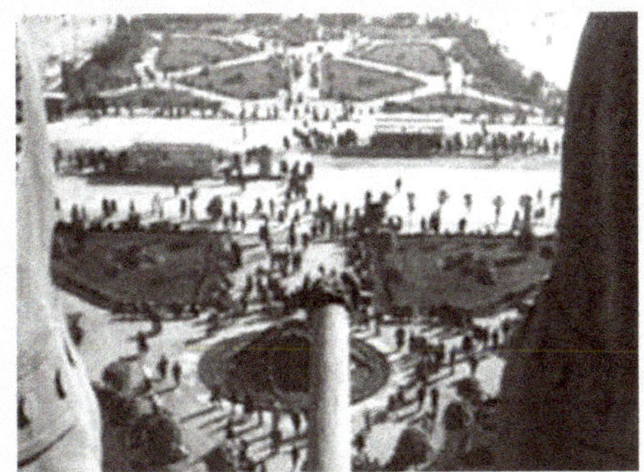
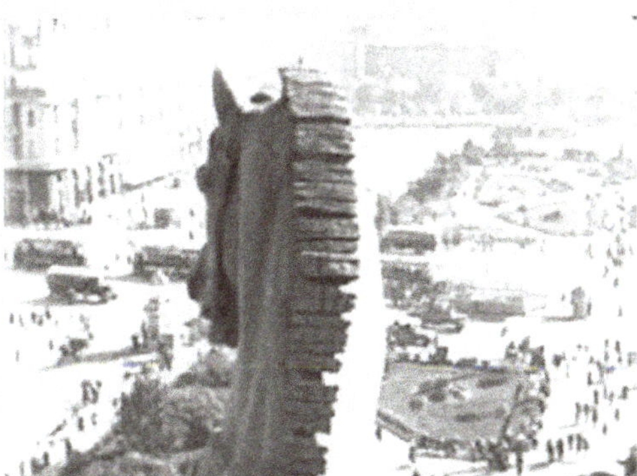
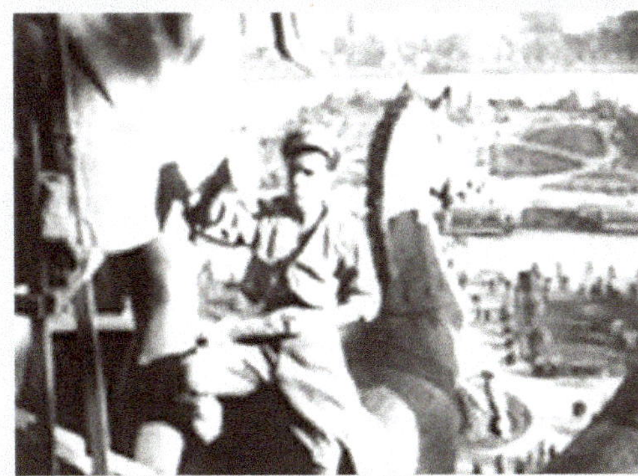
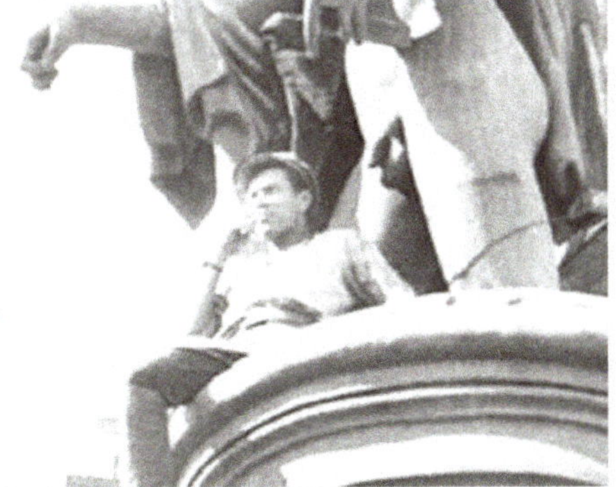

Images © 1927 Sovkino

THE GIRL WITH A HATBOX/ DEVUSHKA S KOROBKOI (1927)

Kazansky Railway Station

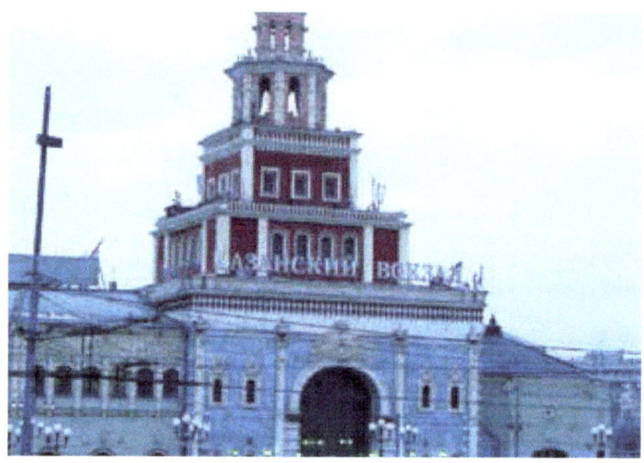

NATASHA KOROSTELEVA (Anna Sten) lives with her grandfather (Vladimir Mikhailov) in a small cottage in the Moscow suburbs. They earn their living as milliners, and each morning Natasha endures a lengthy commute to Moscow, both on foot and by train, in order to sell their hats at the shop of Madame Irène (Serafima Birman). On the crowded train one morning, Natasha meets the good-natured but clumsy Ilya Snegirev (Ivan Koval-Samborsky), who is relocating to Moscow to continue his studies. Ilya unwittingly puts his sizable foot through Natasha's hatbox, and she is overcome with fluster. She rushes off as soon as the train arrives in Moscow – seemingly at Kazansky Station – and leaves Ilya bewildered and stranded at Komsomolskaya Square (until 1933 known as Kalanchëvskaya Square). As he looks about, we see the two other grand railroad stations housed at this square: Leningradsky Station, built by Konstantin Ton; and the fantastic art nouveau building of Yaroslavsky Station, designed by Fëdor Shekhtel. Due to the Moscow housing shortage, poor Ilya has nowhere to stay, so he spends his nights back at Kazansky Station. The film finally now shows us this station, an impressive, sprawling pile designed by Alexei Shchusev as Russian 'revival-meets-art-nouveau', with its principal multi-tiered tower meant to recall the famed, and leaning, Suyumbike Tower of the Kremlin of Kazan. Ilya again makes a bad impression when Natasha returns to catch her train home. He gives another sad-puppy face, and at this point only they fail to realize that they are meant for each other. **➥ Vincent Bohlinger**

Photo © Polina Zakharova

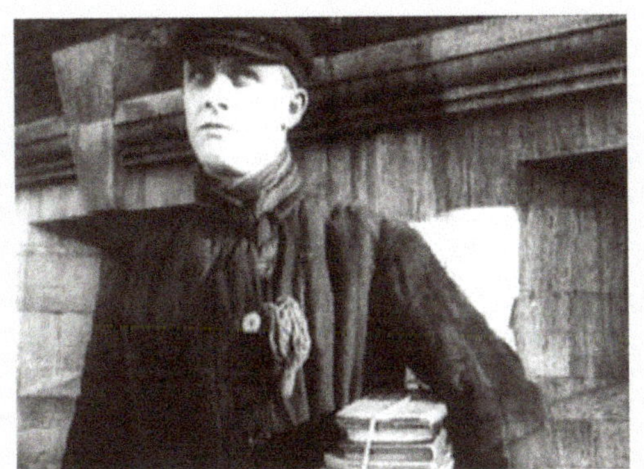
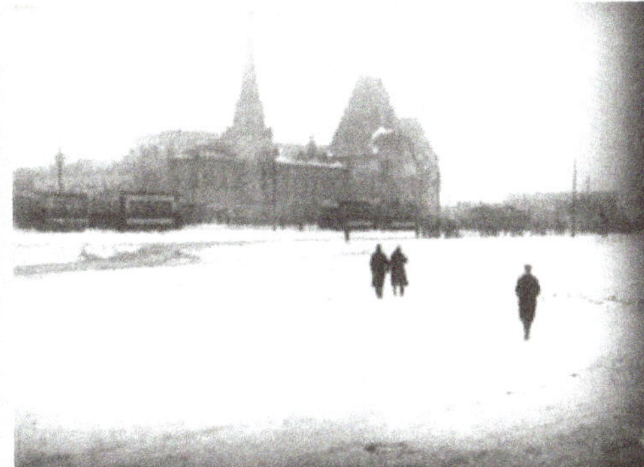
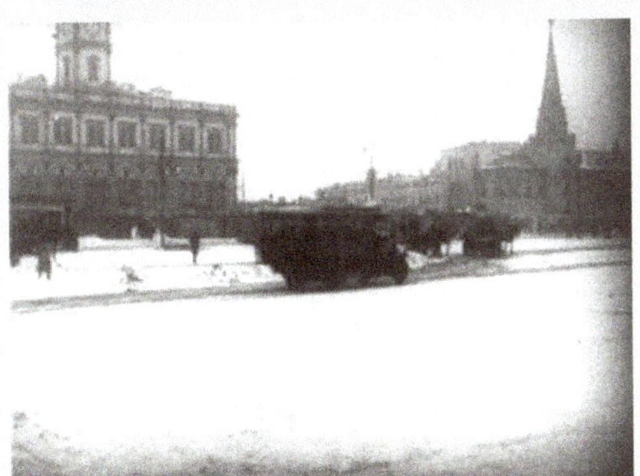
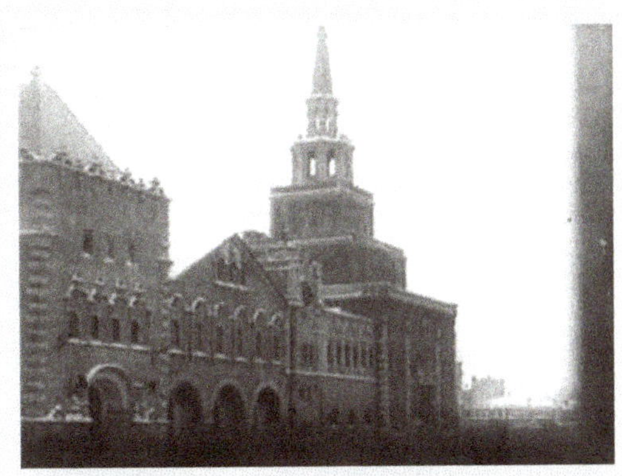
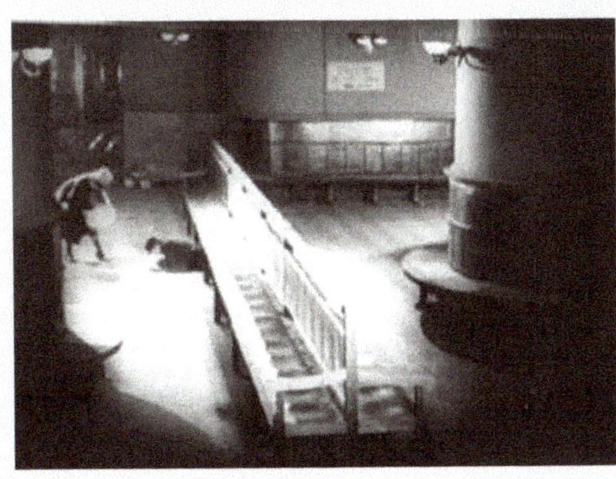
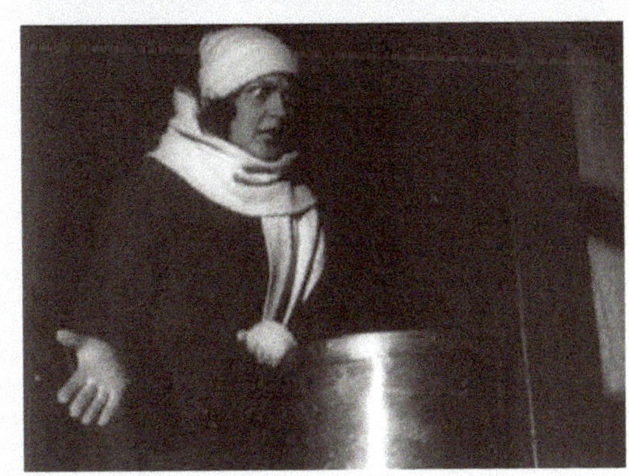

Images © 1927 Mezhrabpom-Rus

THE HOUSE ON TRUBNAYA SQUARE/ DOM NA TRUBNOI (1928)

Yaroslavsky Railway Station

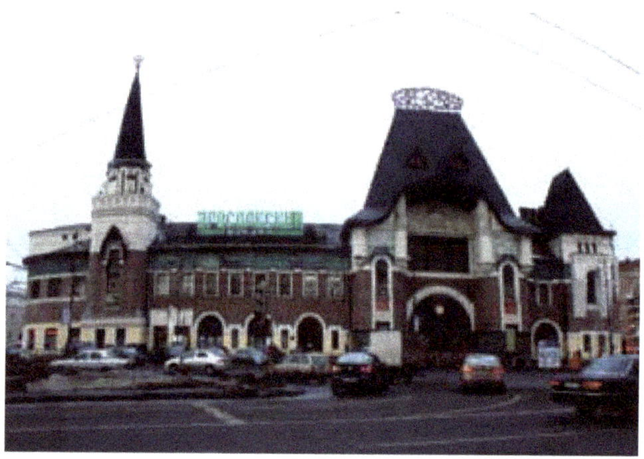

BARNET'S *House on Trubnaya* sees the arrival of a hapless villager, 19-year-old Parasha Pitunova (Vera Maretskaya), in Moscow. Barnet lovingly and painstakingly shows her confusion as she arrives in the big city, trying to find Uncle Fëdor, whose address is scribbled on an envelope. She is unaware that the uncle arrived at the village station the very moment she left for Moscow. The scene of her arrival depicts Moscow in all its architectural splendour as Parasha makes her way from Yaroslavsky Railway Station into various directions, whence she is sent along by passers-by, who seem to have as little knowledge of the city as she does (and she, too, will give equally false directions to another lost provincial who is just as baffled as she). When she finally reaches her destination, she finds a scribbled note from Uncle Fëdor to announce that he has left Moscow. Having almost been run over by a tram as she tries to rescue her runaway goose, Parasha will be recognized by a fellow villager who takes her back to an apartment block at Trubnaya Square, where she ends up in the clutches of a ruthless employer until rescued by Soviet activists. In this gentle satire, Parasha is destined to discover a NEP (New Economic Policy)-era Moscow throbbing with a cussed, petty bourgeois humanity of phonies, rogues and sycophants but also teeming with genuine artistic and revolutionary enthusiasm. Her bewilderment after her entry to the city is set to continue. **◆Giuliano Vivaldi**

Scene description: *Parasha arrives at the Yaroslavsky Railway Station*
Timecode for scene: *0:09:28 – 0:11:01*

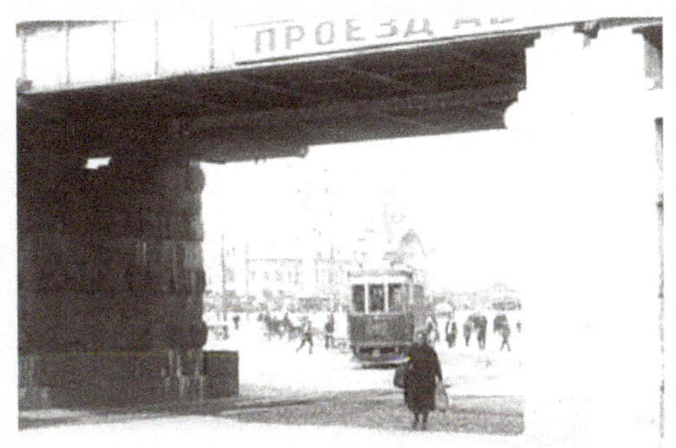
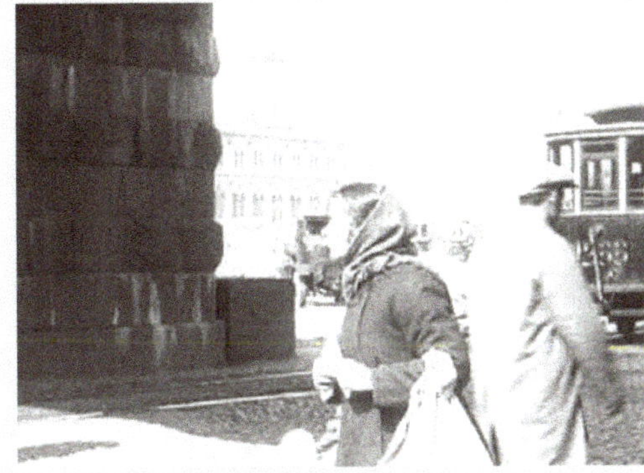

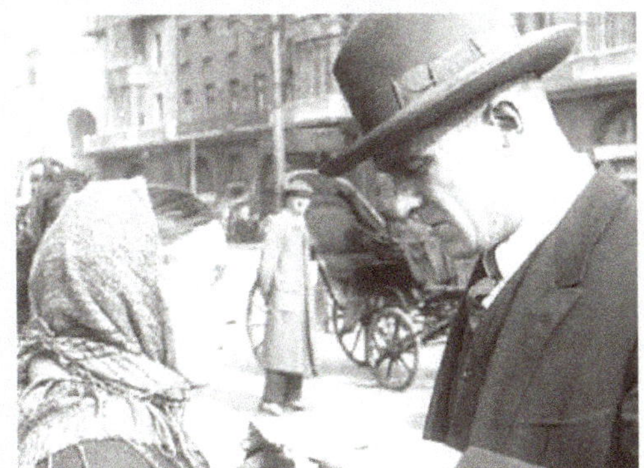
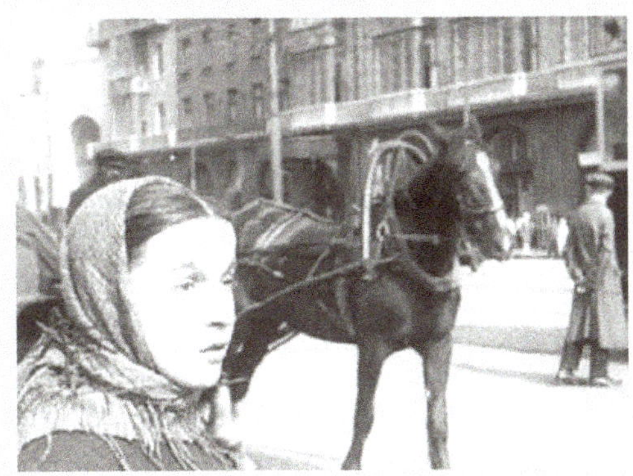

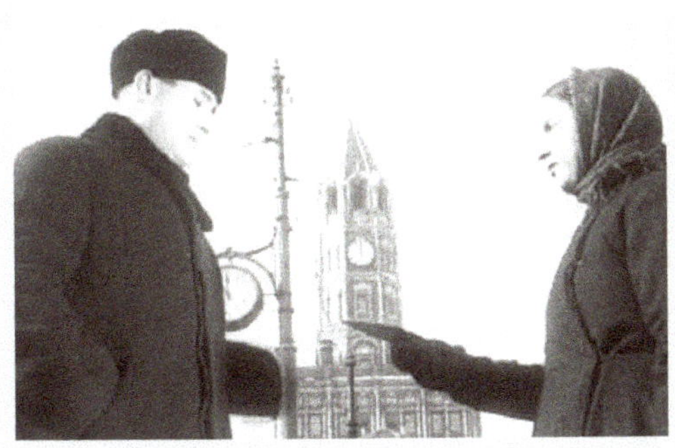
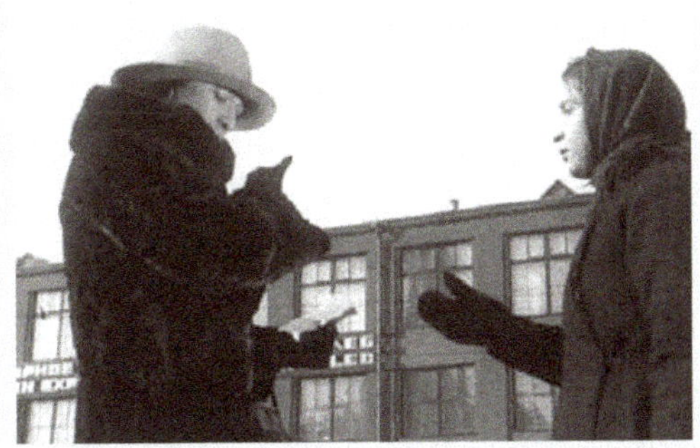

Images © 1928 Mezhrabpomfilm

CINEMATIC JOURNEYS ON THE MOSCOW METRO

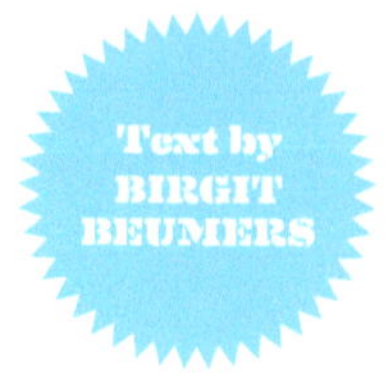

MOSCOW'S METRO was built in the 1930s, with the first stretch opening on 15 May 1935 between Sokolniki and Park Kultury. The stations were designed as palaces for the people, creating a grand Moscow Underground, while the surface of Moscow was being redesigned and reconstructed according to Stalin's General Plan. Many stations resembled museums, lavishly decorated with marbles from all over Soviet Russia, along with bronze statues and mural decorum. Although the metro was in the first place not a transport system but an architectural achievement, its subsequent representation on screen partly contradicted the discourse on the metro as 'the grandest' and 'the best'.

The metro made its first screen appearance in Alexander Medvedkin's *Novaia Moskva/New Moscow* (1938), which follows the journey of the engineer Alësha to Moscow to present his animated model of the capital and its development following Stalin's plans for the reconstruction of Moscow. When the visitors from the province arrive in the capital, they encounter chaos on the streets: heavy traffic, shifting houses, large

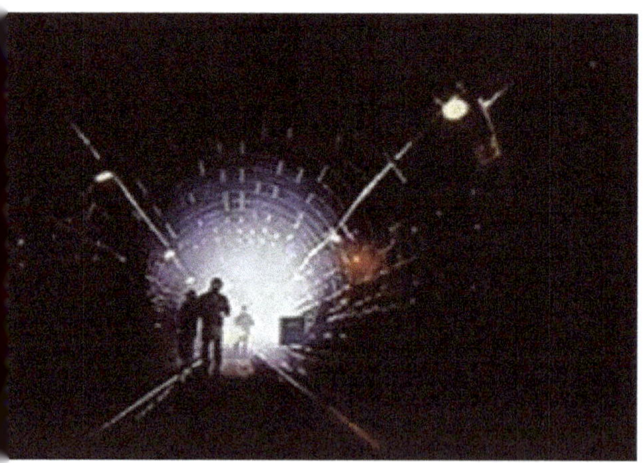

crowds and numerous cars. They need to get to their destination fast, and do so by using the metro. They travel one stop only, but Medvedkin draws attention to the positive aspects of the new transport system: it is cheap, orderly, finely decorated and beautifully lit: the chandelier in the street-level pavilion is the first object that the camera captures before panning the glittering marble. However, Medvedkin refrains from demonstrating the metro as a palatial museum, but turns his attention to its functionality, pioneering the metro as a transport system at a time when cars, boats, trains, and above all planes were the preferred means of transport on the Soviet screen.

During the war, many metro stations served as bomb shelters and are rarely featured on celluloid. The metro stations built under Khrushchev and Brezhnev in the 1960s and 1970s offer a much simpler design. Khrushchev's architectural plans extended to the periphery, where he built housing estates, creating accommodation for the people to live in, rather than palaces for the people. The stations on the radial lines connecting to these districts were plain and practical, but often identical in design. They had a long, central platform with trains running either side, and the stations were fitted with plain white tiles rather than marble. Films of the Thaw and Stagnation periods therefore focus largely on the construction rather than the architectural features of the metro. Thus, in *Dobrovol'tsy/The Volunteers* (Yuri Yegorov, 1958) the metro construction site is the place where relationships are formed. No actual journey is made on the metro, but the static quality of the achievement rather than its functionality as a transport system is emphasized. The hero Kolka of Georgi Daneliya's 1963 blockbuster *Ia shagaiu po Moskve/Walking the Streets of Moscow* also works as a metro construction worker. He knows Moscow better than the born Muscovites travelling on the tube. The old is replaced by the

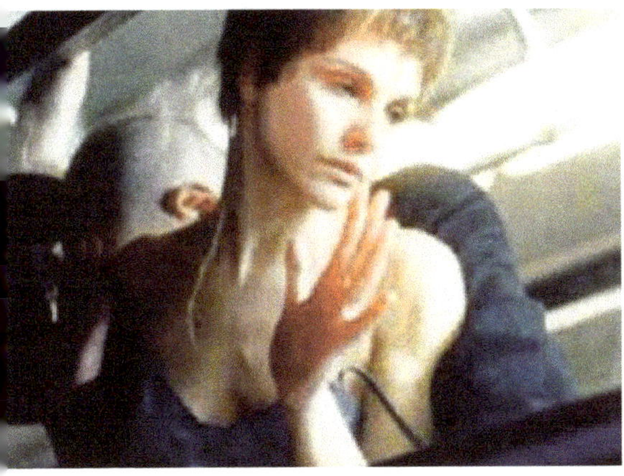

new, the native citizen no longer knows his city, which changes so fast. This echoes the problem encountered by the painter in Medvedkin's *New Moscow* who cannot even manage to paint the buildings in the centre, so fast are they moved or destroyed and replaced.

Throughout the Stagnation era, there are few references to the metro in films, reflecting the decline in construction activity during this period. Trains, suburban trains, planes, motorcycles and cars are more common means of transport than the metro. This underscores the drive away from the metro as an object of pride to a common means of transport, unworthy of depiction on screen.

Russian culture of the 1990s tried to establish a new image of Russia built on the splinters of the Soviet empire and its imperial past. The reconstruction of the Cathedral of Christ the Saviour coincided with the renaming of streets and metro stations in 1990, returning – along with the original names of stations renamed in the 1960s – pre-Revolutionary names and cancelling out all references to the Communist past. At the same time the underground was turned into a shoppers' (capitalist) paradise: shopping malls, such as Okhotny Ryad, are examples.

In the films of the 1990s the metro features as a scene of crime, mystery and sex, in fact making it look worse on-screen than it is in real life. Thus, the plot of Andrei I's *Nauchnaia sektsiia pilotov/Scientific Section of Pilots* (1996) evolves around the metro and prominently features the underground as a place of crime. The Moscow Underground is being terrorized; murders happen without explanation. There is no pattern, no system behind the attacks, which stop as abruptly as they begin. The film begins with three incidents in the metro: blood is dripping from a chandelier; fresh meat is left in a suitcase on a station leaving a trace of blood; and finally the body of a man who suffered an epileptic fit is discovered in a pool of blood. All three incidents happen at Komsomolskaya Station, and all involve a blood substitute with the leukocytes replaced through genetic manipulation. The absence of leukocytes points at an immune deficiency: the metro is bleeding, it is sick. The metro system is a living organism: its limbs (trains) are ailing; its brain (system) is corrupted.

Alexander Zeldovich's *Moskva/Moscow* (2000) is a postmodernist parody of Anton Chekhov's *Three Sisters* (*Tri sestry*, 1900): Irina, Masha and Olga lead a dull existence in post-Soviet Moscow. Their promiscuous relationships with the psychiatrist Mark, the businessman Mike and his business partner Lev culminate in Mark's suicide and Mike's murder, leaving Lev to marry both Olga and Masha. Moscow is a city of crime and sexual perversion, where no relationship has any stability. The film explores the chief tourist sites as locations of death (the Bolshoi Theatre, the ski jump on Sparrow Hills), while other sites are presented to the autistic Olga in a 'guided tour' by Lev that culminates in the metro as the main sight: it is no longer a palace for the people, nor a means of transport, but an estranged location for its own citizens and a place for rape. Lev takes Olga on the 'dernier metro', which goes to the depot; once they leave the station he undresses her and has sex with her. *Moscow* represents the capital as a mere facade behind which crime and perversion are hidden.

On the cinematic screen of the 1990s the metro is no longer the object of pride, but of crime and sex. The metro is an open wound, an ailing patient, a sick mind, forcing its inhabitants into darkness for hours each day. It is no longer a mere location, but abused and reduced to an object of manipulation and perversion. In reality, the metro – with nine lines extending over 313 kilometres and 188 stations, transporting 9 million passengers every day on trains running at 60–90-second intervals – is one of the most efficient transport systems in the world. ✣

The stations were designed as palaces for the people, creating a grand Moscow Underground, while the surface of Moscow was being redesigned and reconstructed according to Stalin's General Plan.

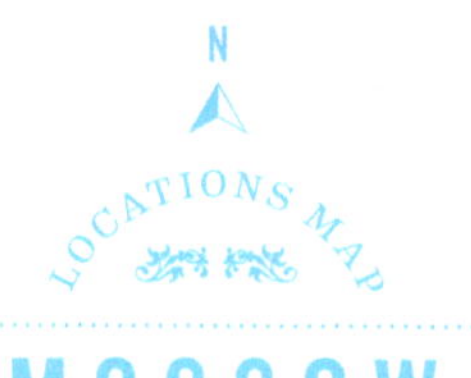

N
LOCATIONS MAP
MOSCOW

maps are only to be taken as approximates

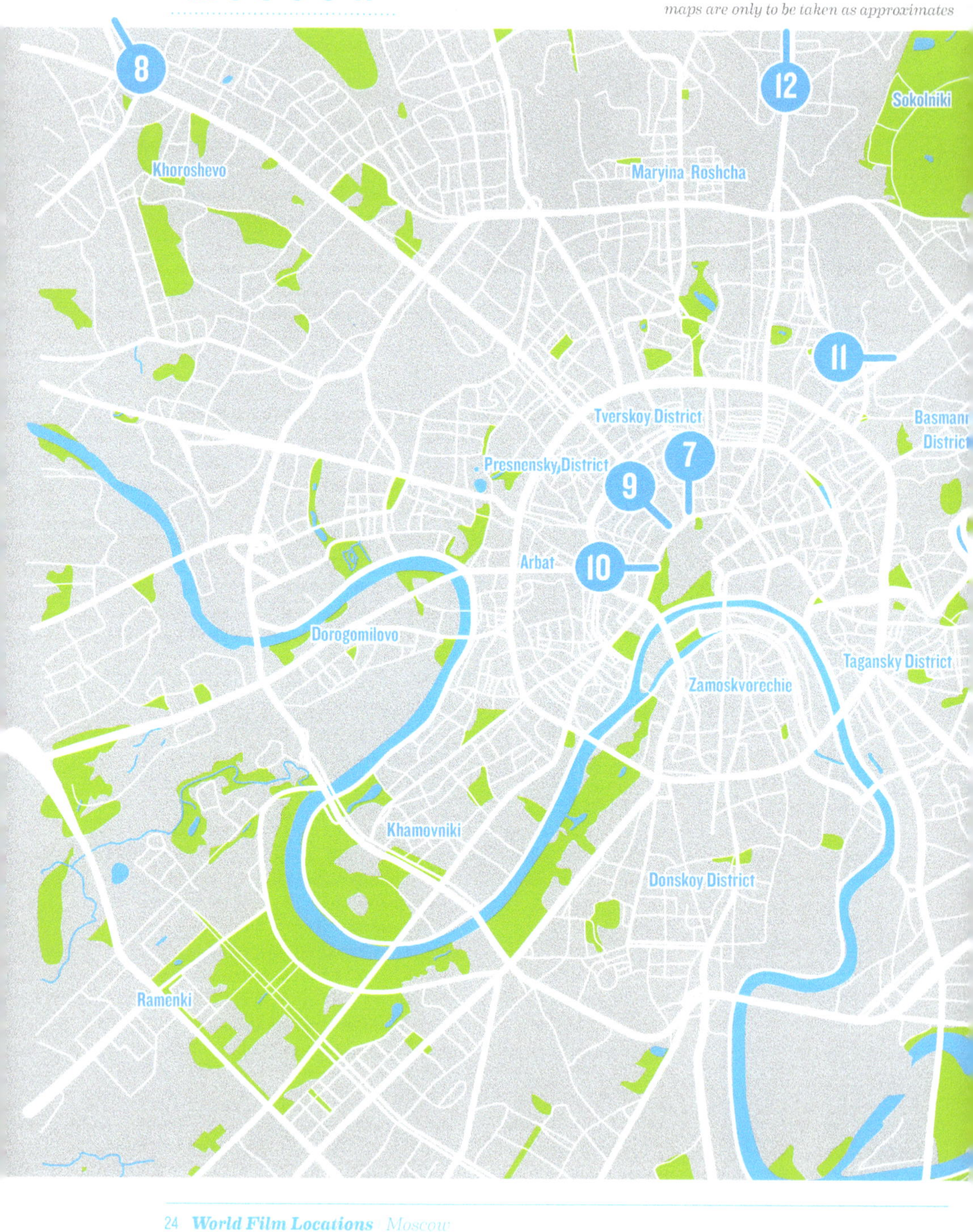

8
12
Sokolniki
Khoroshevo
Maryina Roshcha
11
Tverskoy District
Basmann District
Presnensky District
7
9
Arbat
10
Dorogomilovo
Tagansky District
Zamoskvorechie
Khamovniki
Donskoy District
Ramenki

MOSCOW LOCATIONS
SCENES 7-13

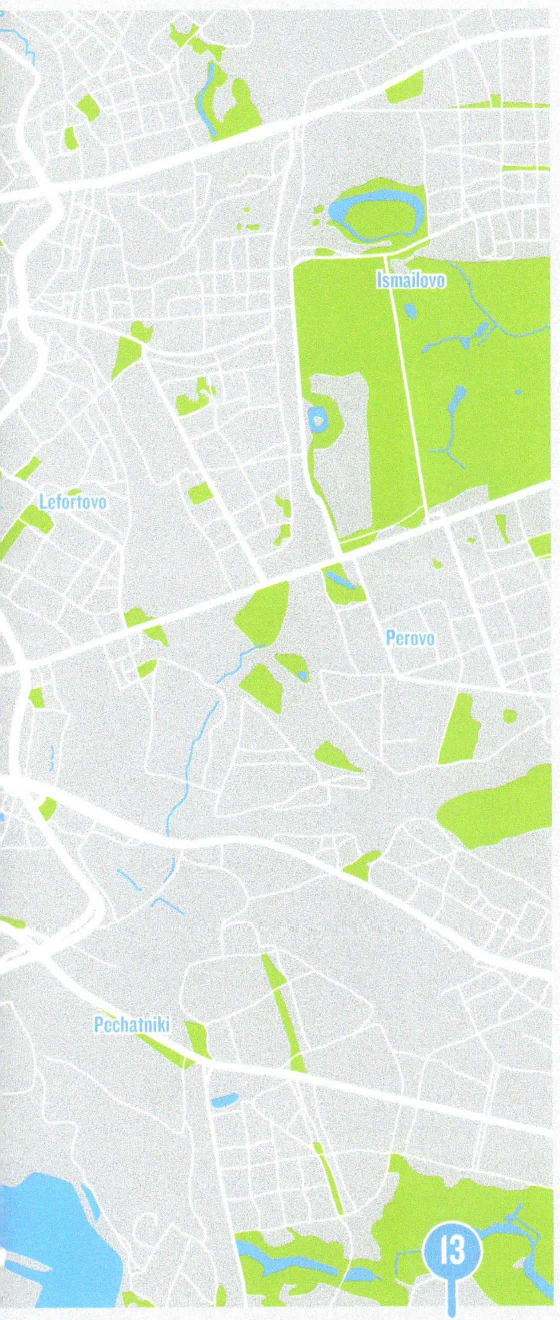

JOLLY FELLOWS/VESELYE REBIATA (1934)

Bolshoi Theatre

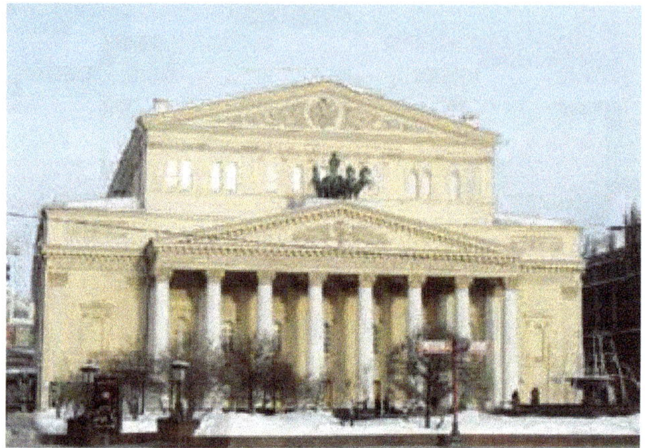

ONE OF THE FIRST Soviet musical comedies, *Jolly Fellows* follows the journey of two musically talented individuals – a shepherd, Kostya (played by the jazz musician Leonid Utësov) and a maid, Anyuta (played by Lyubov Orlova in her first film role) – from a small village to Moscow. This journey is not only geographic, but cultural as well, and the film's climax, a performance by the two of them at the Bolshoi Theatre, marks their ascent to the centre of the new Soviet state. If the presence of a shepherd and a maid in this centre indicate the egalitarian social aspirations of that state, the content of their performance suggests a kind of cultural egalitarianism as well. The concert begins with a gag: the band braved a rainstorm on the way to the theatre and when they attempt to play their instruments only water comes out. Setting aside their instruments, the orchestra scats their way through a jazz number. Anyuta then sings a love song, which is followed by an upbeat comic folk number. The concert concludes with 'The March of the Jolly Fellows' (1934, composed by Isaak Dunaevsky, lyrics by Vasili Lebedev-Kumach and performed by Leonid Utësov), an example of a new, Soviet genre: the mass song. This on-screen eclecticism was not a terribly faithful rendering of the real-life artistic climate: during the film's shooting its scriptwriters, Nikolai Erdman and Vladimir Mass, were arrested, demonstrating that – contrary to the refrain of 'The March of the Jolly Fellows' – it was far from certain that 'If you sing your way through life, You'll never lose your way'. **Chip Crane**

Photo © Birgit Beumers

Scene description: Kostya and Anyuta perform on stage at the Bolshoi Theatre
Timecode for scene: 1:14:40 – 1:29:41

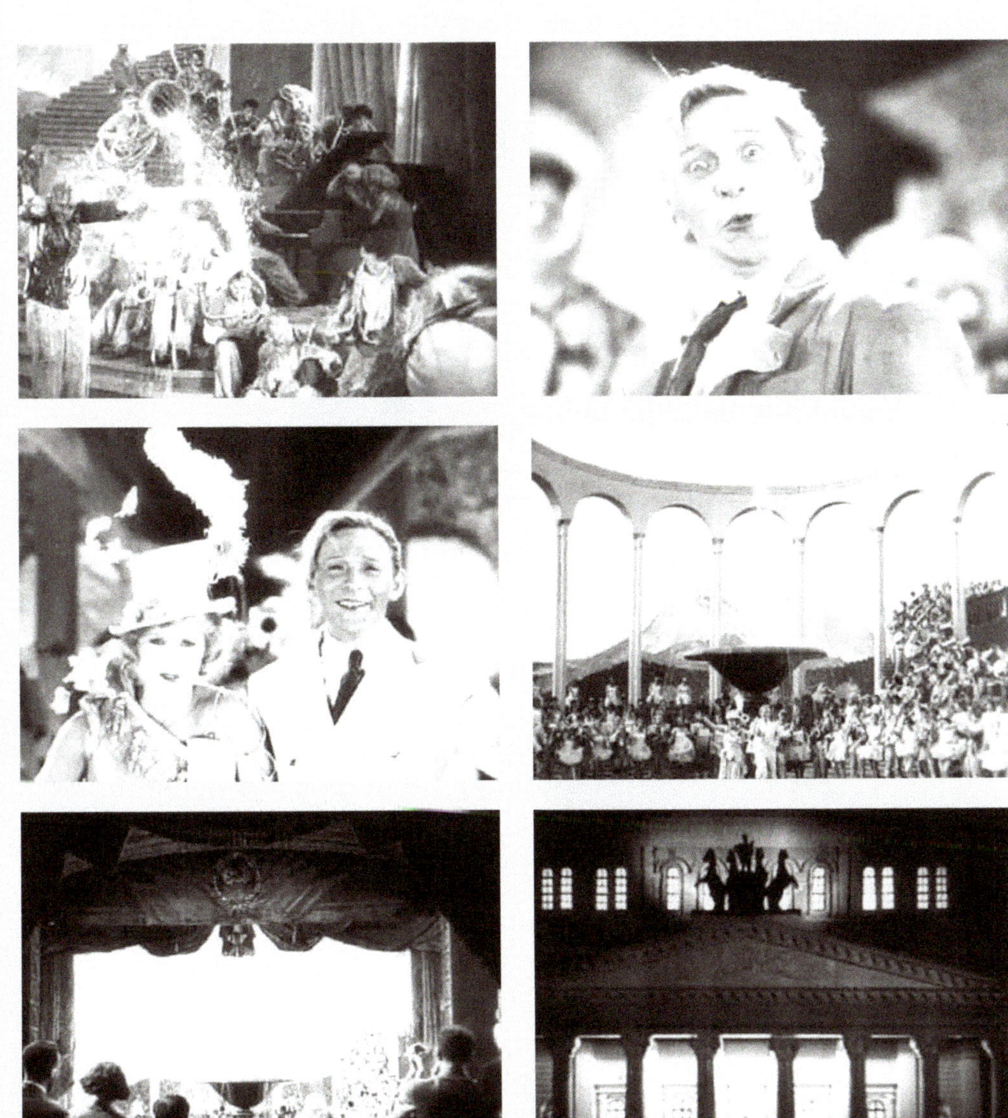

CIRCUS/TSIRK (1936)

Hotel Moskva

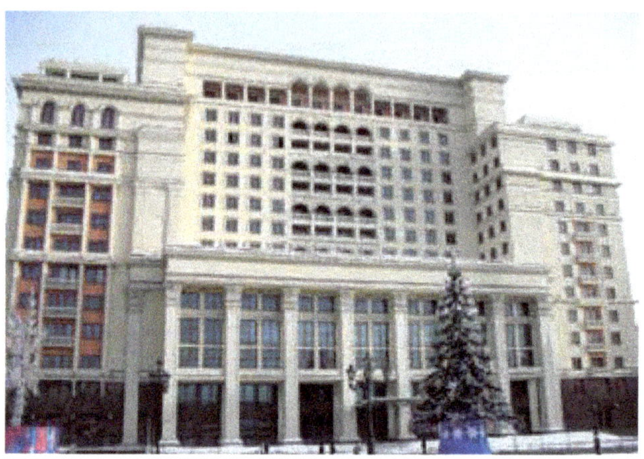

GRIGORI ALEXANDROV'S *Circus* is a Stalin-era musical about an American woman, Marion Dixon (Lyubov Orlova), who runs away to Moscow after being threatened in the United States for having a child with a black man. In Moscow, she works as a circus performer, where she meets Ivan Petrovich Martynov (Sergei Stolyarov). In this scene, they meet in Marion's hotel room, where Martynov teaches her the 'Song of the Motherland', a song (composed by Isaak Dunaevsky with lyrics by Vasili Lebedev-Kumach, written specially for the film) that reappears several times during the film and became widely popular following the film's release. As the scene opens and Martynov sings the first verse, which begins 'From Moscow to the furthest outskirts', the camera shows Moscow's Red Square through Marion's window. The view from her window offers a glimpse of Red Square in a moment of transition. There is St Basil's Cathedral, which had been transformed from church to museum at that point, and Lenin's recently completed mausoleum. The scene shows the Kremlin's Spasskaya Tower, also known as the clock tower, bearing the tsarist double-headed eagles which would be replaced with red stars later in 1935 after this scene had been filmed. On the left is the GUM department store building, which served as a governmental office building at the time. Next to it is the top of the Kazan Cathedral, which would be demolished in 1936. The film returns to this setting in the finale, when Marion and her child, having been accepted by the Soviet citizens, march in a parade through the square, singing the same 'Song of the Motherland' as in this scene. **•➤ Erin Alpert**

Scene description: *Ivan Martynov teaches Marion Dixon the 'Song of the Motherland'*
Timecode for scene: 0:21:38 – 0:25:48

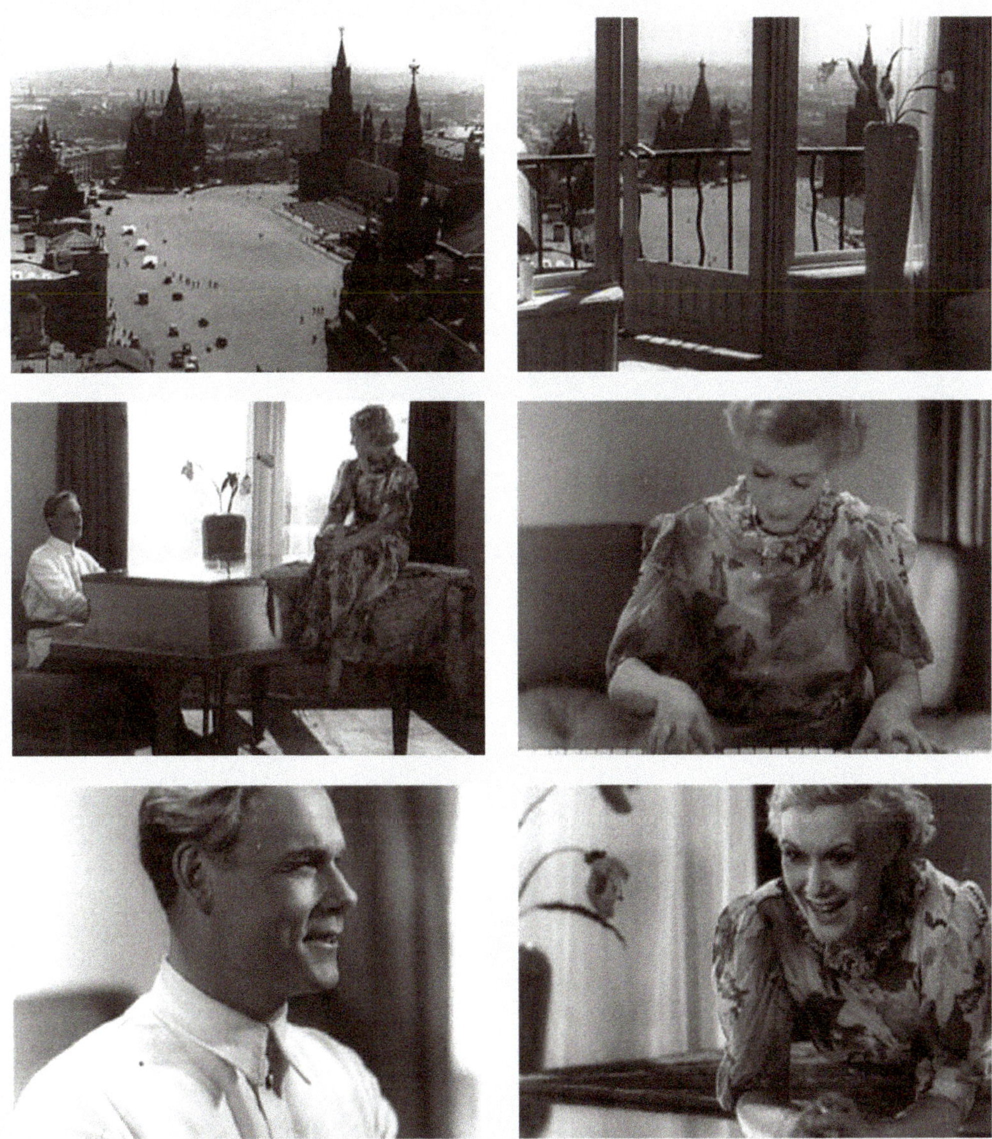

VOLGA-VOLGA (1938)

Northern River Station (Rechnoi vokzal)

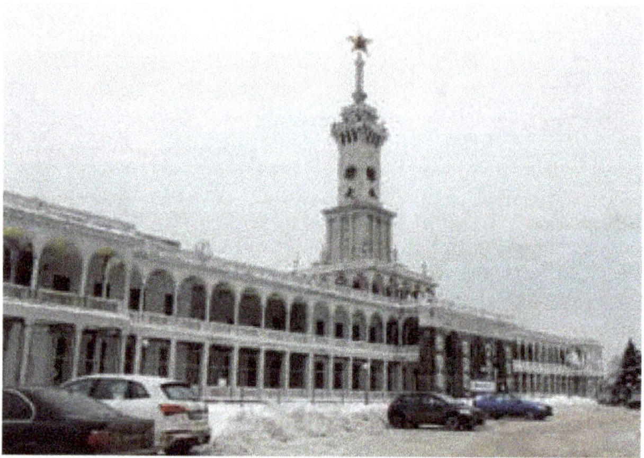

GRIGORI ALEXANDROV'S musical comedy *Volga-Volga* follows two competing groups of musicians travelling from Melkovodsk to Moscow, hoping to compete in the Moscow Musical Olympiad. The two groups, one led by a mail carrier nicknamed Strelka (Lyubov Orlova) and the other by her boyfriend Alësha Trubyshkin (Andrei Tutyshkin), eventually resolve their differences, join forces and arrive in Moscow together. Unfortunately, as they approach the city, they discover everyone they pass singing the song that they had prepared for the competition. The music, written by Strelka's 'friend' Dunya, actually Strelka herself, had been blown overboard in a storm a few nights before. The pages of the composition were then discovered by a variety of different people. Everyone thinks that Dunya stole the music and worries about what to perform in the competition now. In the course of the ship's journey, Alexandrov showcases several newly constructed marvels. In the film, which was released in 1938, the boat travels down the Moscow Canal, completed in 1937, passing many of its landmarks, including the massive statue of Lenin, built in 1937 at the intersection of Volga River and the Moscow Canal and the series of locks leading up to Moscow. In this scene, the boat arrives at the impressive Northern River Station, constructed simultaneously with the Moscow Canal and also completed in 1937, located on the Khimki Reservoir. With the station in the background, a sign that the competition is imminent, Strelka explains to Alësha that Dunya did not steal the music, but rather it was stolen from her. ⟿***Erin Alpert***

Photo © Polina Zakharova

Scene description: Musicians from Melkovodsk arrive in Moscow
Timecode for scene: 1:15:30 – 1:21:15

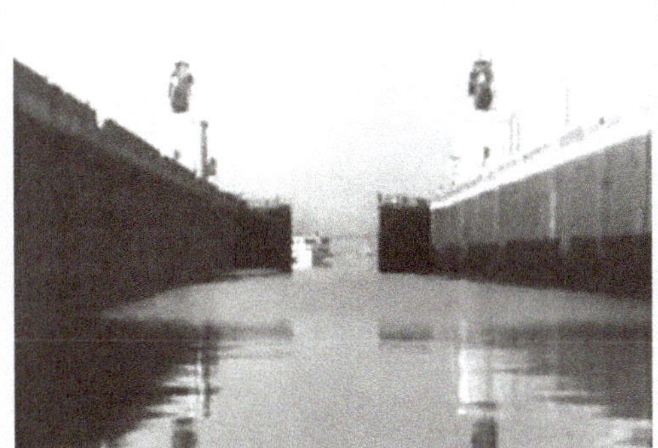

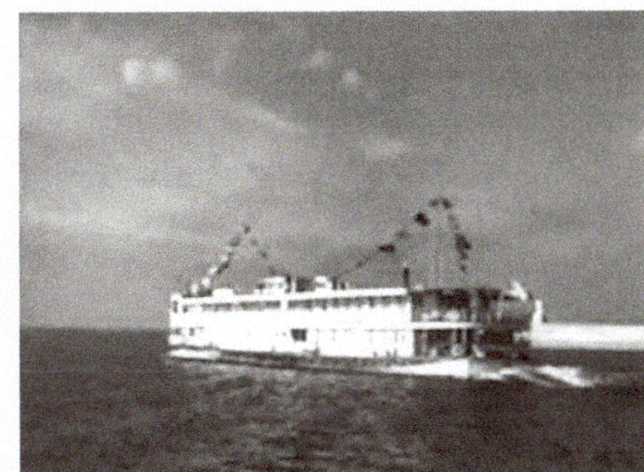

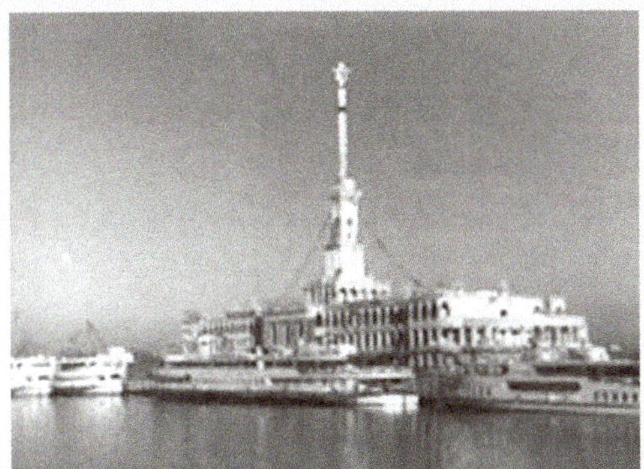

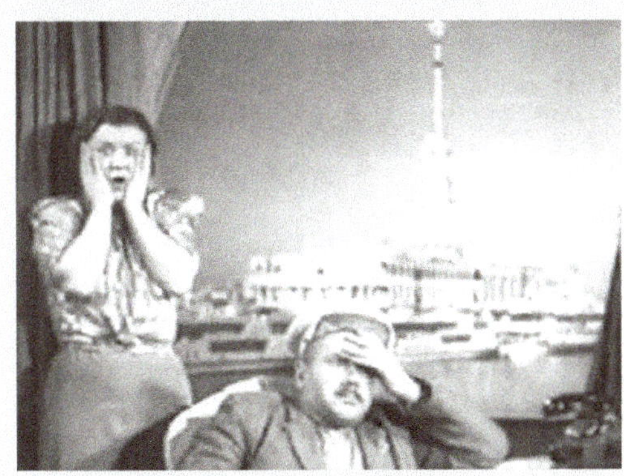

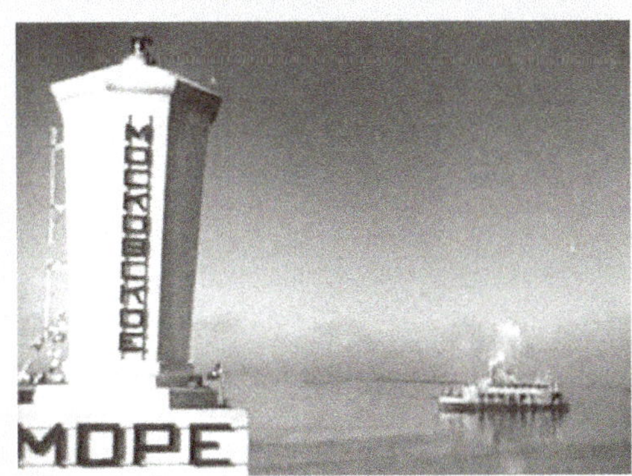

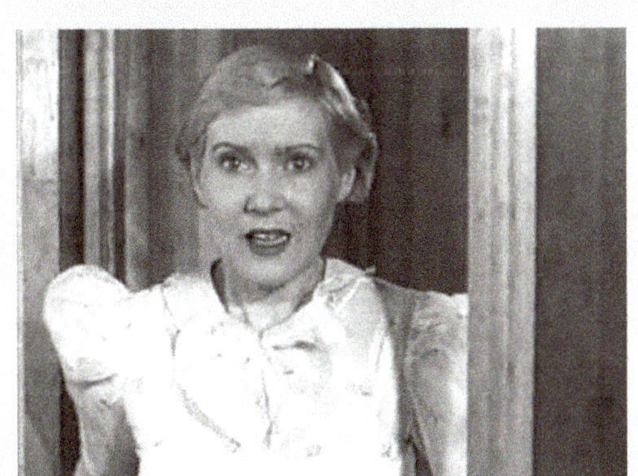

NEW MOSCOW/NOVAIA MOSKVA (1938)

Cathedral of Christ the Saviour

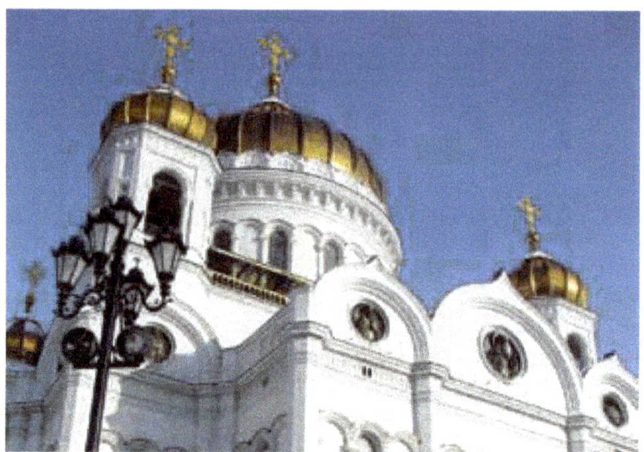

ALEXANDER MEDVEDKIN'S *New Moscow* is a comedic response to the Stalinist reconstruction of the capital: would-be landscape painters are frustrated as buildings are demolished faster than they can be put to canvas, and grandmothers are frightened by the view from the window as their apartment block is moved to widen streets. A group of young engineers have invented a device capable of keeping up with this rapid change: a 'Living Model' of Moscow. When the model is publicly unveiled, something goes terrifically wrong: the model begins moving in reverse and the cityscape of the recent and not-so-recent past reappears: monasteries' cupolas rise over the city, high-rise buildings disappear, and the massive Cathedral of Christ the Saviour (demolished in 1931 to make room for the Palace of Soviets) is reborn as documentary footage of its destruction is shown in reverse. The engineers quickly right the situation and the model turns toward the future. Through a combination of animation and montage the new city appears before our eyes: the magnificent River Station replaces an old factory, a steady stream of cars pass under Mayakovsky Square, and the Palace of Soviets, planned to be the tallest building in the world, succeeds the demolished cathedral as a squadron of aeroplanes flies triumphantly overhead (in reality, the building was never finished). Simultaneously serving as a demonstration of the utopian power of Stalinist architecture and urban planning and an uncomfortable reminder of what was being lost, this scene was central to the decision to ban the film.
⊷ Chip Crane

Photo © Birgit Beumers

Scene description: The 'Living Model' shows the reconstruction of Moscow
Timecode for scene: 1:00:12 – 1:05:47

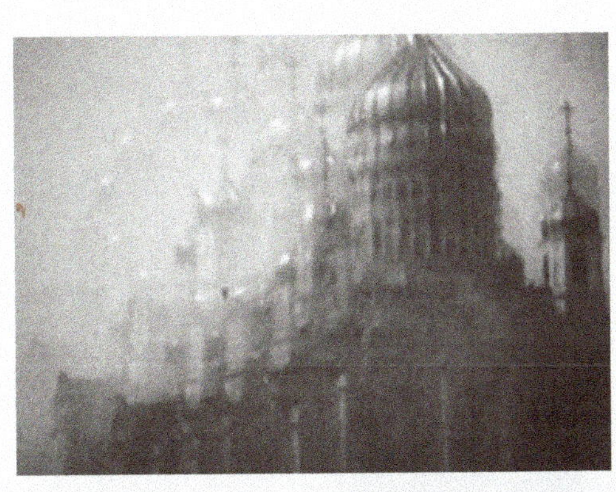
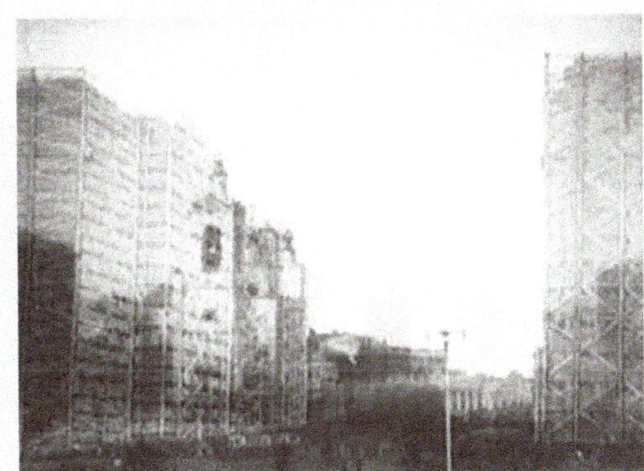
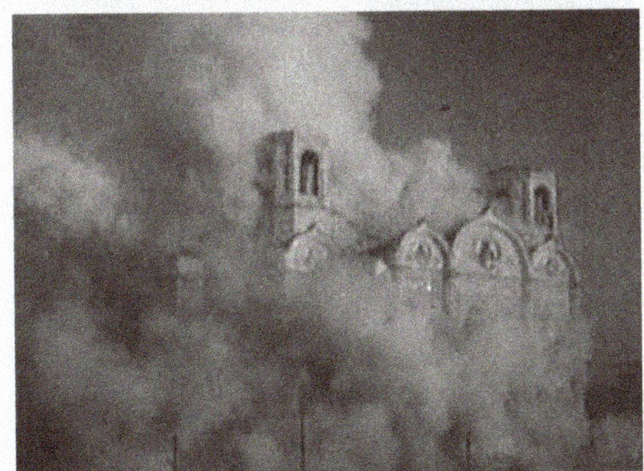
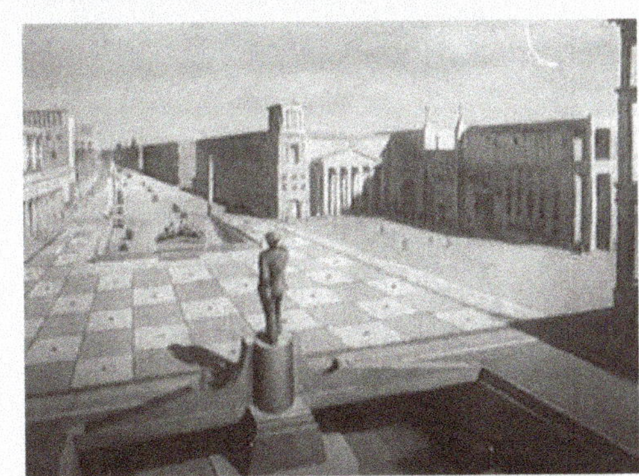
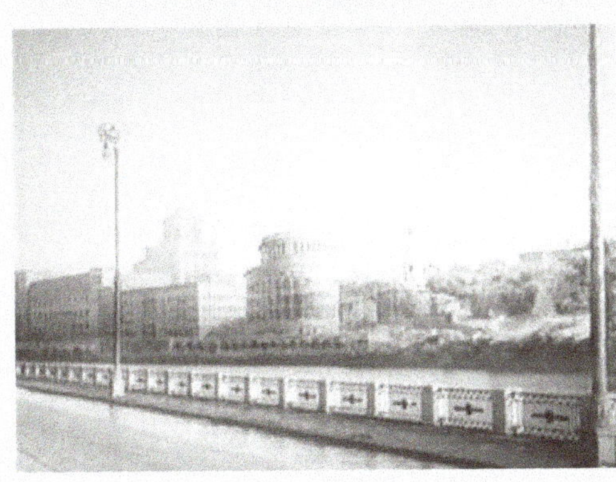
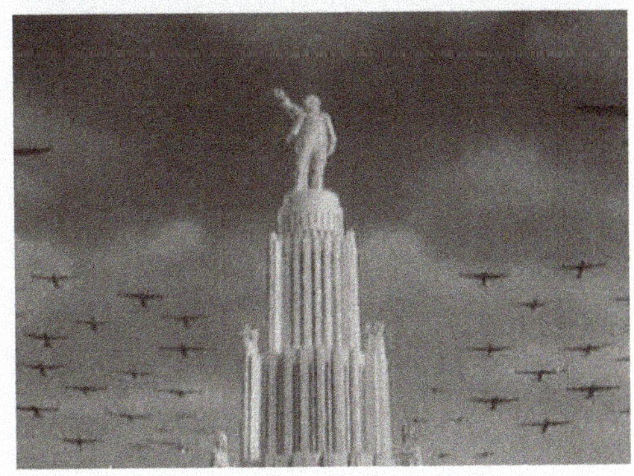

Images © 1938 Mosfilm

A GIRL WITH CHARACTER/ DEVUSHKA S KHARAKTEROM (1939)

Yaroslavsky Railway Station, Komsomolskaya Square

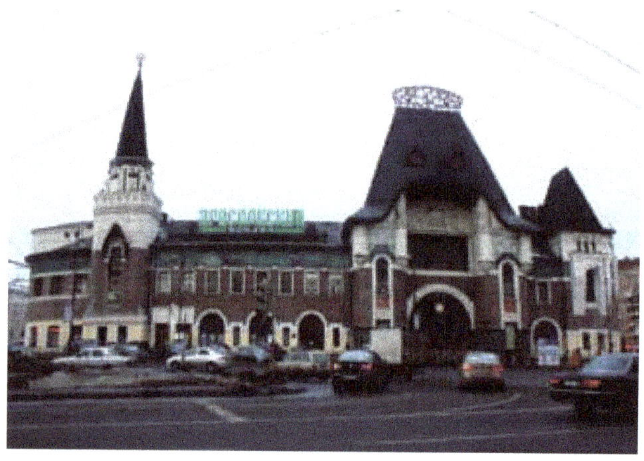

A GIRL WITH CHARACTER tells of Katya Ivanova's journey from the Soviet Far East to Moscow to seek justice over her incompetent fur farm boss. This journey from the periphery to the centre was made by millions of Soviet citizens as they gravitated towards the capital in search of work and opportunities in the 1930s. One of the main points of arrival would have been Komsomolskaya Square (until 1933 known as Kalanchëvskaya Square), where three main railway stations are located: the Yaroslavsky, Leningradsky and Kazansky stations. Katya finds herself at Yaroslavsky Station on the Square and is in awe at the majestic view of Moscow that stands before her. But her first act is to file an official complaint against her boss to the Complaints Bureau. While her protest is being dealt with, Katya experiences the glamorous working girl's lifestyle in the big city. Initially, she works as a sales assistant in a luxurious furs department store, learning that 'the Soviet salesperson must always speak the truth'. She is trained to encourage culture, knowledge and taste among her customers. Subsequently, she finds herself in a factory testing the quality of gramophone records. However, her stay in Moscow is short: she soon finds herself back at Komsomolskaya Square. The boss has been dismissed – and Katya replaces him. She has persuaded some city girls to return to work with her in the Far East. So Katya's return home is triumphant: she has gained justice and moral approval from the heart of Soviet power, experienced the fruits of mass luxury and is now ready to apply this to the developing periphery. **Jamie Miller**

Photo © Polina Zakharova

Scene description: Katya arrives in Moscow to make her complaint and experience the big city
Timecode for scene: 0:38:20 – 0:40:56

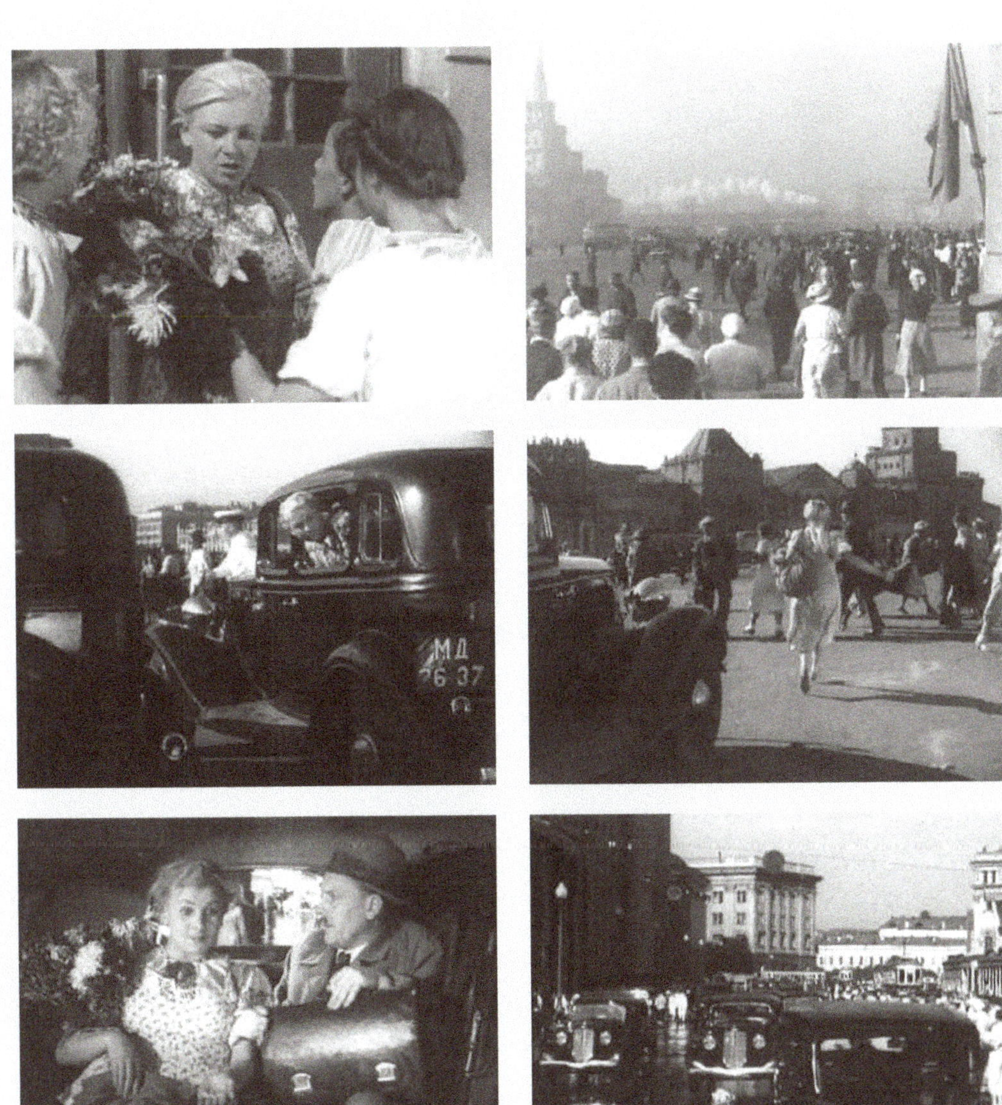

THE RADIANT PATH/SVETLYI PUT' (1940)

All-Union Agricultural Exhibition (VDNKh)

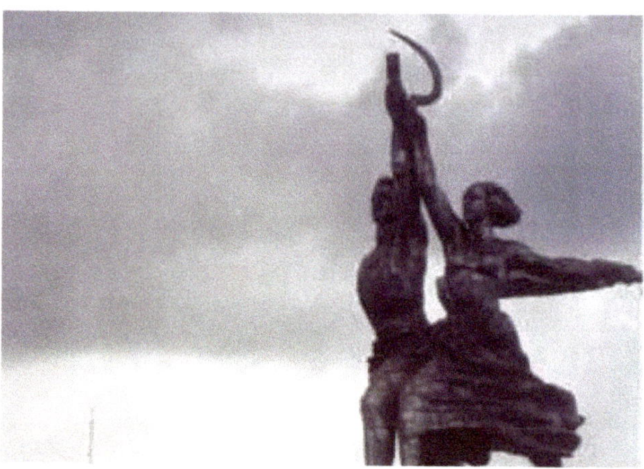

THIS LAST MUSICAL comedy by Grigori Alexandrov is a vivid example of high Stalinist culture. It tells a Soviet Cinderella story, in which the main heroine, Tatyana Morozova (Lyubov Orlova), undergoes a magical transformation from an illiterate domestic servant to an engineer and deputy of the Supreme Soviet. After joining the Stakhanovite movement as a textile worker, she sets a labour record for which she is awarded the highest prize, the Order of Lenin. In the final scene, Morozova, now a hero and a truly transformed Soviet Cinderella, is reunited with her Prince Charming, an engineer and former mentor (Yevgeni Samoilov). The couple wanders the All-Union Agricultural Exhibition in Moscow, past monumental sculptures, fountains, and a bas-relief glorifying Soviet labour until they reach the famous monument of the Worker and Kolkhoz Woman. The two steel figures were created by Vera Mukhina in 1937 for the Soviet Pavilion at the World Exhibition in Paris; the male figure holds aloft a hammer, the female figure a sickle, forming the Soviet emblem. The film's finale symbolically portrays the couple as the New Soviet Man and Woman, transformed by the 'radiant path' of communism. The All-Union Agricultural Exhibition was established as an exhibition space in 1939, where each Soviet republic would display its achievements in individual monumental pavilions, showcasing agricultural and industrial achievements under the watch of giant statues of Stalin and of Vera Mukhina's 'Worker and Kolkhoz Woman'. The latter statue is a famous landmark located today in the Russian Exhibition Centre and was adopted as Mosfilm's logo in 1947.
➻Sasha Rindisbacher

Photo © Birgit Beumers

Scene description: Morozova and Lebedev at VDNKh
Timecode for scene: 1:25:34 – 1:36:05

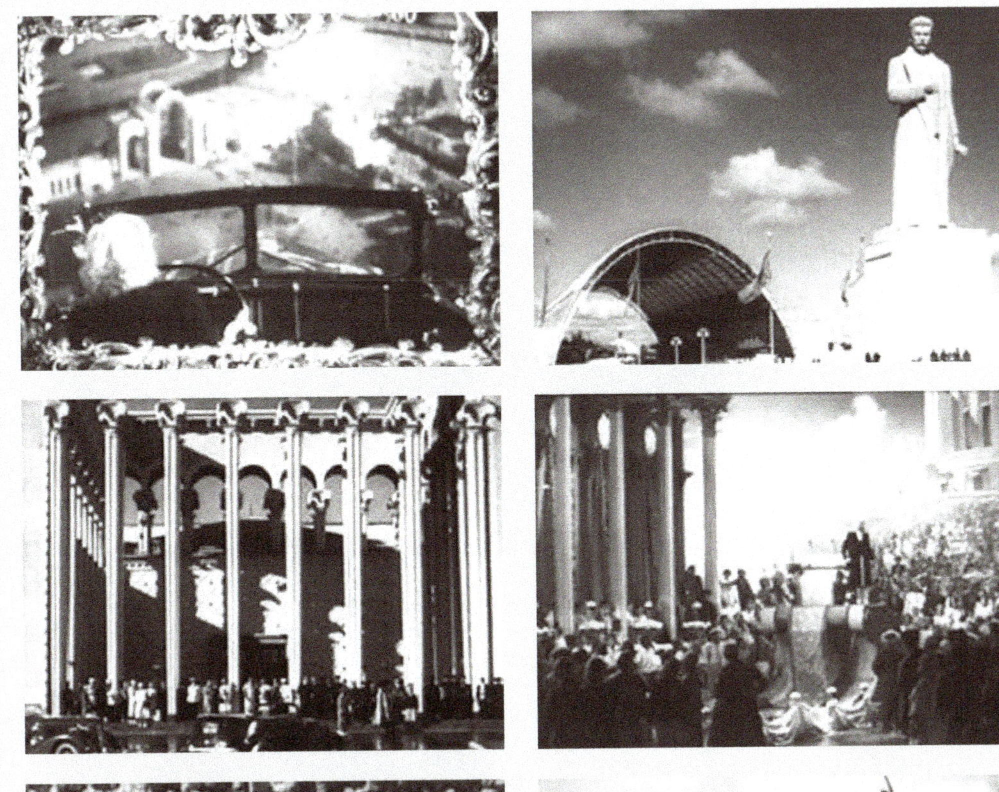

Images © 1940 Mosfilm

THE VOW/KLIATVA (1926)

Gorki Leninskiye Estate

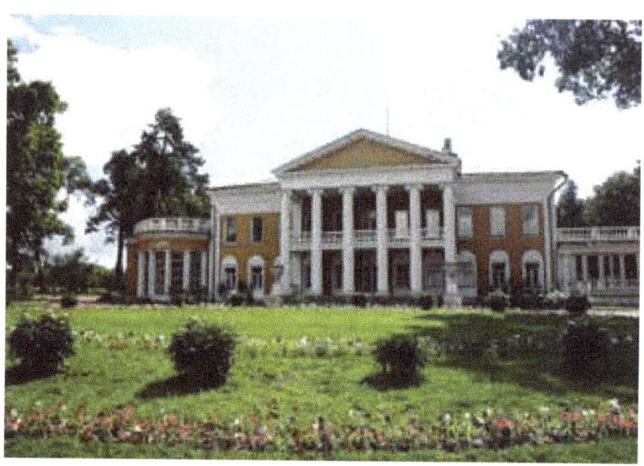

ONE OF THE MAJOR THEMES in Mikhail Chiaureli's *The Vow* is the transition of power from Lenin to Stalin. In this scene, Varvara (Sofia Giatsintova), whose husband was murdered by kulaks, arrives in Gorki after first trying to find Lenin in Moscow. She has journeyed to deliver her late husband's letter to Lenin. When she arrives in Gorki, she learns that Lenin has died and is grief-stricken. As Nikolai Bukharin and Lev Kamenev concern themselves with how to maintain power and what to write in Lenin's obituary, and Stalin's supporters worry about how to ensure that Stalin will succeed Lenin, Stalin (Mikhail Gelovani) himself takes a walk and remembers the departed great leader. The location of this scene, the estate at Gorki (renamed Gorki Leninskiye after Lenin's death), served as Lenin's dacha while he was in power. He died there in January 1924. This scene acts as a crucial link between the two leaders. Stalin walks the estate and stops to look at an empty bench, a reminder of Lenin. Lenin was famously photographed on this bench and the symbol of Lenin's empty bench is recognizable from Dziga Vertov's film *Tri pesni o Lenine/Three Songs about Lenin* (1934), which features an almost identical shot of Lenin's bench in the snow, as well as images of the empty bench throughout the seasons.

❧ Erin Alpert

Directed by Mikhail Chiaureli
Scene description: The widow Varvara arrives in Gorki where Stalin mourns the passing of Lenin
Timecode for scene: 0:17:50 – 0:21:40

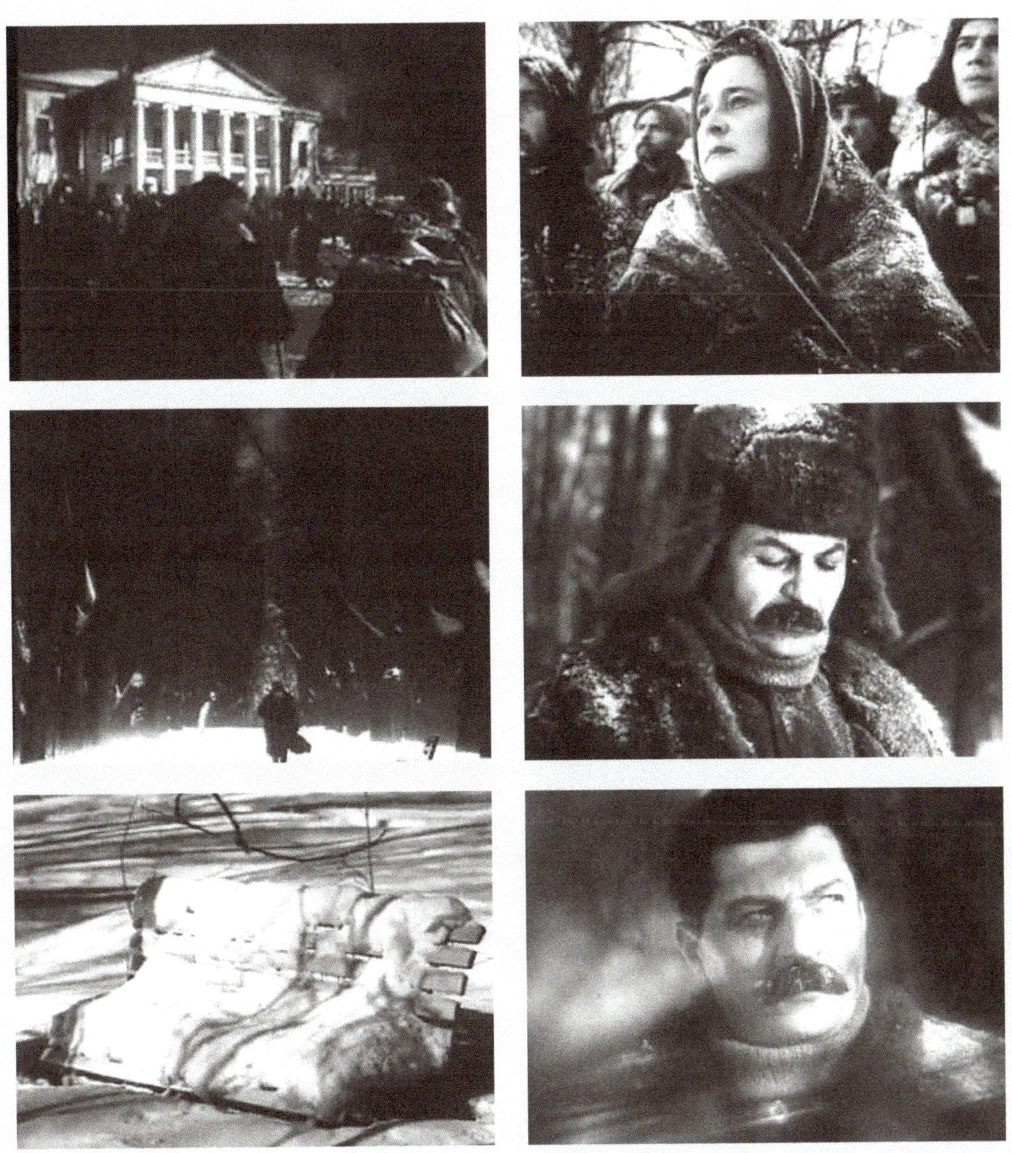

THE PALACE OF SOVIETS

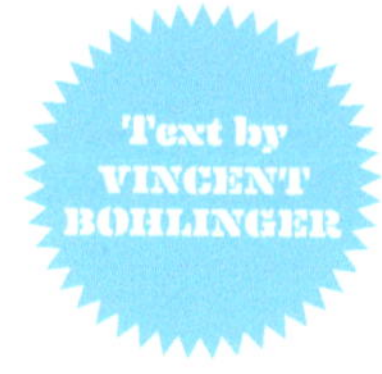

HAVING NEVER actually been built, the Palace of Soviets has served as something of a signifying absence in the Moscow landscape. If its real-life nonexistence reminds us of any shortcomings in Soviet or Stalinist industry, economy and culture, then that is likely due to the very real presence and exuberant symbolism the Palace maintained in several Russian films and in the imagined geography of what was to be an improved and more advanced Moscow.

The Palace was to be built on the site of the Cathedral of Christ the Saviour, the largest Orthodox cathedral in the world. The cathedral had been commissioned by Tsar Alexander I in 1812 in honour of Napoleon's retreat from Russia, but it took many decades for the cathedral, its interiors and its surrounding square to be designed and constructed. It was finally consecrated in May 1883 – four tsars later – on the day of Alexander III's coronation. Rising on the embankment along the Moskva River less than half a kilometre from the Kremlin, this hefty mass with squat domes – the seat of the Orthodox Church in Moscow – dominated the skyline and was a pronounced landmark seen throughout much of the city. It took more than a year to dismantle the cathedral, with its ultimate ruin realized by a series of explosions in December 1931. The demolition was filmed by the young Vladislav Mikosha, and additional footage of one of the explosions is featured during a sequence of celebratory destruction in *Novaia Moskva/New Moscow* (Alexander Medvedkin, 1938).

The Soviets had much cultural capital invested in the annihilation and supplanting of the cathedral, and it should be noted that its destruction was undertaken prior to any definitive plans as to what the Palace of Soviets was supposed to look like. The cathedral was a highly visible emblem of the union of tsarist and church wealth and power, as well as – considering its origins – nationalist aggression and war. The Palace of Soviets was to be altogether different: a grandiose meeting place in honour of a new social order. As the cathedral was being demolished, an international contest for its replacement was held. After several rounds of competition and many adjustments, the winning design, announced in 1933, came from the combined effort of two teams, one headed by Boris Yofan and the other by Vladimir Shchuko and Vladimir Gelfreikh. The Palace would showcase an enormous auditorium, with a seating capacity of well over 20,000, and function itself as a giant high-rise pedestal for a colossal statue of Lenin, based on a model sculpted by Sergei Merkurov. A lighting scheme was planned so that even at night the Palace could be seen as far as 40 kilometres from Moscow.

The proposed dimensions of the Palace reveal the Soviet preoccupation with defining and positioning itself both against and in terms of western paradigms. The total height of the Palace was to be 415 meters, almost four times taller than the cathedral it was to replace. The Palace would surpass New York's Empire State Building (with a height of 443 meters in total, but only 381 meters

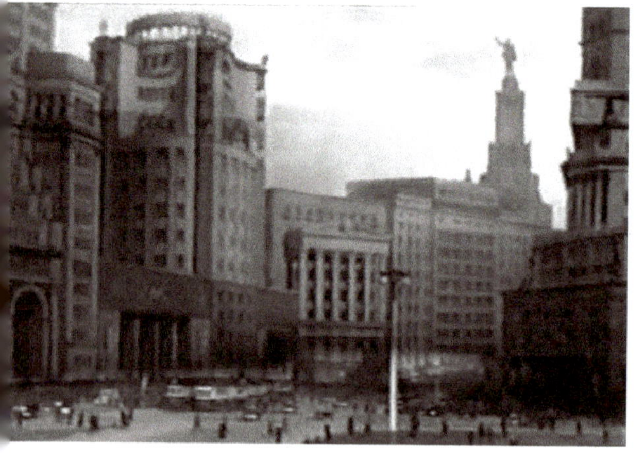

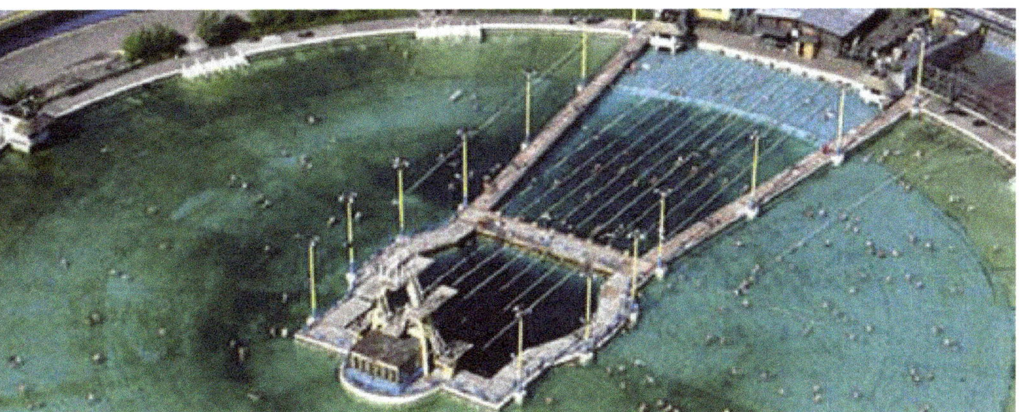

excluding its spire) to become the tallest building in the world. Almost a full quarter of the Palace was to comprise the Lenin statue, itself standing at 100 meters, over 30 storeys tall. Lenin alone therefore would be taller than the Statue of Liberty (at 93 meters), but atop the Palace, Lenin would positively dwarf Liberty.

The Palace was part of the everyday political and cultural discourse of the 1930s, and its appearance in the occasional film gives prime example of the blurring of mythology, history and reality to be found in works adhering to the principles of socialist realism. In *New Moscow*, the Palace is shown in several shots as a key, recognizable indicator of the city that will soon be. Lenin's upraised arm is an iconic gesture, and for the Palace of Soviets it was to be raised more prominently upward to the sky in a challenge for development and success in aviation, a contemporaneous Soviet obsession. A memorable low-angle shot in *New Moscow* highlights this challenge as going-to-be-met by flaunting squadrons of aeroplanes flying overhead neatly in formation on either side of Lenin atop the Palace. In the science fiction film *Kosmicheskii reis/ Space Journey* (Vasili Zhuravlëv, 1935), the Palace is instantly spotted in the opening and closing shots of the film. The Palace is merely a part of the background cityscape and we are instead supposed to admire the stately architecture of the space institute and the recently built giant launching ramp that rockets people to the moon. The film is set in a near and seemingly utopian future – the year 1946 – and already we see the over-fulfilment of Lenin's challenge: not only is the Palace long completed, but we have also moved beyond dominion of the sky with mere aeroplanes to adventures in outer space with our own lunar rockets. The Palace of Soviets in these films is framed to serve as both a thrown gauntlet and a rewarded trophy, as both the challenge and the promised realization of Soviet success. With a contemporary film such as *Shpion/ The Spy* (Alexei Andrianov, 2012), the Palace represents a nostalgic even if troubling what might have been.

The outbreak of World War II proved fatal to the already long-complicated construction of the Palace, and some materials that had already been used in its foundation were repurposed in defence of the city. After the war, the gapping emptiness and aborted attempts to restart construction were perhaps continual reminders of naïve Soviet overreaching. Between 1958 and 1960, the site became the Swimming Pool 'Moskva', the largest outdoor pool in the world – a beautiful massive circle of bright blue water, steaming in winter and reminiscent of a giant hot spring. By August 2000, the Cathedral of Christ the Saviour had been fully resurrected on this site. If the Palace survives now as more than just imagined memory, it is in its influence on the architectural style – neoclassical and eclectic – found in other monumental buildings constructed during the Stalin era, particularly the 'Seven Sisters' high-rises that command the Moscow cityscape to this day. ✣

The proposed dimensions of the Palace reveal the Soviet preoccupation with defining and positioning itself both against and in terms of western paradigms.

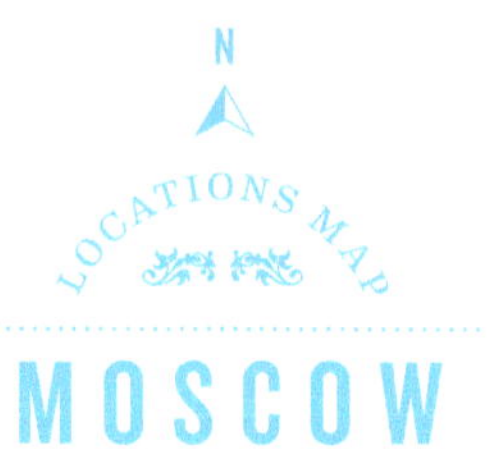

N
LOCATIONS MAP
MOSCOW

maps are only to be taken as approximates

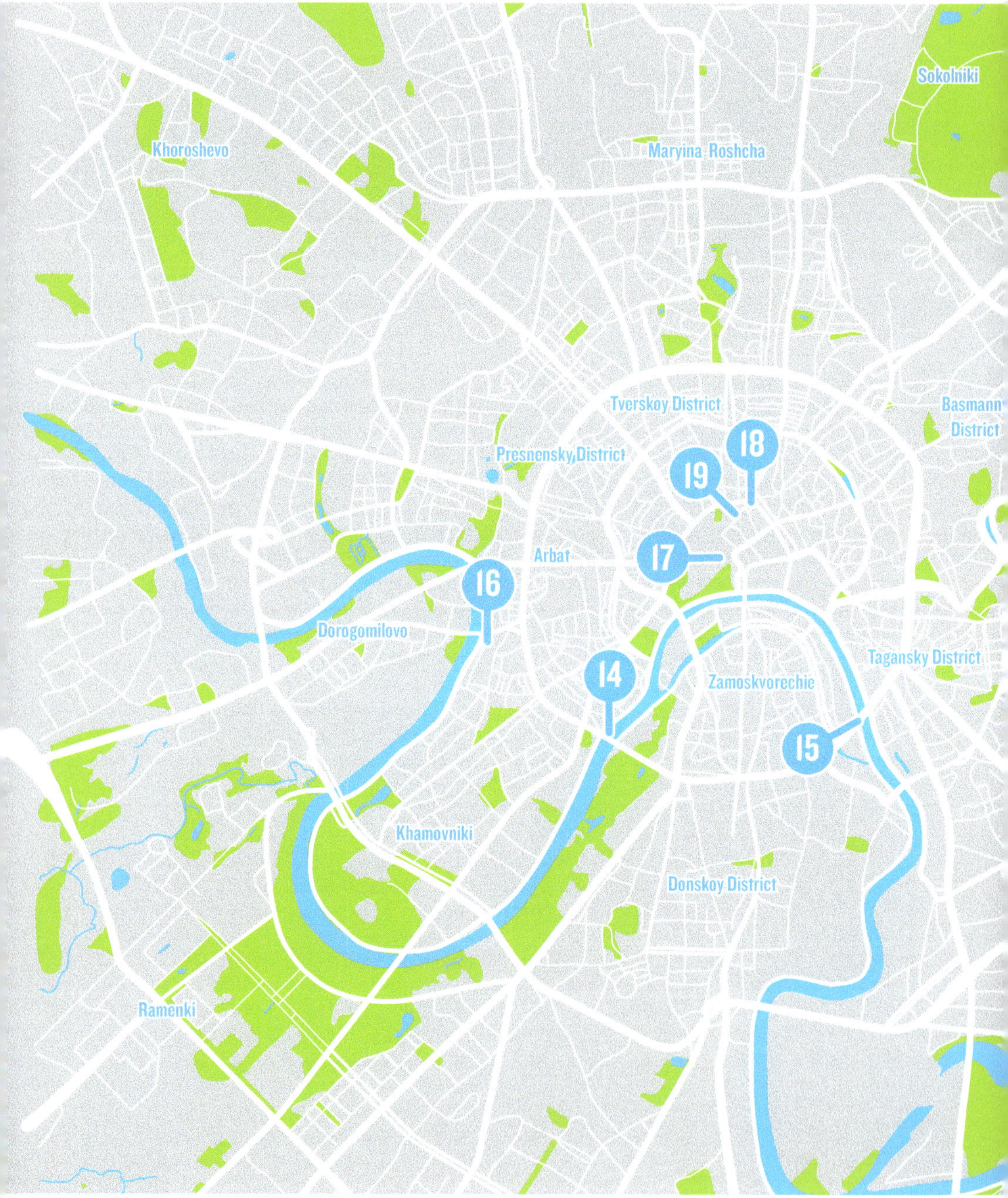

Sokolniki
Khoroshevo
Maryina Roshcha
Tverskoy District
Basmann District
Presnensky District
19
18
Arbat
17
16
14
Tagansky District
Zamoskvorechie
15
Dorogomilovo
Khamovniki
Donskoy District
Ramenki

MOSCOW LOCATIONS
SCENES 14-19

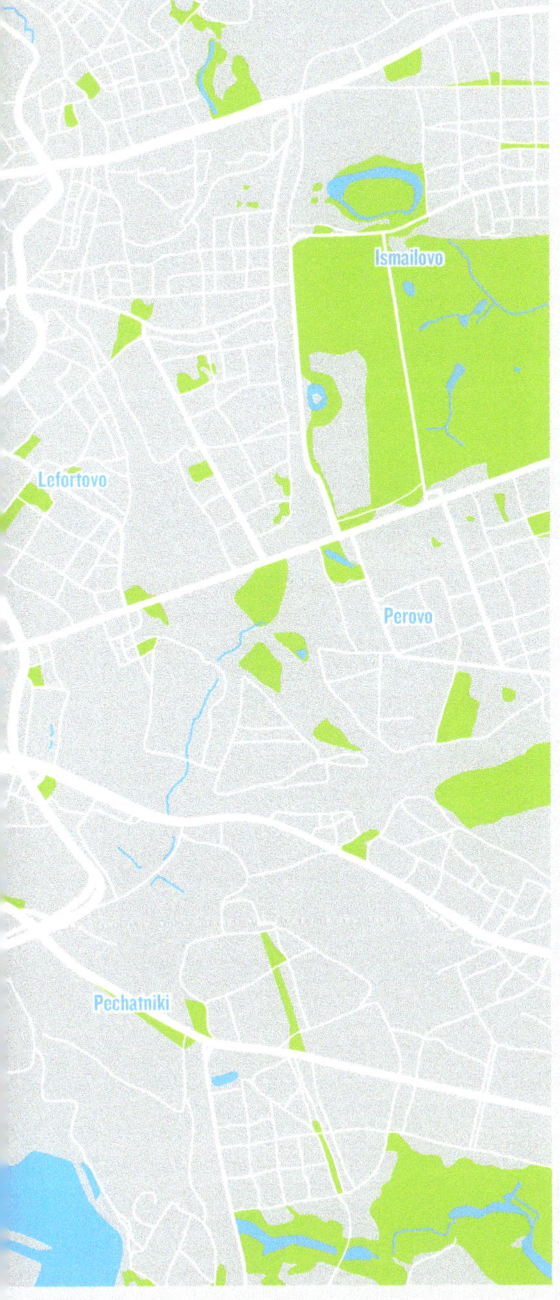

THE CRANES ARE FLYING/LETIAT ZHURAVLI (1957)

Krymsky Bridge

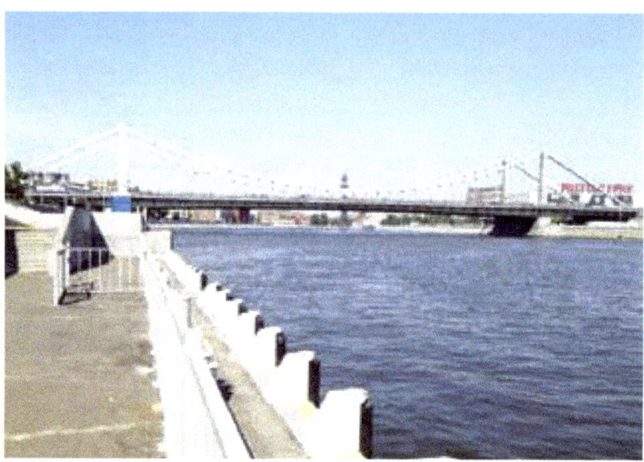

MIKHAIL KALATOZOV'S *The Cranes Are Flying* is the first Soviet film to deal with the human – rather than patriotic and ideological – dimensions of World War II. Boris, a young man in his twenties, volunteers for combat within days of Nazi Germany's invasion of the USSR in June 1941. Departing for the front, he leaves his girlfriend Veronika behind in Moscow. Veronika is soon orphaned during an air raid and goes to live with Boris's family; there, she is raped by Boris's cousin Mark who has an exemption from army service. With no news from Boris, Veronika reluctantly weds Mark and the two are evacuated into the Russian interior, where she, haunted by her unfaithfulness to Boris, eventually learns of Boris's death. The film opens with Boris and Veronika skipping along one of the Moskva River embankments before dawn: the war has already begun, but its start has not yet been announced. Standing by the Krymsky (Crimean) Bridge, opened in 1938 during Stalin's massive reconstruction of central Moscow, Boris points to a flock of cranes overhead and the couple, distracted, is sprayed by water from a street sweeper. Later, Veronika returns to the same spot by the bridge to wait for Boris only to encounter Mark, who, with anti-tank defence structures (called 'hedgehogs' because of their shape) visible in the background, begins his advances on her. Both scenes by the suspension bridge capture and foretell the personal loss, separation, and betrayal that will dominate this look at the war.

⤙Sasha Senderovich

Directed by Mikhail Kalatozov
Scene description: *Veronika with Boris, later with Mark, at the bridge*
Timecode for scene: *0:00:00 – 0:10:52*

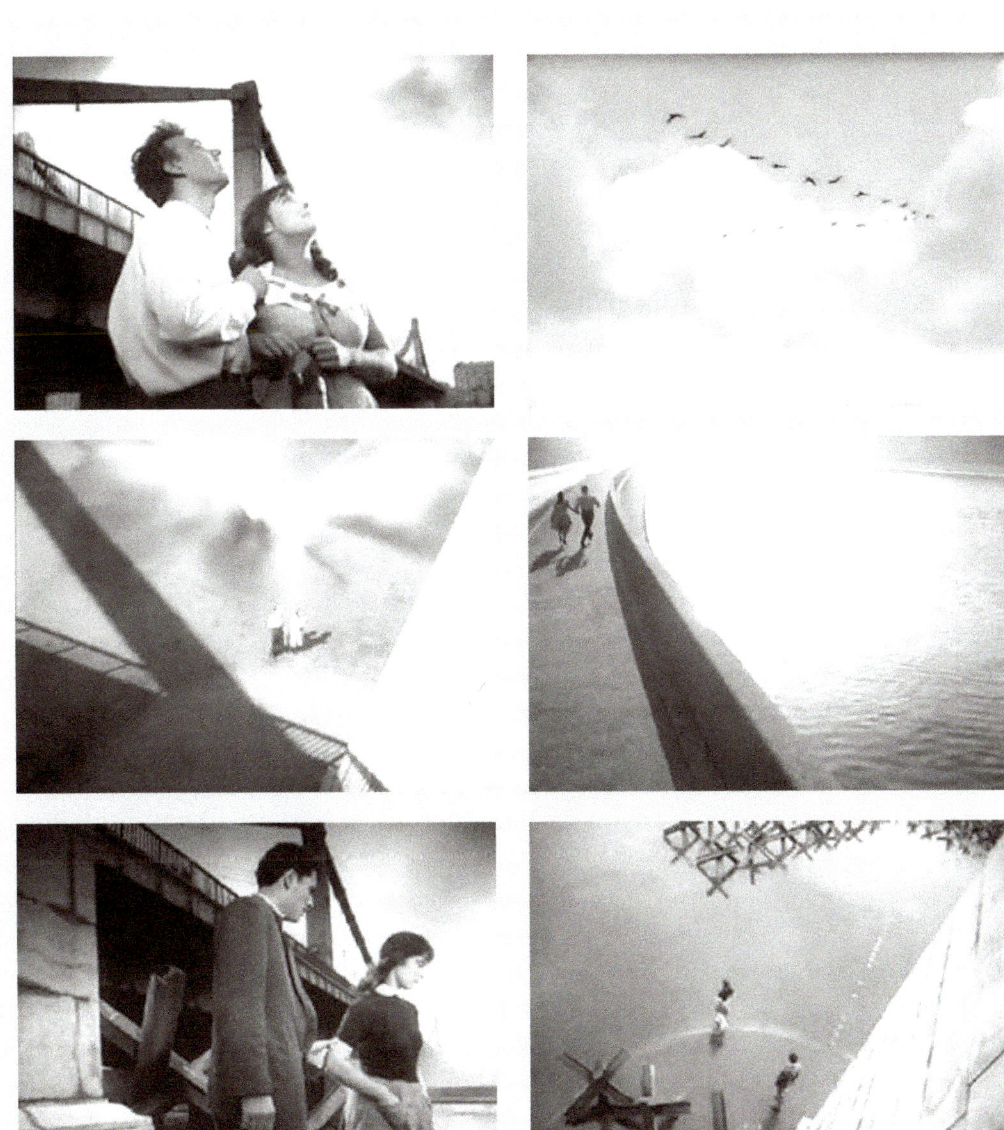

Images © 1957 Mosfilm

THE HOUSE I LIVE IN/ DOM, V KOTOROM IA ZHIVU (1957)

Embankment and Bolshoi Krasnokholmsky Bridge

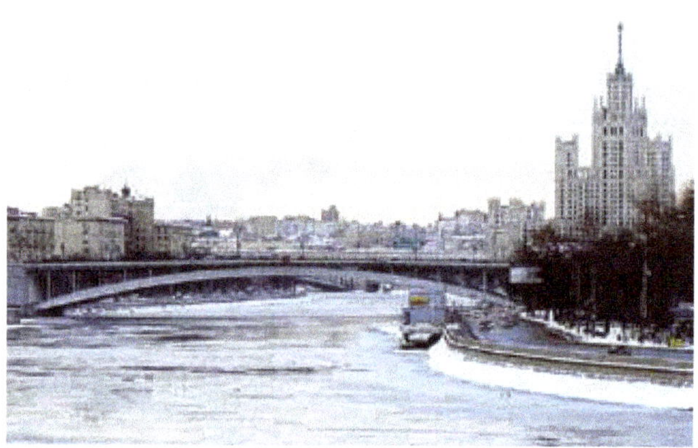

THE HOUSE I LIVE IN appeared in Soviet cinemas during the Thaw, a period that introduced a relative and temporary relaxation of the strict rules that mandated what is artistically permissible in the Soviet Union. The film's plotline follows the lives of two families over a period of ten years, starting with their relocation to a newly-built apartment on the outskirts of Moscow in 1935 and ending with the conclusion of World War II. As the Davydov and Volynsky families settle down and make plans for their future, Sergei (Vladimir Zemlyanikin) and Galya (Zhanna Bolotova) grow up and become romantically involved. Serëzha, from a working-class background, and Galya, from a well-to-do family, have their differences but the appearance of normalcy and the pursuit of romantic dreams are poignantly disrupted by the Nazi invasion. On the eve of the war, Serëzha and Galya go out for a stroll along the embankment of the Moskva River and stop at the Bolshoi Krasnokholmsky Bridge, while in the background we can hear the song 'Silence at Rogozhsky Gates' (music by Yuri Biryukov, lyrics by Alexei Fatyanov, 1957), the historical name for the area. The directors show the vast, empty spaces and the silence of the city that are to be filled with the hopes and aspirations of the new generation, aspirations cut short by the war. The film draws attention to the shaping of individual lives by historic events and although many of the characters disappear or die, as does Galya, Serëzha survives the war and returns to his Moscow home, ending the film on an optimistic note. ➻ ***Rad Borislavov***

Scene description: *Sergei and Galya take a walk down the embankment on the eve of World War II*
Timecode for scene: *0:47:00 – 0:48:38*

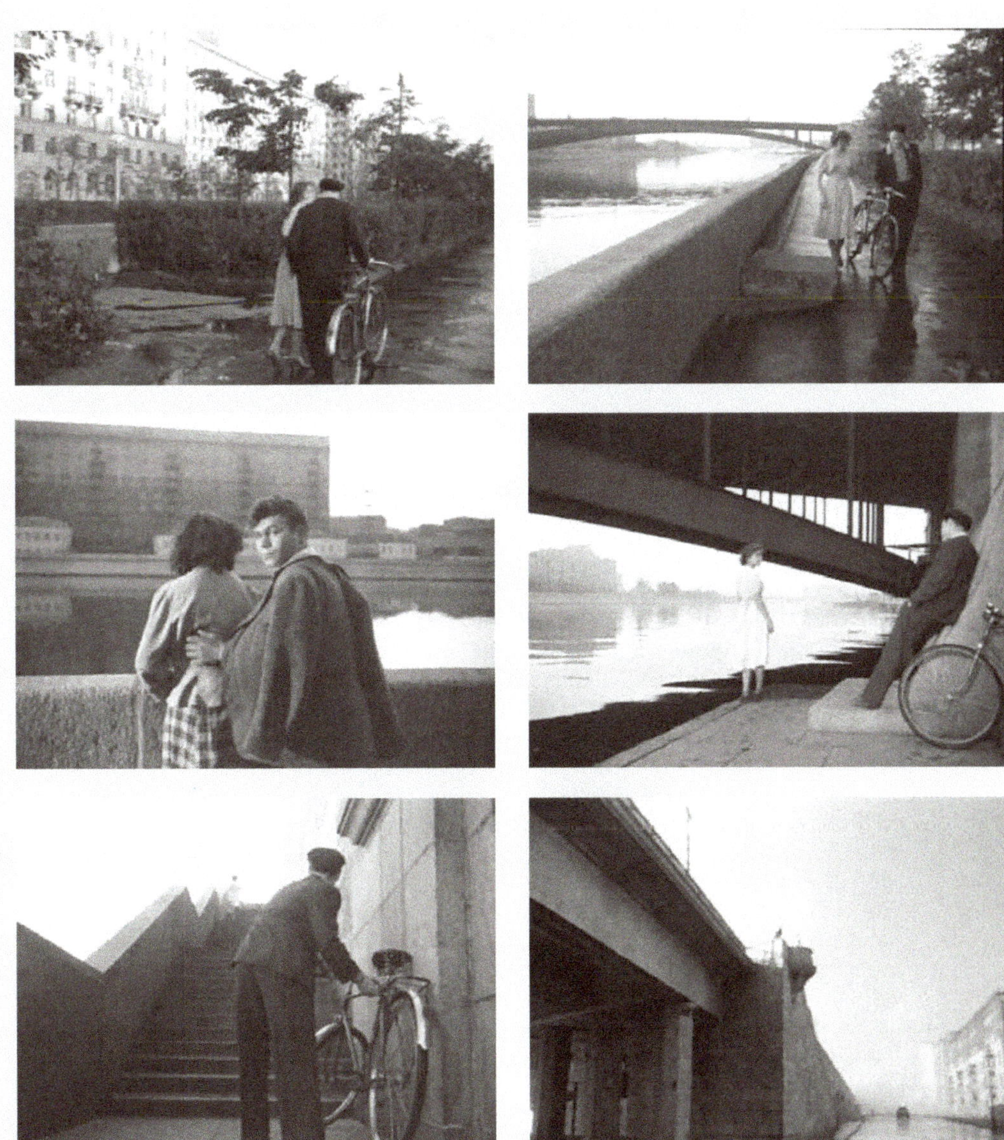

THE STEAMROLLER AND THE VIOLIN/ KATOK I SKRIPKA (1960)

LOCATION

Rostovskaya Embankment 5

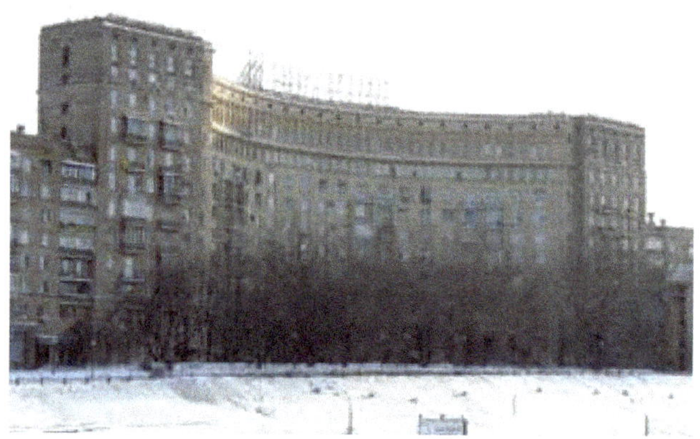

ANDREI TARKOVSKY'S short film *The Steamroller and the Violin*, set in the Moscow of the early 1960s, was his diploma project for the All-Union State Film Institute (VGIK). Co-written with Andrei Konchalovsky, it chronicles the bond between a steamroller, Sergei (Vladimir Zamansky), and the young violinist Sasha (Igor Fomchenko). Set on an early spring day, most of the film's action occurs in the yard of Alexei Shchusev's so-called 'house of architects' on Rostovskaya Embankment, overlooking the Moskva River and the Kiev Railway Station that was built by Ivan Rerberg, the grandfather of Georgi Rerberg, who would later work as cinematographer on Tarkovsky's *Zerkalo/Mirror* (1974). Later, on the way from his house to the music school, the 7-year-old pauses, fascinated by the playful gleaming of the sun on the mirrors displayed in the shop window of a store. Looking at the window, he sees multiple reflections of himself, of passers-by, and of nearby buildings, as well as distant buildings, including the Dormition Cathedral and Ivan-the-Great Bell Tower. This familiar view of the cathedral is foregrounded by the construction cranes of the Kremlin Palace of Congresses, which would be completed only a year later. The Kremlin is not near Sasha's music school, and these shots are superimposed. This scene juxtaposes old architecture and Soviet-era buildings through the perspective of a boy who is building a friendship with a constructor of this new Moscow. ➻*Nadja Berkovich*

Photo © Birgit Beumers

Scene description: Sergei takes Sasha for a ride on his steamroller
Timecode for scene: 0:12:59 – 0:17:50

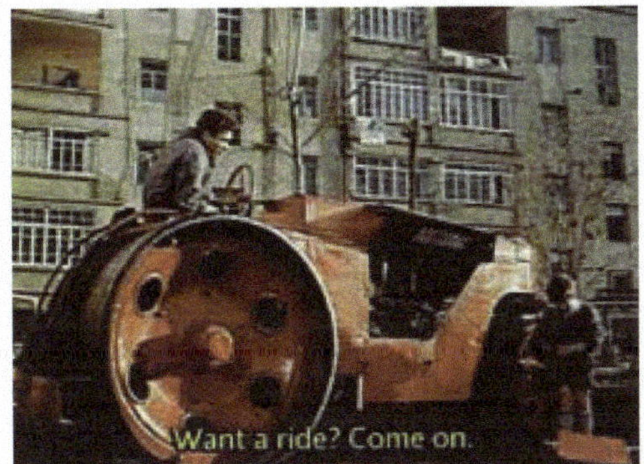

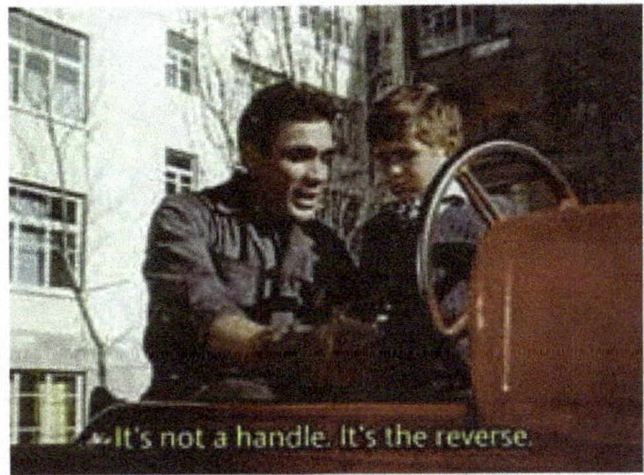

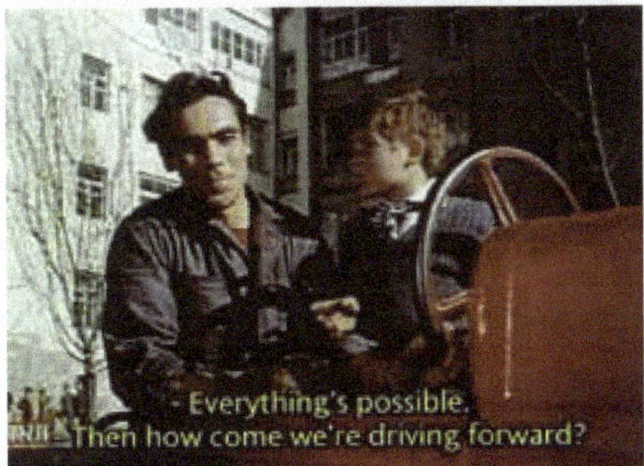

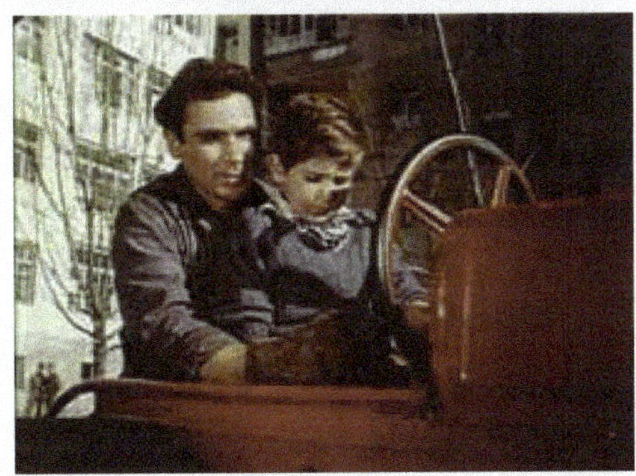

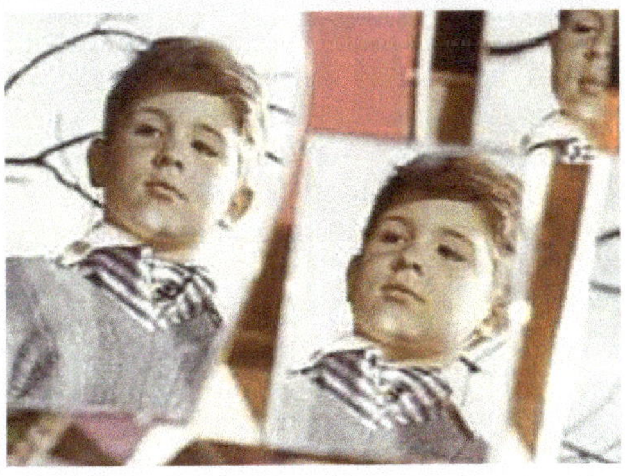

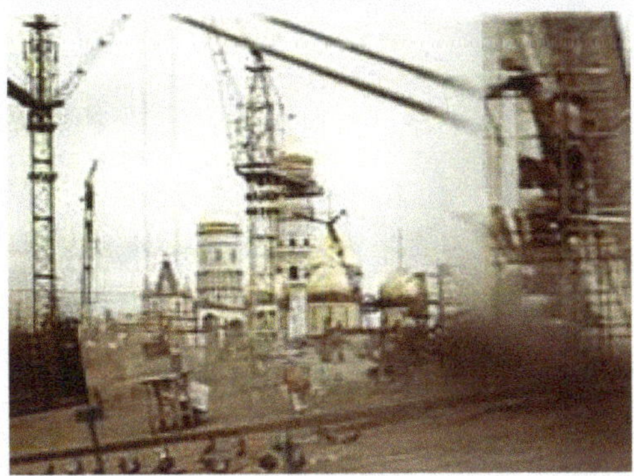

WALKING THE STREETS OF MOSCOW/ IA SHAGAIU PO MOSKVE (1963)

GUM Department Store

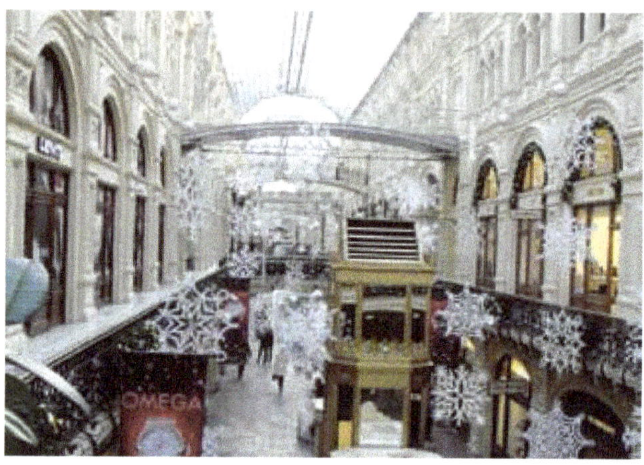

IN *WALKING THE STREETS OF MOSCOW* the young protagonist Kolya (Nikita Mikhalkov) facilitates many new friendships and encounters during a long day that follows his hard night shift building the Moscow metro. On his way home he crosses paths with Volodya (Alexei Loktev), an aspiring writer from Siberia, who has come to Moscow to discuss his work with a famous author. The two young men become friends and Kolya invites Volodya to stay at his apartment. As Volodya goes sightseeing before his appointment with the author, Kolya and his old friend Sasha (Yevgeni Steblov) head to the Department Store GUM to buy a suit for Sasha's wedding. At GUM they encounter Volodya, who is subsequently introduced to Alëna (Galina Polskikh), a music shop salesgirl, and Kolya's love interest. The friends' encounter at GUM, the largest Soviet department store and symbol of Soviet consumer culture on the eastern side of Red Square, was as circumstantial as it was unsurprising. The department store was famous for the best selection of consumer goods in the USSR and therefore became a major attraction of the capital, along with Red Square, St Basil's Cathedral, and the Lenin Mausoleum. The building was constructed between 1890 and 1893, creating three trading rows under an enormous glass ceiling-skylight engineered by Vladimir Shukhov. Following the 1917 Revolution GUM was nationalized and first continued to serve as a department store, before being converted into an office building in 1928. In 1953 it became a department store again.
⮡ Sasha Rindisbacher

Photo © Birgit Beumers

Directed by Georgi Daneliya
Scene description: *Volodya, Sasha and Kolya at GUM*
Timecode for scene: *0:22:30 – 0:24:30*

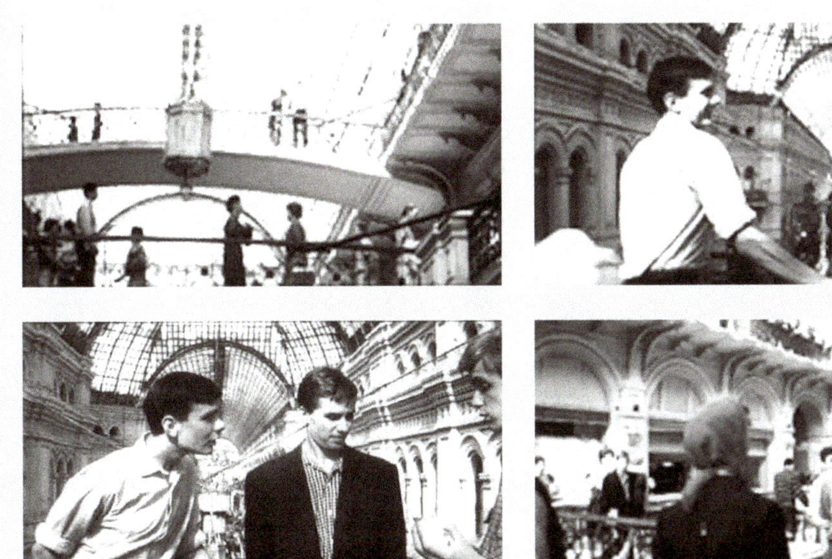

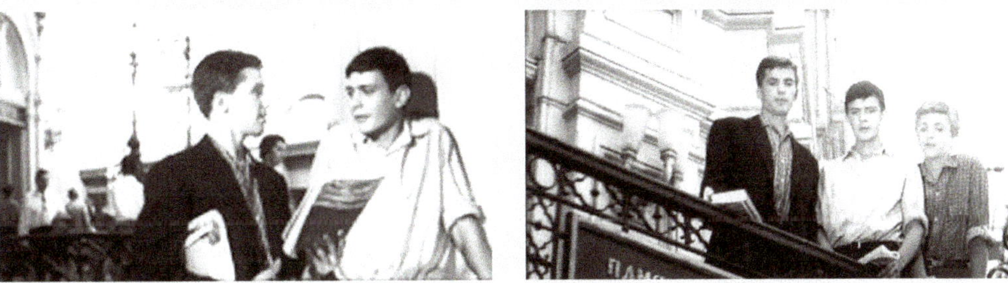

ILYICH'S GATE (AKA I AM TWENTY)/ ZASTAVA IL'ICHA (AKA MNE DVADTSAT' LET) (1965)

Lubyanka Square, towards Okhotny Ryad

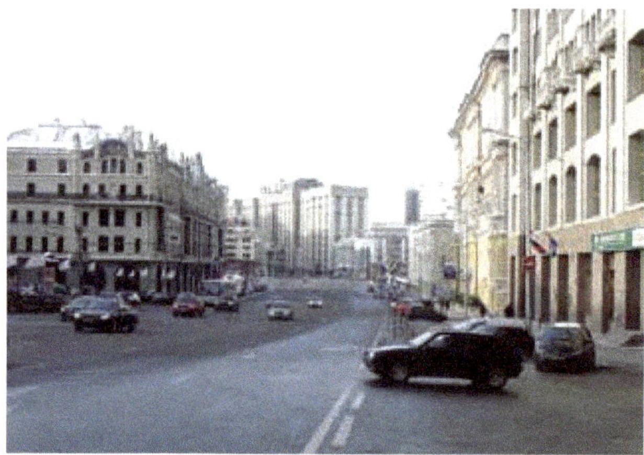

ILYICH'S GATE may be regarded as a film-encyclopaedia of early 1960s Moscow, including – as it does – so many small details of that period. It portrays a Moscow of communal courtyard scenes containing a vitality that seems almost uncharacteristically southern and is reminiscent of Marlen Khutsiev's native Tbilisi or of Odessa, where he shot his early films. Demolition works point to how the city of Moscow is on the cusp of immense transformations, while the scenes of the poetry reading at the Polytechnical Museum indicate the hopes and the spirit of the Thaw. Generational issues and the theme of the war are given especial emphasis both at the beginning and the end of the film. The early morning scenes in Moscow are some of the most lyrical cinematic images of this period. The May Day demonstration symbolizes a Moscow in motion, where private and public spaces still converge, representing neither the perfect regimentation of Stalinist parades nor the apathy and cynicism of the Stagnation. The optimism of the poetry reading and the May Day parade give way to a more sombre and melancholic mood, where conscience and ideals struggle with self-doubt. The often unprincipled compromises of the older generation symbolize the pressures under which Sergei (Valentin Popov) and his friends are destined to live. Even the May Day parade makes its way through Lubyanka Square and past the KGB headquarters. ⊷*Giuliano Vivaldi*

Scene description: May Day parade
Timecode for scene: 0:52:49 – 0:57:21

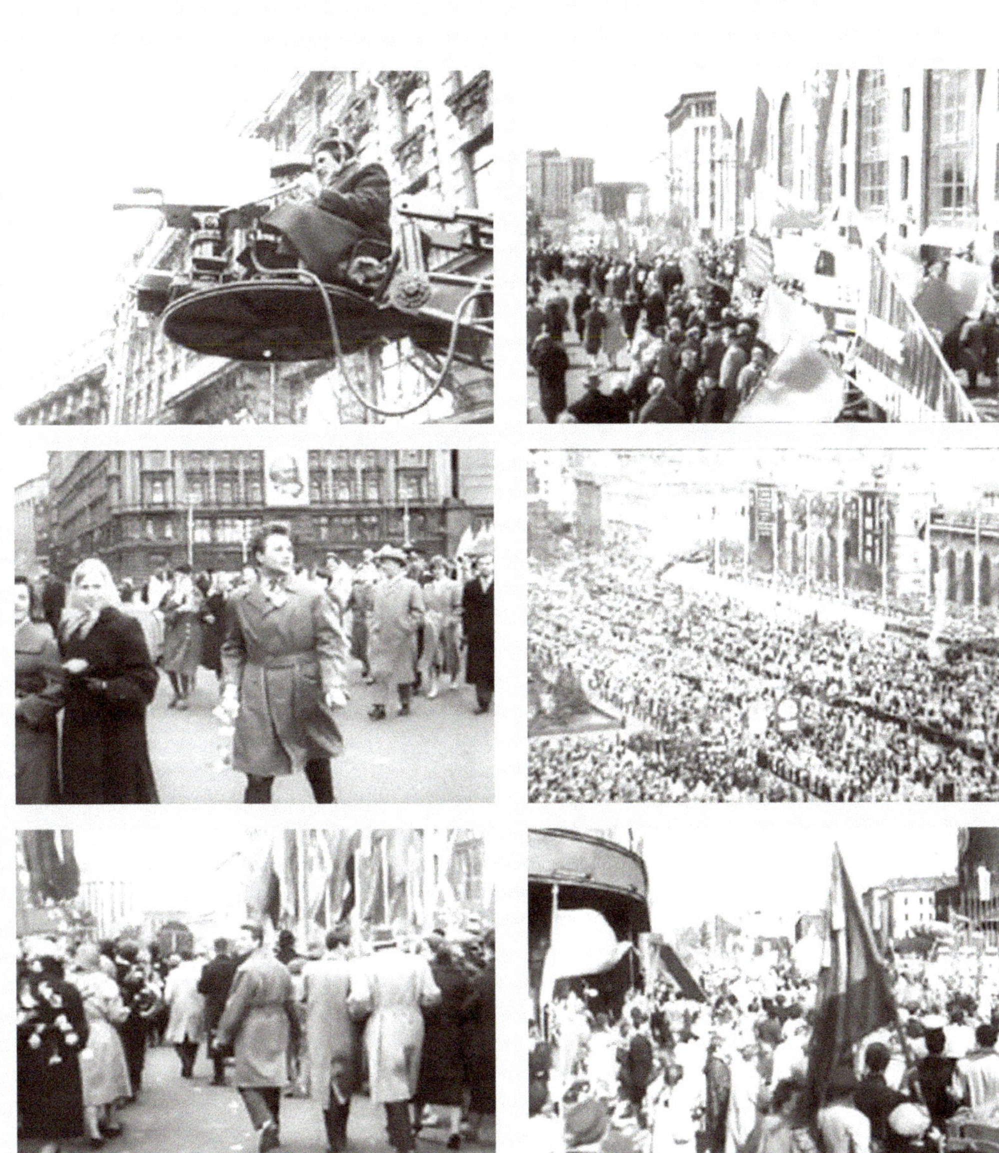

Images © 1965 Gorky Film Studio

JULY RAIN/IUL'SKII DOZHD' (1966)

Red Square and Theatre (Sverdlov) Square

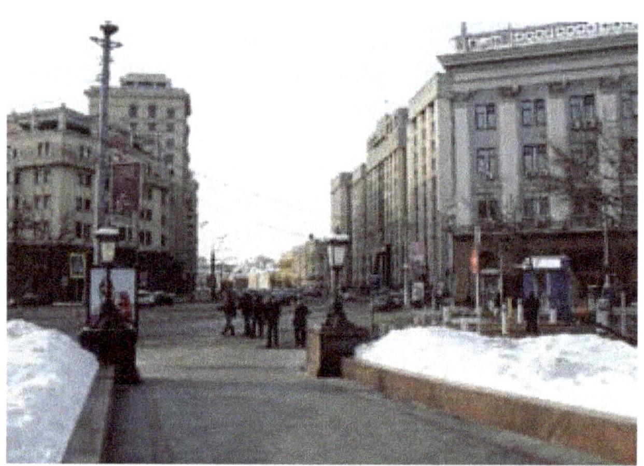

MARLEN KHUTSIEV'S *July Rain* portrays Moscow as a vibrant backdrop to the lives of the stylish twenty- and thirty-somethings at the centre of its narrative. Quintessential 'Thaw-era' cinema, *July Rain* begins with a long series of tracking shots down a bustling Moscow street, while the film's midpoint features travelling shots through many of Moscow's streets, all set to a jazzy a cappella version of Bach. But it is at the film's end when Moscow and its people truly shine, as Lena (Yevgeniya Uralova), having finally resolved a major ambiguity in her life by rejecting a marriage proposal, walks out of a pedestrian tunnel and into the spring air of central Moscow and the Alexander Gardens by the Kremlin. After purchasing apples from a street vendor, she wanders past the entrance to Red Square, where workers are setting up for Victory Day celebrations. It is indeed 9 May and Lena finds herself at a gathering of aging veterans on Theatre Square (then called Sverdlov Square) by the Bolshoi Theatre. With Leonid Utësov's rendition of World War II-song 'The Road to Berlin' (1945) ringing out the veterans embrace and Lena walks by, perhaps contemplating her own personal victory but also admiring the passion and heroism of those who defended their city and the country from the Nazis. The film ends amidst a crowd of young people who have also gathered at the entrance to the Bolshoi. Khutsiev's camera fixates on these young faces, revealing a new generation that has its own, less heroic battles to fight. **•> Tim Harte**

Scene description: *Lena strolls through central Moscow amidst Victory Day celebrations*
Timecode for scene: *1:36:02 – 1:43:05*

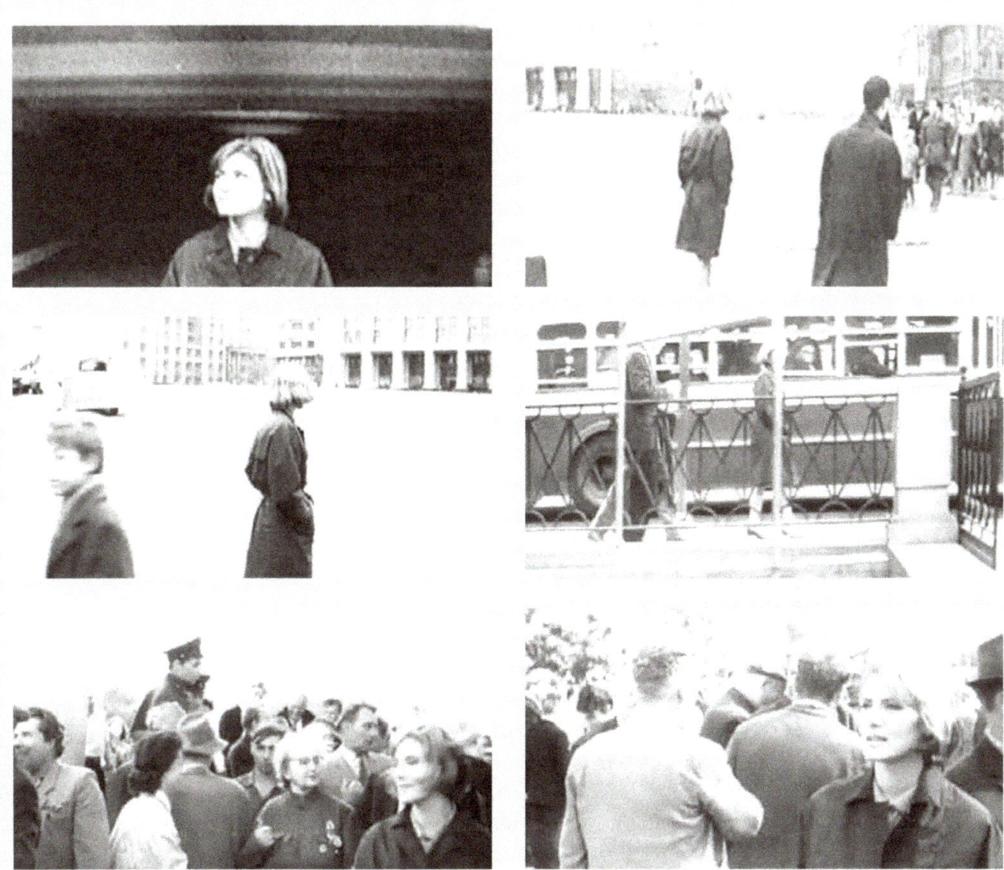

SITES OF PRODUCTION AND DEMONSTRATION

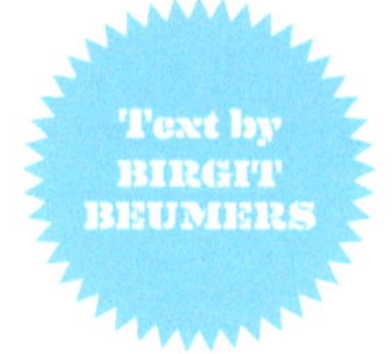

CINEMA MADE its debut in France on 28 December 1895 at the Grand Café in Paris, presented by Auguste and Louis Lumière. A few months later, the Lumières toured their new invention across Europe and the United States, including Russia's capital, St Petersburg. First presented on 4 May 1896 at a fairground in the Aquarium Park (nowadays the territory of the city's film studio, Lenfilm), the 'cinematograph' arrived in Moscow at a fair in the Hermitage Theatre and Gardens on 26 May.

The cinematograph then embarked on a tour of Russia, presenting the new attraction to the masses and providing cheap entertainment. Films were mostly shown in booths at fairs and exhibitions rather than in stationary venues. In 1903 two 'electric theatres' opened in Moscow, thereby attracting a different audience: the urban middle class and bourgeoisie. By 1913 Moscow boasted around 70 cinemas, and the exhibition sector was even larger in St Petersburg. However, production soon centred in Moscow, which had fifteen studios.

The first film studio was opened in 1907 in St Petersburg by Alexander Drankov, an official Duma photographer. Then the former army captain Alexander Khanzhonkov opened a trading company in Moscow in 1908, which became one of Russia's leading production studios. From a merchant family, Iosif Ermoliev had studied and worked in the finance section of Pathé Moscow before venturing into film production in 1914.

By the time of the Revolution, there were a number of studios operating in Moscow, and many of them moved south, into the territories still held by the Whites, in the hope the Bolsheviks could not hold on to power. On 4 March 1918 the closure of cinemas was prohibited in order to stop the disappearance of projection equipment, and on 27 August 1919 the film industry was fully nationalized. With this final closure, many producers, but also actors and directors, emigrated.

Goskino, the State Film Department, was established in 1922 with the remit to distribute films; it was replaced in 1924 by Sovkino. At the same time, the company Mezhrabpomfilm continued to receive support from the German-based International Workers' Aid. By the 1920s, only different 'factories' of Sovkino and Mezhrabpomfilm were operating in Moscow: the premises of the former Khanzhonkov Studio on Zhitnaya Street were occupied by the first factory of Goskino.

In 1930 Soyuzkino was established as the sole body to produce and control films. The Film Institute VGIK (All-Union State Institute of Cinematography), originally founded in 1919 as a film school (GTK, State Film Technicum) – established directors' courses in September 1932, which were directed by Sergei Eisenstein after his return from Hollywood; in 1934 the Film Institute became a college.

On the basis of Mezhrabpomfilm, which was dissolved in 1936, the children's studio Soyuzdetfilm was established in 1936; it was transformed into the Gorky Film Studio in 1948, and renamed in 1963 as Gorky Film Studio for Children and Youth Film. It is located on the northern edge of the city, next to the Film Institute.

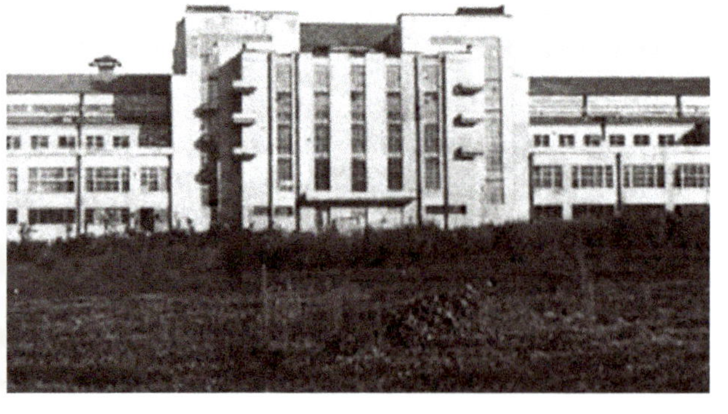

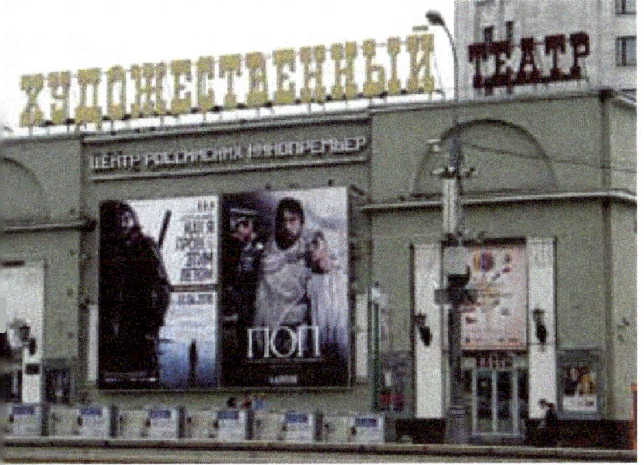

In the 1920s a decision had been taken to build a cinema city, Moskinokombinat. On 20 November 1927 the foundation was laid for a new complex on Sparrow Hills (then Lenin Hills), and the 1st and 3rd factory moved to the new site in January 1931; the studio was named Mosfilm in 1935. In 1947 the studio acquired as its logo the image of Vera Mukhina's sculpture 'Worker and Kolkhoz Woman', created for the Paris World Exhibition of 1937. During the war the studio, along with other crews from Leningrad and Kiev, was evacuated to Alma-Ata to form the Central United Film Studio (TsOKS). Mosfilm boasts a number of technical innovations and patents, from colour to kinopanorama and 3D.

After the war, the film-maker Ivan Pyriev became head of Mosfilm, leading the studio from 1954–57 and using his influence to support young film-makers who had just graduated from the Film Institute. Mosfilm, as well as other studios, was run with an artistic council that vetted all scripts and films, and with 'creative units' that decentralized film production. Pyriev, who went on to found the Film-makers' Union, was succeeded by the officials Vladimir Surin (1959–70) and Nikolai Sizov (1970–86). Not until perestroika did film-makers again take the headship: Vladimir Dostal (1987–98) and Karen Shakhnazarov (since 1998).

Moscow had several historical purpose-built cinemas, such as the 'Kinofon' in the Solodnikov Arcade in Moscow which opened as early as 1903. The 'Arts' ('Khudozhestvenny') Cinema on Moscow's Arbat opened in 1909 with 400 seats; it was refurbished and designed by the leading architect of the period, Fëdor Shekhtel (Franz Schechtel, b.1859–d.1926) in 1912–13, now with 900 seats. In 1921 it became the first cinema of Goskino, and the public premiere of Eisenstein's *Bronenosets Potemkin/The Battleship Potemkin* (1925) took place here. In 1931 the cinema hosted the first sound film (Nikolai Ekk's *Road to Life*); and the first colour film (Ekk's *Grunia Kornakova*) was also shown here in 1936. In 1955 it became the first widescreen cinema in Moscow. Nowadays the Khudozhestvenny Cinema is part of the Moscow cinema network Moskino, and has one auditorium with 609 and another with 50 seats.

During the Soviet era, many cinemas were built in the fast-growing suburbs; they were mostly large, single-auditorium buildings. One of the largest cinemas was the October, which – after its refurbishment – is a multiplex with eleven screens owned by the Karo network. When it originally opened in 1968, the October was equipped with a special 3D screen: the small hall with 442 seats was truly universal, fitted with advanced film projection and sound equipment for the demonstration of 70 mm, widescreen, standard and 3D films. The hall had two screens: a large aluminium screen for the demonstration of 3D films in the Polaroid method, which could be raised to uncover a lens raster screen for the demonstration of 3D films without glasses.

The Rossiya was built in 1961 on the site of the Strastnoy Monastery and opened with Georgi Daneliya's *Ia shagaiu po Moskve/Walking the Streets of Moscow*. In 1997 it underwent reconstruction and became the Pushkinsky, part of Karo Film and for many years a main site for the Moscow International Film Festival with its impressive screen of 10 by 20 meters. In 2012 the building was sold to Stage Entertainment for musical performances.

The Cinema Centre (Kinotsentr) was built for the Film-makers' Union of the USSR in the 1970s. After a dispute over ownership following the collapse of the Soviet Union between the Confederation of the Film-makers' Unions of the former Soviet republics and the Russian Film-makers' Union, the building was put to commercial exploitation. This meant, among other things, that the Museum of Cinema had to vacate the purpose-built premises it had occupied there since 1984. Today, offices and a multiplex with 22 screens occupy the building. The Museum of Cinema remains without an exhibition space. ✛

> **Mosfilm, as well as other studios, was run with an artistic council that vetted all scripts and films, and with 'creative units' that decentralized film production.**

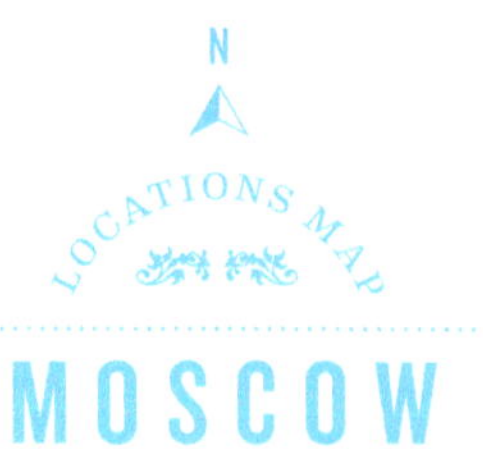

N
LOCATIONS MAP
MOSCOW
maps are only to be taken as approximates
Sokolniki
Khoroshevo
Maryina Roshcha
21
Tverskoy District
Basmann District
Presnensky District
26
25
24
Arbat
23
Dorogomilovo
Zamoskvorechie
Tagansky District
20
22
Khamovniki
Donskoy District
Ramenki

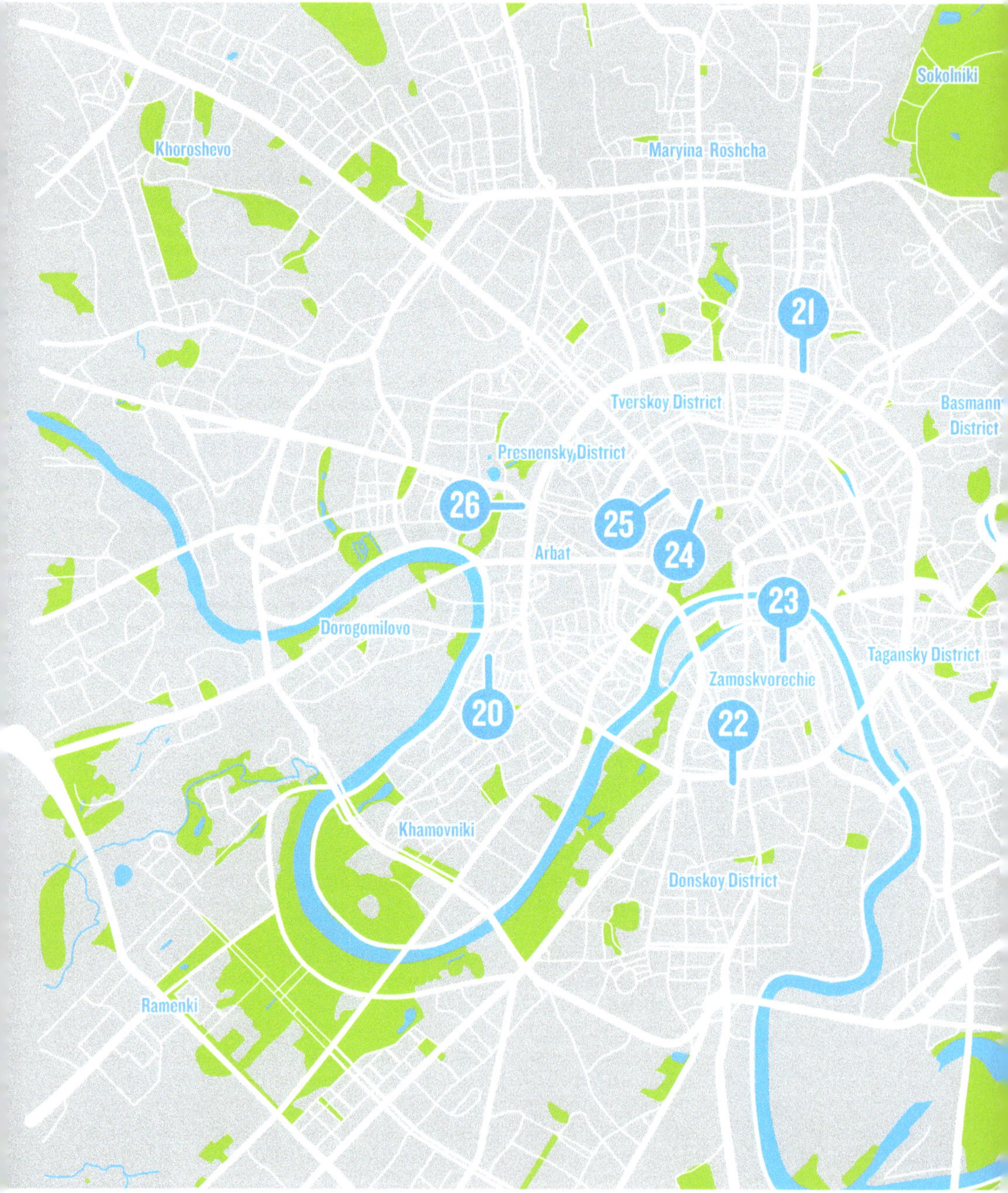

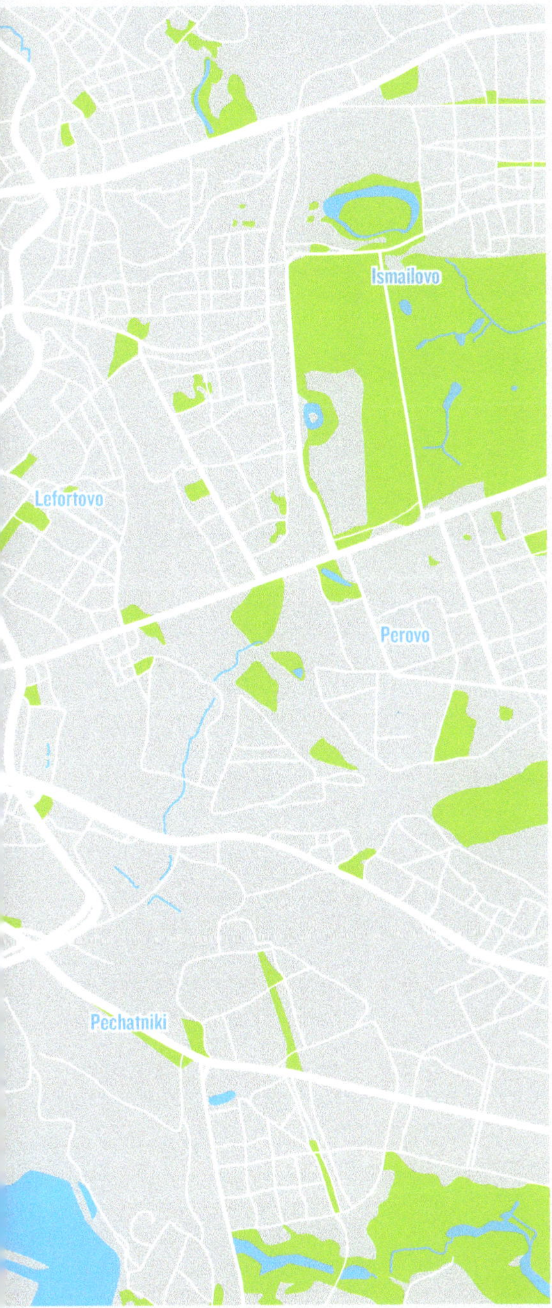

Ismailovo
Lefortovo
Perovo
Pechatniki

THREE POPLARS ON PLYUSHCHIKHA STREET/ TRI TOPOLIA NA PLIUSHCHIKHE (1967)

 Rostovskaya Embankment 5

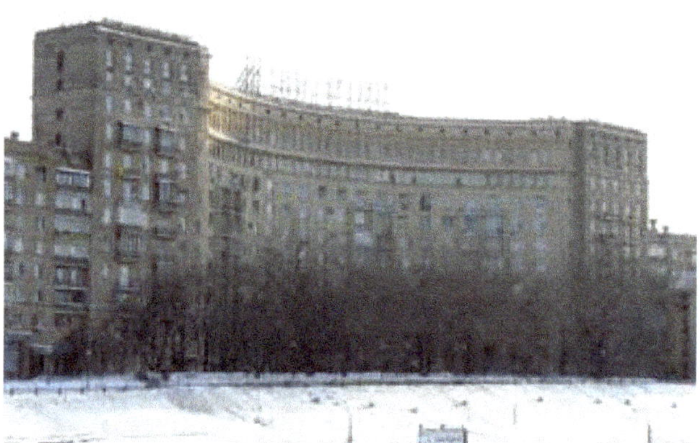

THREE POPLARS ON PLYUSHCHIKHA STREET was shot in the vicinity of Plyushchikha, a cosy Moscow street situated near Smolensk Square, between the Moskva River and the Garden Ring. The exact filmic location, Rostovskaya Embankment 5, is also known as 'House of Architects', which was projected in the 1930s by Alexei Shchusev, the chief architect of Stalin's 'Empire Style'. Shchusev's building on the high banks of the Moskva River is famous for its peculiar semi-circular shape. The house was originally planned as part of a more grandiose residential complex. The project was only realized after the architect's death. Shot from the north-western angle, the film features the building's backyard, not its recognizable front. This is where a taxi drops off the protagonist Nyura (Tatyana Doronina), who has just arrived in the capital from a village to visit her sister-in-law. The taxi driver Sasha (Oleg Yefremov) asks Nyura out on a date and waits for her near the 'Three Poplars' cafe, hence the film's title. Nyura decides to go out with the driver, but then she fails to open the door. The scenes in Three Poplars cafe were filmed on the set, which created the replica of an actual cafe on Shabolovka Street, where the original story by Alexander Borshchagovsky was set. However, in the 1960s, Shabolovka was irrevocably associated with the television centre located there, and Tatyana Lioznova suggested substituting it for the more neutral Plyushchikha neighbourhood, a typical residential area of the old Moscow. **➻Sasha Razor**

Scene description: The peasant Nyura comes to Moscow to visit her sister-in-law
Timecode for scene: 0:53:26 – 0:55:35

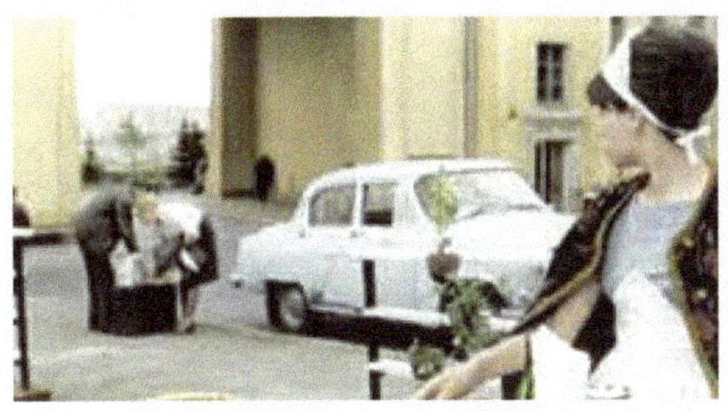
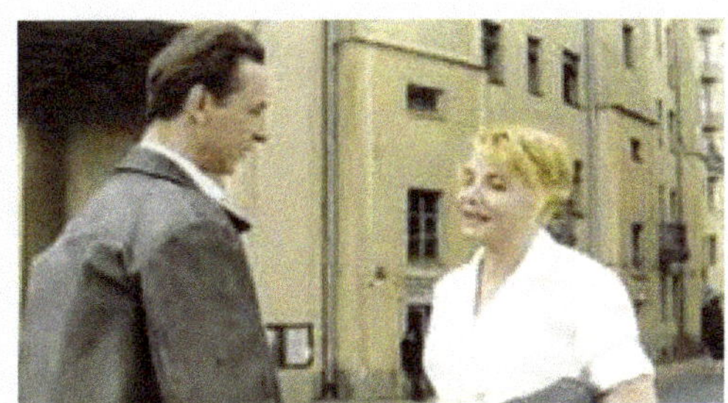

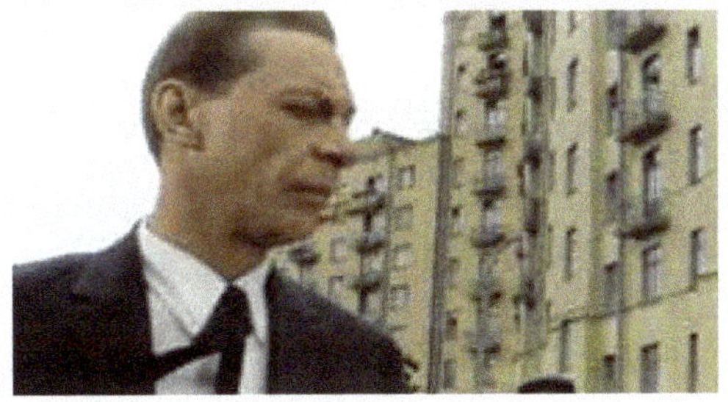
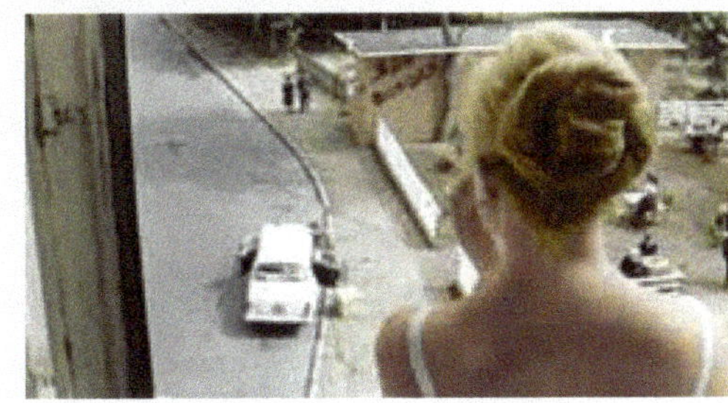

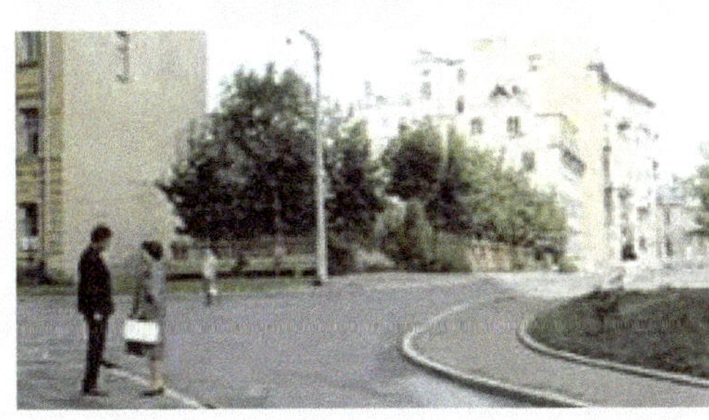
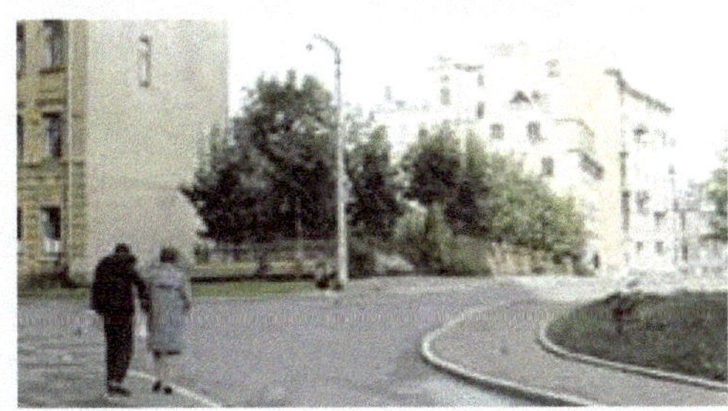

BELORUSSIAN STATION/ BELORUSSKII VOKZAL (1970)

Sklifosovsky Hospital

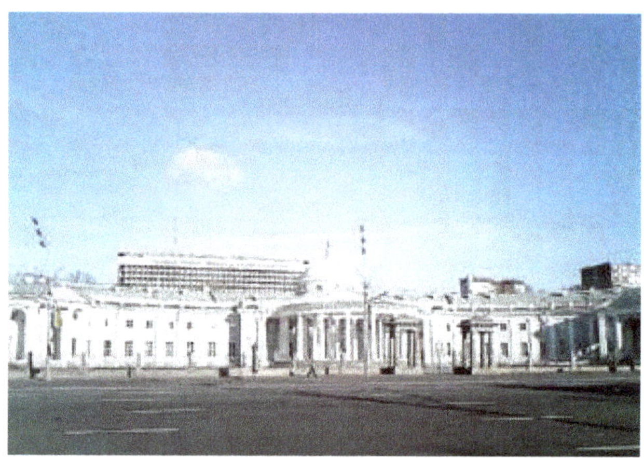

BELORUSSIAN STATION portrays a conflict between the older generation of Soviet people who lived through the trauma of World War II and the new, carefree and materialistic youth raised in the relative prosperity of Brezhnev-era socialism. The narrative focuses on four World War II veterans who reunite at the funeral of a fifth veteran, 25 years after the war. They recall their old camaraderie and collectivist spirit, and lament over the new generation's empty and thoughtless lives. The most dramatic moment in the film occurs when the four friends find a badly injured young man who needs to be taken to the emergency room. They hitchhike in the hope that somebody would drive him to the hospital, but nobody stops. When finally they form a human barricade and force one car to stop, the driver refuses to take any passengers. The four friends kick him out of the car, and one of them – together with the driver's girlfriend, who seems to have remorse about her friend's behaviour – delivers the injured young man to the Sklifosovsky hospital. While the patient receives treatment, the driver and the girl wait for the doctor's diagnosis in tense silence. The film condemns the new Soviet materialism and highlights the older generation's discontentment about the lost spiritual values of the past. The reception room of Sklifosovsky hospital featured in the film is located in the older part of the building that was built in 1803 as a shelter and hospital for the poor. In 1923 the hospital began specializing in emergency medicine, and in 1929 was named after the renowned Russian surgeon and physiologist Nikolai Sklifosovsky. **↪Larissa Rudova and Sasha Rindisbacher**

Scene description: The injured young man is brought into the hospital
Timecode for scene: 0:54:30 – 0:55:40

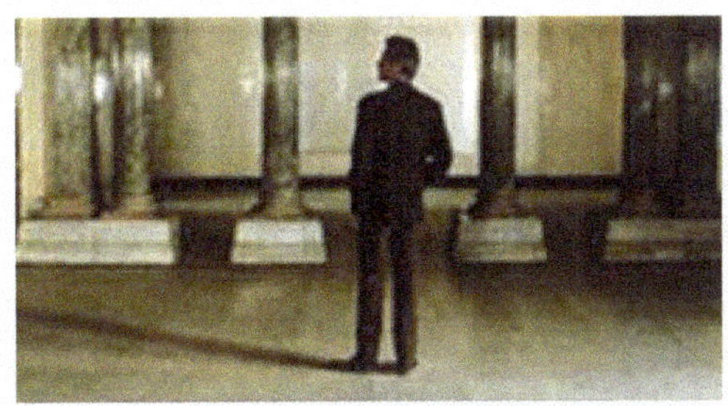
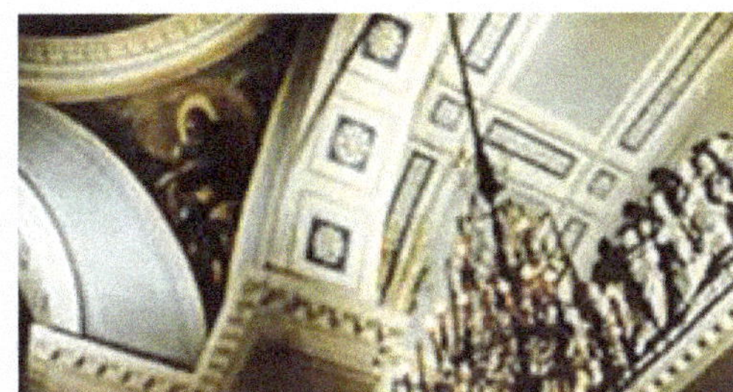

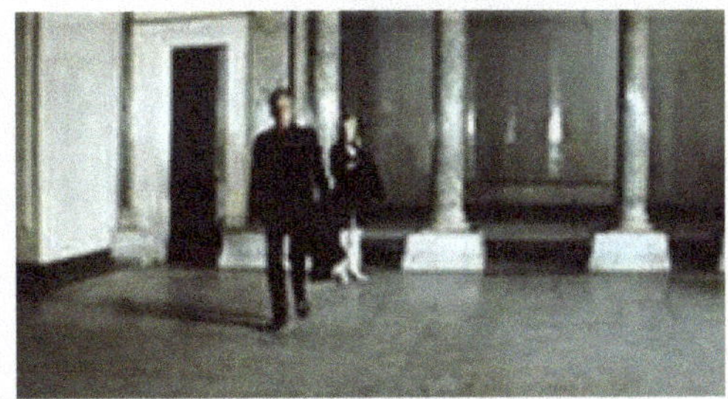
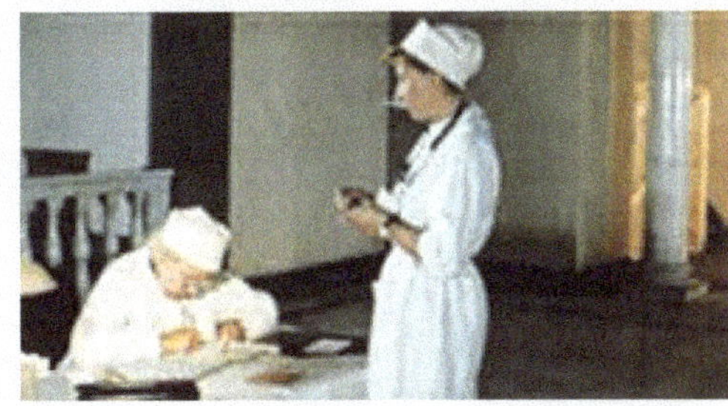

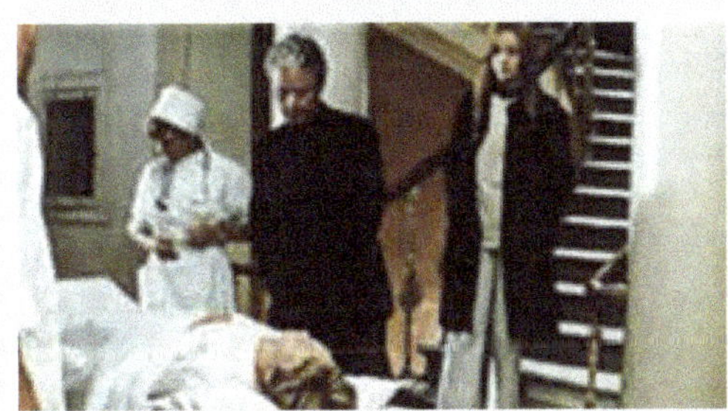
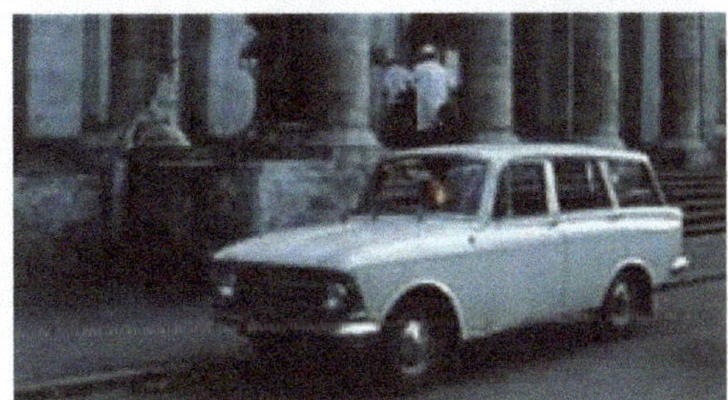

Images © 1970 Mosfilm

HAPPY-GO-LUCKY/PECHKI-LAVOCHKI (1972)

Dobryninsky department store, Korovy val 1

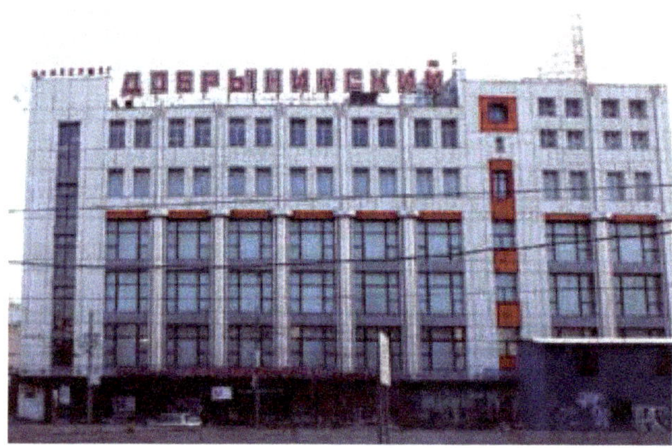

IN VASILI SHUKSHIN'S *Happy-Go-Lucky* the main character, Ivan Rastorguev (Shukshin), is indelibly marked by his identity as a country bumpkin: he is uneducated, gullible and ingenuous, which leads to many comic situations. Ivan, however, is also an honest, hard-working and decent person employed in a kolkhoz, and his mishaps are a commentary on the deep rift between the intelligentsia and the people, with Moscow as the symbolic centre of Soviet civilization and of its backwater peripheries. Venturing outside their Altai village to go on vacation on the Black Sea, Ivan and his wife Nyura encounter a professor of ethnography (Vsevolod Sanaev), who invites them to visit his home in Moscow. The professor is well-intentioned, but his milieu is clearly intellectual, and Ivan and Nyura are ill at ease. The visitors go out shopping with the professor's daughter-in-law (Lyubov Mysheva) in the south of Moscow, an area called Zamoskvorechie (literally, 'beyond the Moskva River'). They visit a famous department store on Dobryninsky Square and mingle with the crowds of shoppers. The professor's daughter-in-law is polite but bored and when she darts into a phone booth, Ivan is visibly tired and glum; he squats next to a kiosk and smokes, reminiscing about happier times in the village. As he gets up to go, he forgets one of the packages and is chided gently by his wife, while in the background viewers can see the imposing department store, an icon of Soviet consumerism, and Ivan's discomfort in the urban setting. **⦿ Rad Borislavov**

Scene description: Ivan and Nyura go out shopping with the professor's daughter
Timecode for scene: 1:13:11 – 1:16:43

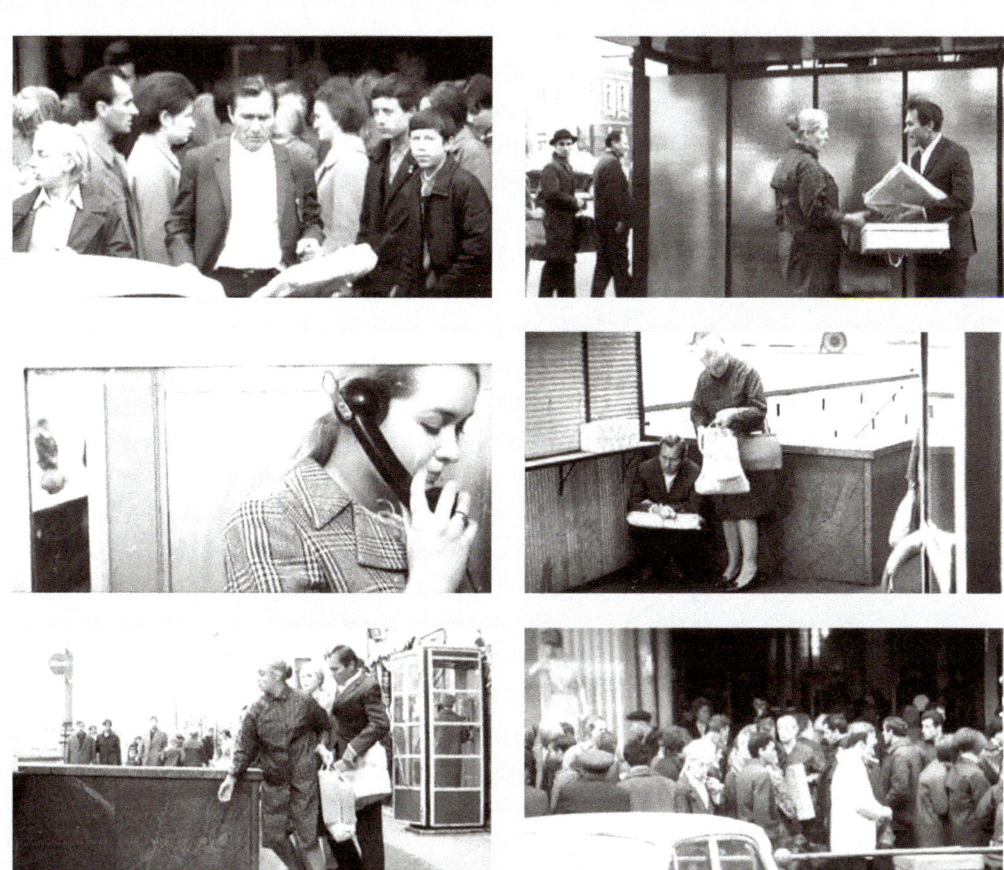

IVAN VASILIEVICH CHANGES PROFESSIONS/ IVAN VASIL'EVICH MENIAET PROFESSIIU (1973)

 Novokuznetskaya Street 13, Bldg 1

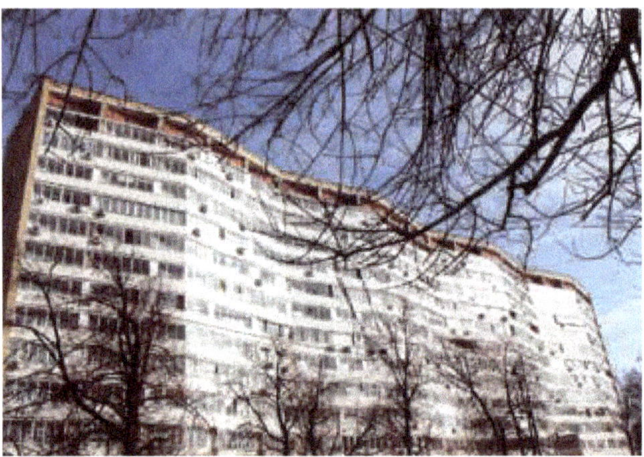

LEONID GAIDAI'S COMEDY *Ivan Vasilievich Changes Professions* is a tale of time travel and mistaken identity in two very different Moscows. After inventing a time machine in his apartment, Engineer Alexander (Shurik) Timofeev (Alexander Demyanenko) sets the machine to travel to Moscow during the reign of Ivan the Terrible. When the portal to the past opens, Tsar Ivan Vasilievich (Yuri Yakovlev) and his guards attack the intruders, damaging the time machine in the process. This traps Tsar Ivan in contemporary Moscow and the superintendent of Shurik's building, Ivan Vasilievich Bunsha (Yuri Yakovlev) in the past. Both Ivans not only have the same name and patronymic, but also look identical to each other. Bunsha assumes the role of Tsar, while Tsar Ivan is mistaken for the building superintendent. In this scene, Tsar Ivan steps out onto the balcony of Shurik's apartment on Novokuznetskaya Street and looks at the cars on the road and the high-rise apartment buildings down the street. He declares the scene beautiful, using the archaic word *lepota*!, further contrasting the ancient Tsar with his modern setting. As he watches the city from the balcony, he is discovered simultaneously by Bunsha's wife Ulyana (Natalya Krachkovskaya) and Shurik's neighbour Anton Shpak (Vladimir Etush), who both mistake him for Bunsha. When Ulyana enters Shurik's apartment to persuade Ivan to come home, insisting that he must be drunk, he calls her a witch and chases her away. Shpak then asks for Ivan's help in finding the man who robbed his apartment, but is also forced out by a knife-wielding Ivan. **•►*Erin Alpert***

Scene description: Tsar Ivan the Terrible looks out over Moscow
Timecode for scene: 1:03:24 – 1:05:11

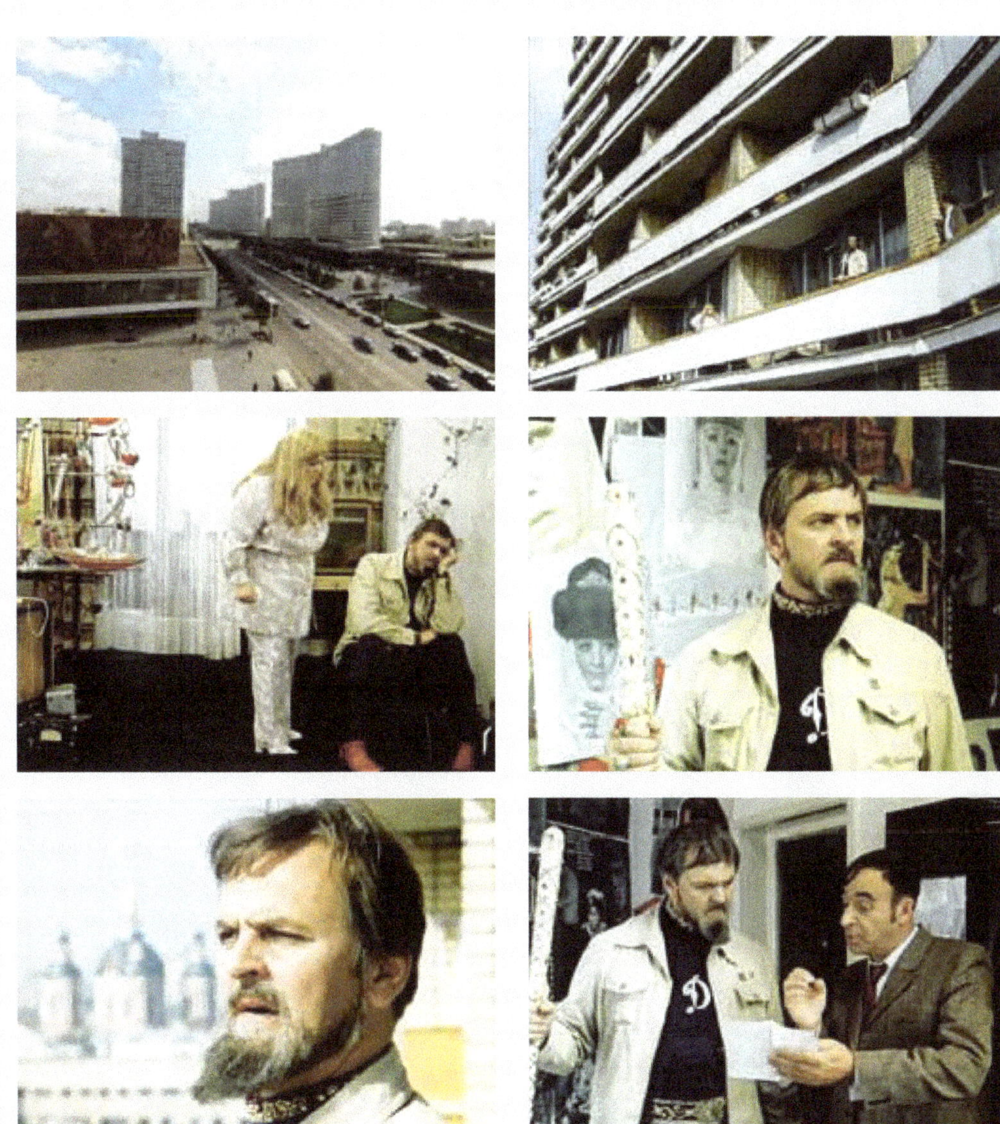

OFFICE ROMANCE/ SLUZHEBNYI ROMAN (1977)

New Arbat; Teatralny proezd; Samotechka; Ploshchad' Nogina; Kuznetsky most 3/6; Bolshoi Gnezdikovsky lane 10 (GITIS)

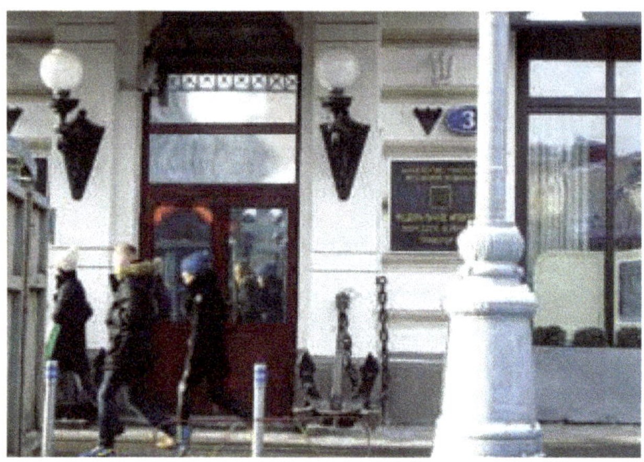

THE FILM'S OPENING SCENE serves up an apt metaphor for the main concerns: a dreary arterial road on a smoggy autumn day sees atomized Soviet commuters hurry to work in an overcrowded Moscow. The grand architecture of the Kremlin and its environs are only glimpsed and the uplifting and triumphalist use of the Moscow skyline elsewhere is undercut by steeply-angled crane shots that emphasize the alienation of the individual in the unfeeling crowd. Lines of workers hurrying through the rainy streets look like mindless ants. They are absorbed in their quotidian cares and the only human contact is the shove in the back of the person blocking the entry to a sardine-crammed trolley-bus. Eldar Ryazanov's *Office Romance* continues the director's preoccupation with the ethical person and love in an increasingly materialistic and callous society. How can the meek, the lonely and the unloved make their way if people lack compassion or simply fail to have regard for others? The result is a characteristically sensitive, funny and sentimental melodrama – the genre which Ryazanov made his own. Similar scenes to the opening are shown throughout the film and are used to cut away from the claustrophobic interior setting – the petty office intrigues, backbiting and final blossoming of romance. However, with one exception – a freak September snowfall that throws autumnal colours into relief and which the director decided to include for posterity – such external scenes do not provide vistas of relief; the cityscapes all reinforce the same questioning mode about the loss of the individual's worth in society's eyes. **➼Jeremy Morris**

Photo © Birgit Beumers

Directed by Eldar Ryazanov
Scene description: *People make their way to work in central Moscow*
Timecode for scene: 0:00:00 – 0:01:40

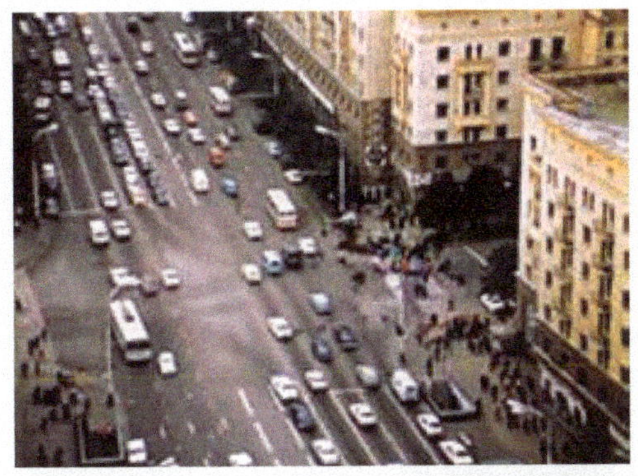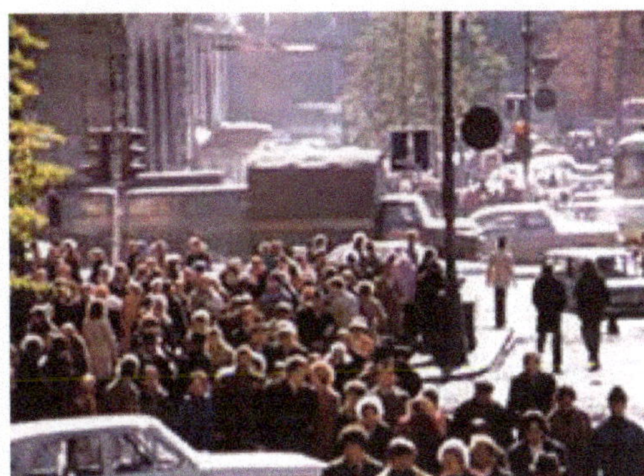

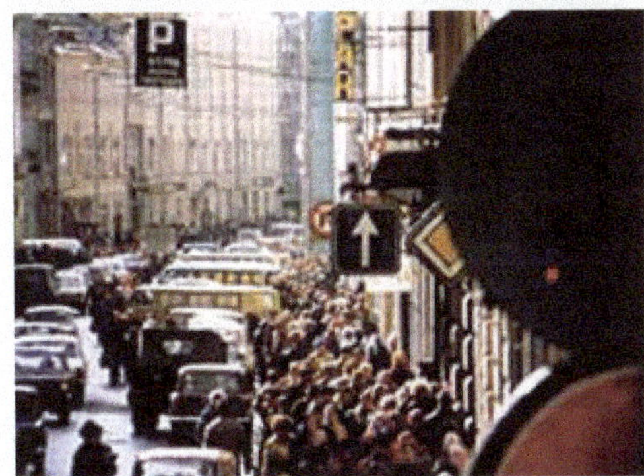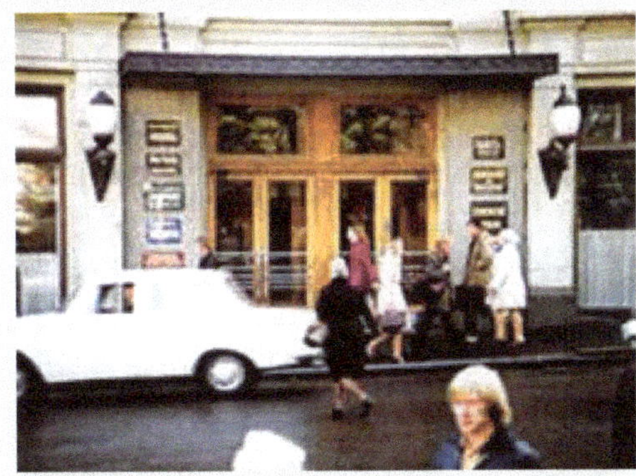

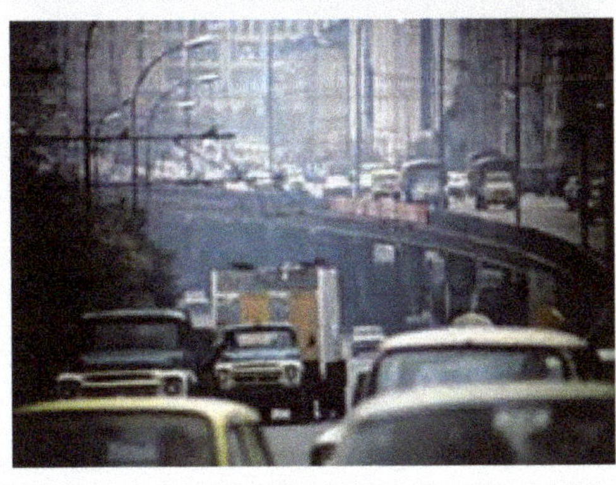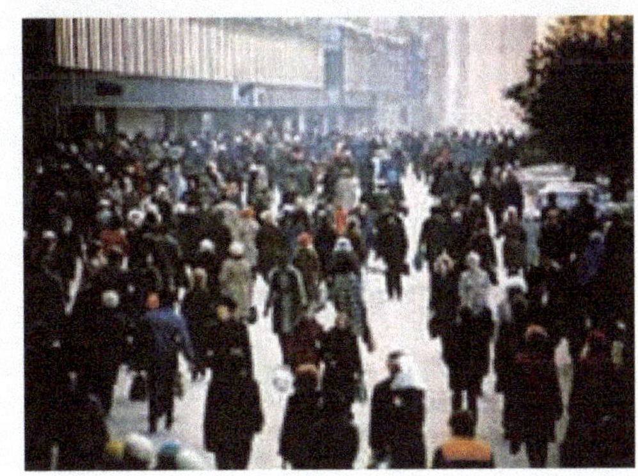

MIMINO (1977)

Bolshoi Theatre, Theatre Square

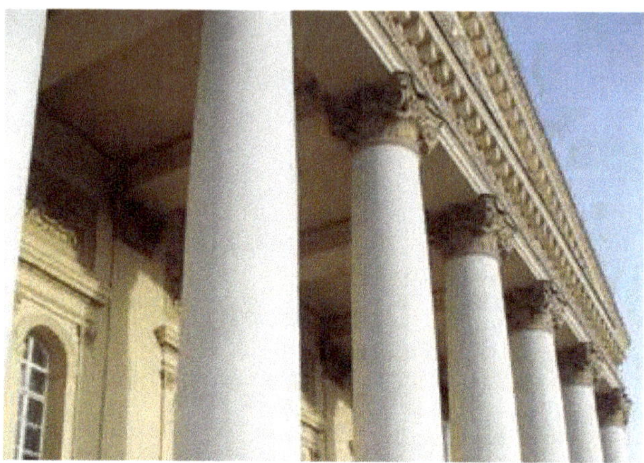

GEORGI DANELIYA'S *Mimino* features a small-time helicopter pilot, Mimino (Vakhtang Kikabidze), from the Georgian mountains. Frustrated by his colleagues' comical ineptitude, Mimino moves to Moscow in search of work as an airline pilot. The film begins and ends in Georgia, juxtaposing sweeping shots of the USSR's idyllic hinterland with dense close-ups of a dark and freezing Moscow. We catch fleeting glimpses of Moscow's landmarks as Mimino struggles to succeed in a crooked city at odds with his naïve amicability. Arrested for an altercation with an old enemy, rejected from the airline and evicted from his lodgings, Mimino is at rock bottom. In this scene, he has arranged to attend an opera with Larissa, a stewardess he briefly met on the runway. She, however, deliberately stands him up. Mimino waits in the icy gloom outside the Bolshoi Theatre, Moscow's most renowned theatre and the epitome of high culture in the capital. We now understand that Moscow is not the city of dreams Mimino believes it to be for outsiders. Daneliya cuts from the disconsolate protagonist on the street to a performance of Verdi's *Il Trovatore* (1853). Mimino attends with a fellow Caucasian, but cannot understand the opera's complexities or Italian libretto anyway. He eventually obtains work as a pilot through a chance case of mistaken identity. Nevertheless, he remains homesick and returns to Georgia's beautiful pastures. *Mimino* highlights a man's attachment to his homeland and snubs the idea of Moscow as a place for every Soviet citizen to aspire to.
➠Ian Garner

Photo © Birgit Beumers

Scene description: Mimino is stood up by his date
Timecode for scene: 0:43:10 – 0:45:20

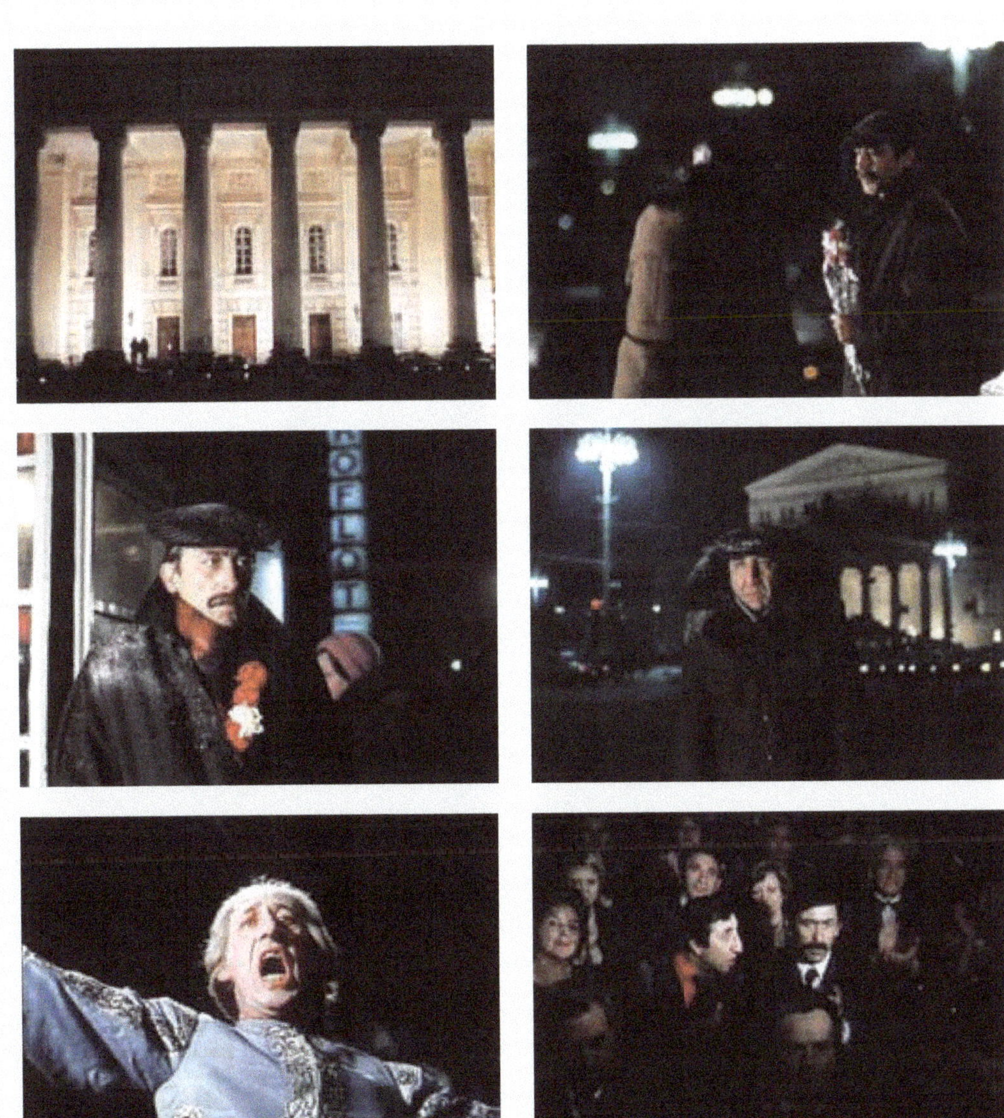

Timages © 1977 Mosfilm

MOSCOW DOES NOT BELIEVE IN TEARS/ MOSKVA SLEZAM NE VERIT (1979)

LOCATION

Vosstanie Square/Kudrinskaya Square (facade); Kotelnicheskaya Embankment (interior)

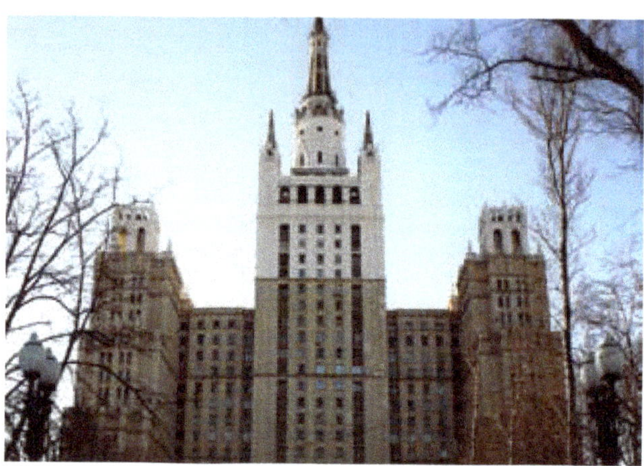

MOSCOW DOES NOT BELIEVE IN TEARS, which won the Academy Award for Best Foreign Language Film in 1980, follows the lives of three female friends over twenty years, from their arrival in Moscow in the late 1950s through their romantic entanglements and professional successes and failures into the late 1970s. Katya, the film's heroine, works her way up the hierarchical ladder to become the director of the factory where she had started as a mechanic in her youth. As the film opens in 1958, Katya's dormitory roommate Lyuba sees life as a lottery: marrying right is the only path to social advancement. She convinces Katya to use Katya's Moscow relatives' apartment, where they have the opportunity to house-sit, as a space for attracting highly-placed, eligible bachelors. The location is key to the scheme: the apartment, on Vosstanie Square, is in one of the so-called 'Seven Sisters' prestigious high-rise buildings erected in the Stalin era. Katya's relatives, like other tenants in the building, are members of the country's cultural elite; the two friends pretend to be their daughters. The ornate structure of the building mirrors the baroque decorations inside the apartment: Soviet society here, despite its professed classlessness, is all about consumerism and class status. The plan ultimately backfires: in the apartment, Katya is seduced and impregnated by Rudolph, a TV cameraman, who believes her to be a professor's daughter and is interested in her as a vehicle for his own social advancement. He abandons her when he learns about her lie and her working-class background.
⤏Sasha Senderovich

Scene description: Katya and Lyuba move into the apartment of Katya's relatives to dog-sit
Timecode for scene: 0:21:54 – 0:28:40

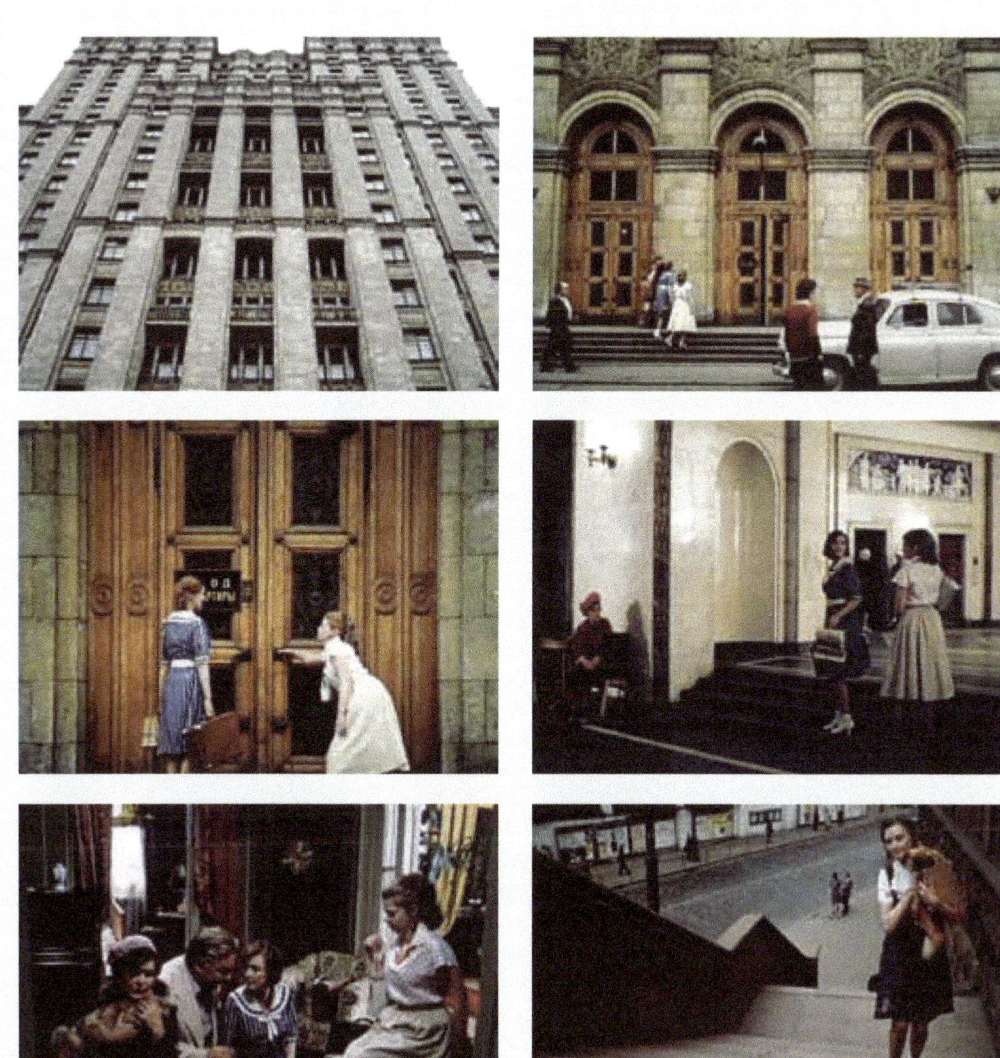

Images © 1979 Mosfilm

URBAN POETICS

Moscow in Films of the 1960s

IN THAW CINEMA, the image of Moscow changes dramatically when compared to Stalin-era films: instead of monumental architecture, private space dominates. Along with an increase in the production of consumer goods and social reforms, Khrushchev launched a campaign to construct five-storey apartment buildings (*khrushchevki*) on the outskirts of Moscow, showing a concern for living standards and placing the individual before industrial progress. These apartments represented the first private spaces many Muscovites ever possessed, and therefore feature in numerous Soviet films, sometimes assuming centre-stage in chamber dramas like Nikita Mikhalkov's *Piat' vecherov/Five Evenings* (1978) or *Bez svidetelei/Without Witnesses* (1982). The 1960s Moscow films, however, paid more attention to the city itself as a reclaimed private space. Streets, squares, parks and even the metro became spaces for chance meetings and romance, for soulful discussions of the human condition, and for long walks at any time of day or night, in contrast to the staid monumentality of Moscow in Stalin-era films. This transformation can be theorized through Henri Lefebvre's distinction between 'dominated' (ideologically created and sustained) and 'appropriated' spaces, produced by lived experience. Such (re)appropriation is evident in a number of Thaw-era films where Moscow was both the setting and a character: *Zastava Il'icha* (aka *Mne dvadtsat' let*)/*Ilyich's Gate* (aka *I am Twenty*) (Marlen Khutsiev, 1961/65), *Ia shagaiu po Moskve*/*Walking the Streets of Moscow* (Georgi Daneliya, 1963), *Iul'skii dozhd'*/July Rain (Marlen Khutsiev, 1966), and Mikhail Kalik's *Liubit'*/*To Love* (1968). These films came to symbolize the Thaw generation with its idealism, vague apprehensions and a fragile sense of newly-found freedom.

The late 1960s saw the ascendancy of the private and the decline of the public in Soviet cinema. The period was also marked by the accentuation of the visual and the devaluation of the verbal. *July Rain* contains an unusually large amount of documentary footage for a fiction film. Moscow of 1966, with its traffic, its throngs of passers-by, its houses and parks and billboards as captured by a travelling camera, plays a prominent part in the film; the city looks genuine and fresh, compared to the vacuous talk of the characters, a loose group of 'golden youths', not all that young, privileged, bored and pretentious. They strive for something larger than everyday life and fail to find it. This film's style has been defined as an 'aesthetic of documentalism'; however, it seems

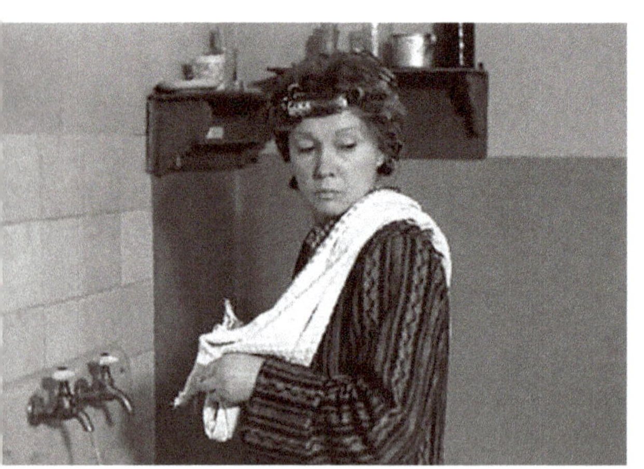

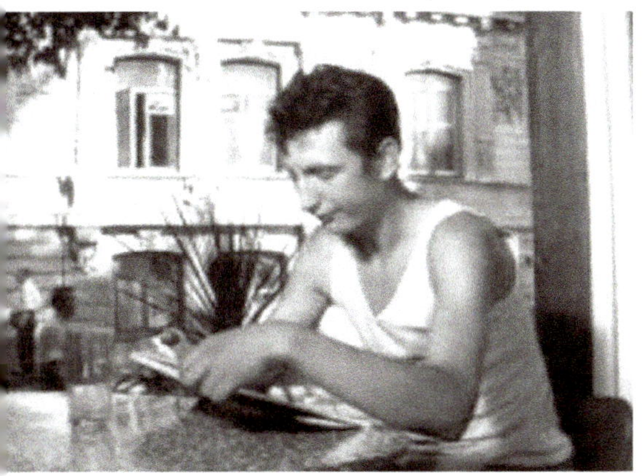

more fitting to define it as 'poetic realism'. What seemed like stark documentation of reality at the time has now acquired a romantic connotation; what looked unpremeditated, spontaneous and raw – like *cinéma-vérité* – looks like calculated narrative segments. In other words, the film shares the fate of the French *nouvelle vague* which it once emulated and referenced, from the camera movement to Charles Aznavour on the soundtrack and the partying habits of its characters doing the twist and talking endlessly in an apartment filled with cigarette smoke. Granted, it is a very Russian Paris, with the shish kebab picnics and all. Aznavour and Jacques Brel exist as disembodied sounds and images, but the Soviet bard Yuri Vizbor is very much present, and sings his own and Bulat Okudzhava's songs throughout the film.

The same mixture can be found in Daneliya's *Walking the Streets of Moscow*, where the city, as the *New York Times* critic Vincent Canby observed in 1966, looks very much like Paris –

The late 1960s saw the ascendancy of the private and the decline of the public in Soviet cinema. The period was also marked by the accentuation of the visual and the devaluation of the verbal.

except that its youthful heroes are 'untouched by existentialism, alienation, the Bomb, Coca Cola, old Humphrey Bogart films and even sex'. What they have instead is an abundance of optimism and hope that things will only get better, as proclaimed in the film's song: 'Sometimes everything feels so good / You don't understand the reason why. / And it is just that the rain has passed, / A normal summer rain.' Rain as a metaphor was obviously important for the 1960's generation, the so-called *shestidesiatniki*.

Obviously, Moscow in poetically heightened films like *Walking the Streets of Moscow* or *July Rain* never existed in reality. Therefore, when the mood turned sour in the late 1960s, this did not mean a sign of changing times but a sign of changing cinematic style. Poetic realism gave way to everyday realism. In Kalik's omnibus film *To Love* the two tendencies exist side by side. In one segment, two out-of-towners – He and She – meet in Moscow and have trouble finding any privacy. They are turned down by hotels with the permanent 'no vacancy' signs, driven out of an apartment building's dark entrance by a sneering cleaning woman, and finally take a taxi out of town to walk through a cold nocturnal forest before they return to the city, where they say a hasty goodbye at a busy train station. The views of Moscow retain the same fashionable New Wave look, but the mood has become stark and unromantic.

An interesting contrast can be drawn between the portrayal of the same Moscow setting in *July Rain* and in Daneliya's *Mimino* (1977). The final scene of *July Rain* takes place at a meeting of World War II veterans against the backdrop of the Bolshoi Theatre with its monumental columns. The scene juxtaposes the unselfconscious joy of the surviving veterans meeting their comrades-in-arms with the vacant expressions of the young people looking at this celebration noncommittally, with a mixture of curiosity and scepticism. The scene is imbued with 1960s pathos: present-day youngsters have to measure themselves against the heroic older generation. Both of these groups, however, are composed of individuals who reveal, in brief close-ups, their unique character. In *Mimino*, the two protagonists from the Caucasus are the only memorable persons in the faceless crowd that flocks to the Bolshoi, leaving them alone and freezing among the columns that dwarf them. The effect is both sad and comical. Everyday Moscow means snowbound streets full of noisy traffic, nondescript interiors of bureaucratic institutions, and cramped *khrushchevki* whose residents are not friendly to strangers. A communion of fellow citizens that already looked wistful in *July Rain* and *Walking the Streets of Moscow* is completely forsaken in the shuffle of the businesslike, materialistic and alienating big city. ✠

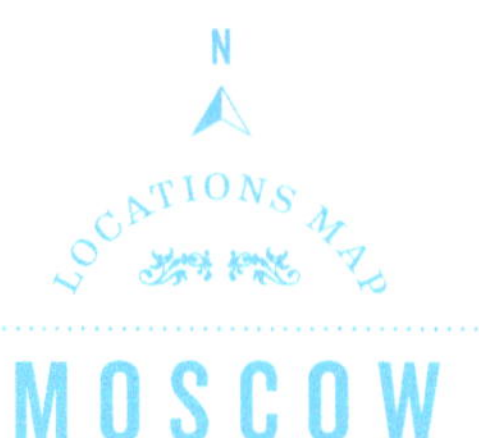

N
LOCATIONS MAP
MOSCOW

maps are only to be taken as approximates

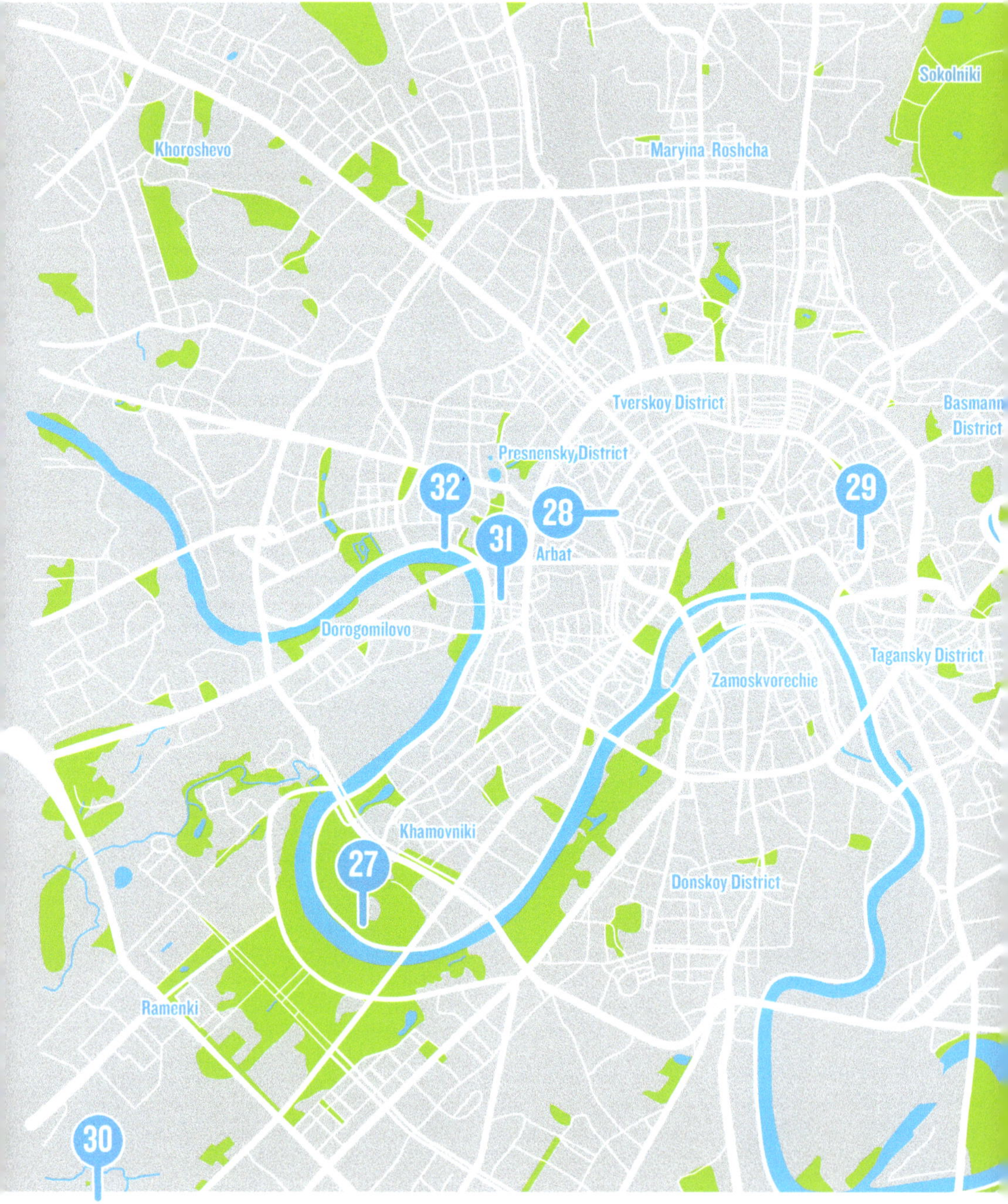

Sokolniki
Khoroshevo
Maryina Roshcha
Tverskoy District
Basmanny District
Presnensky District
32
28
29
31
Arbat
Dorogomilovo
Tagansky District
Zamoskvorechie
Khamovniki
27
Donskoy District
Ramenki
30

MOSCOW LOCATIONS
SCENES 27–32

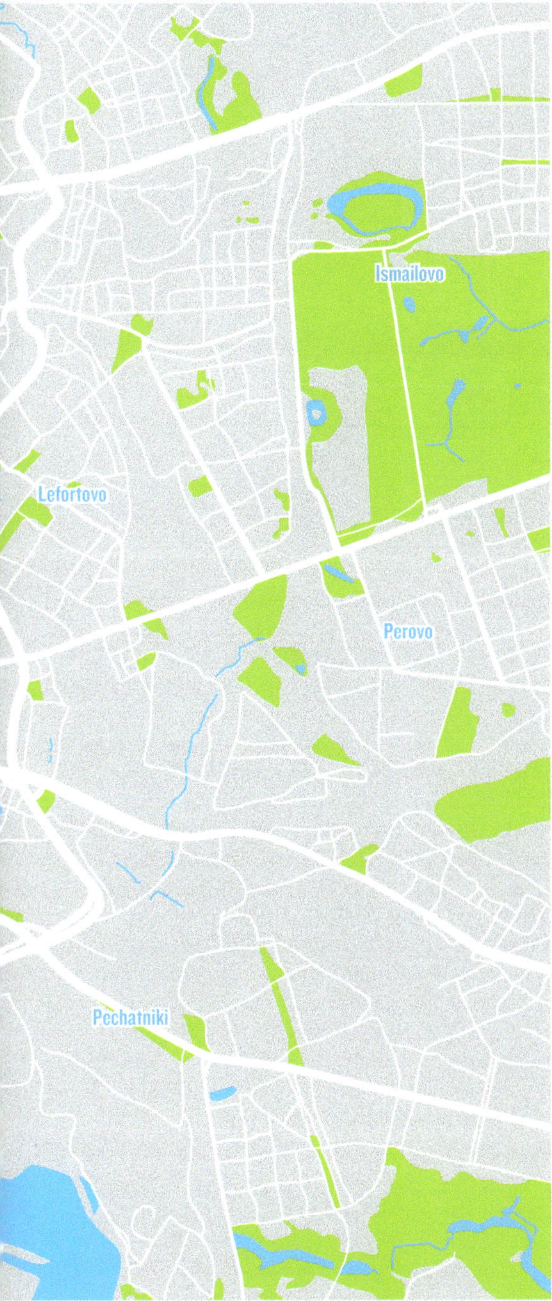

THE MESSENGER/KUR'ER (1986)

 Sparrow Hills

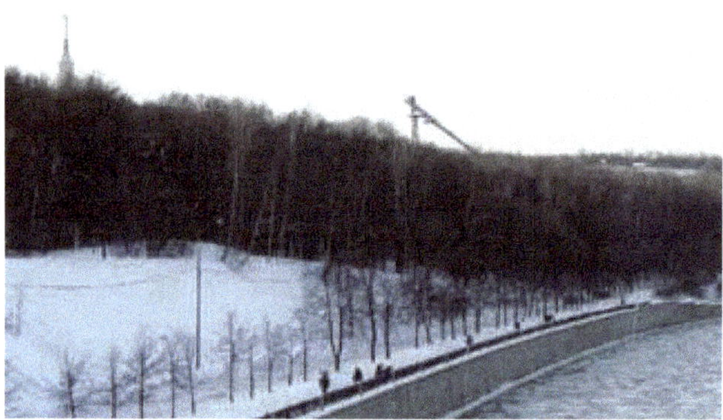

IVAN (FËDOR DUNAEVSKY), an unmotivated youth who is rejected from college, takes a job as a courier for a magazine. He meets his friend Kolya Bazin (Vladimir Smirnov) on the metro and, shirking their respective duties, they go skateboarding in Sparrow Hills. This brief scene captures some of the exhilaration of adolescence. The moving camera sails down from the treetops to a low angle of the back of the boys' feet as they run and skate, then changes to a reverse angle of the same, which soon sweeps up to reveal Bazin's head and shoulders. Then there is a cut to a high angle shot as they make their way down a path that runs parallel with the river. The camera cranes upwards, settling on an elevated view of Moscow. But exhilaration and aimlessness are side by side here. There's only one skateboard, and although the boys are shrieking excitedly, they will soon have to return to their duties. Ivan will be reproached for his lateness by Professor Kuznetsov (Oleg Basilashvili), whose daughter the boy is about to begin a fractious relationship with. This prefigures some of the strangely motivated, counterintuitive decisions Ivan will make later in the film. The scene encapsulates the new mood of glasnost; skateboards, hedonistic whooping and Eduard Artemiev's distinctive, disco-influenced score. 'Head towards Mosfilm!' is the only line of dialogue in this scene. This sequence seems like an announcement that a new mood of exuberance, but also openness to fatalism, was also heading towards Mosfilm.
John A. Riley

Photo © Birgit Beumers

Scene description: Ivan and Bazin neglect their duties to go skateboarding
Timecode for scene: 0:15:07 – 0:15:41

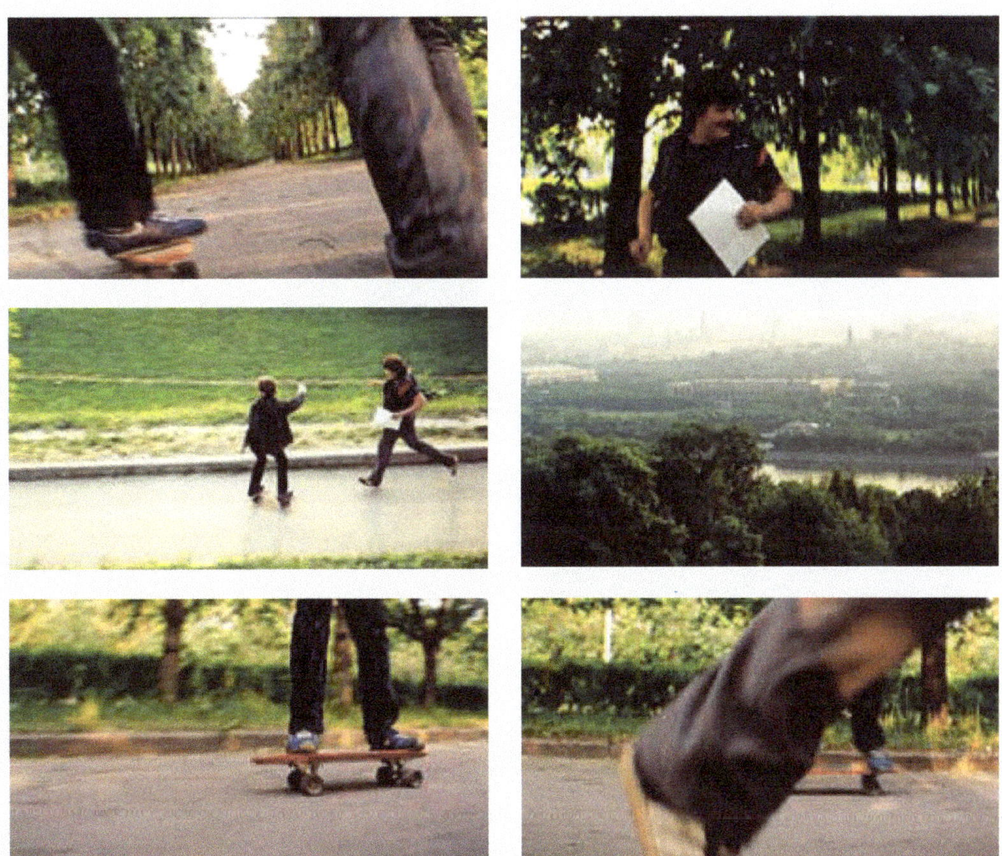

Images © 1986 Mosfilm

A FORGOTTEN TUNE FOR THE FLUTE/ ZABYTAIA MELODIIA DLIA FLEITY (1987)

Bolshaya Nikitskaya Street, Greater Church of the Ascension, and former Cinema of Repertory Films

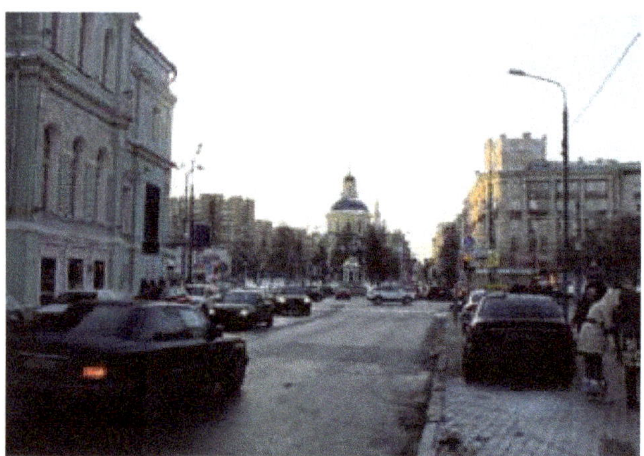

ELDAR RYAZANOV'S satirical comedy *A Forgotten Tune for the Flute* offers a familiar story: a love triangle with an indecisive husband caught between wife and lover. The action takes place during the political turmoil of perestroika. Both contemporary politics and timeless Russian culture lend context to the unfolding story, shaping it into a 'sad comedy', Ryazanov's hallmark genre. Moscow provides the perfect stage for both elements. In a key scene, the protagonist Leonid Filimonov (Leonid Filatov), a former musician, now a frustrated bureaucrat at the Ministry of Culture, drives his love interest Lida (Tatyana Dogileva) to her amateur theatre rehearsal and picks her up afterwards. They begin a clandestine romantic relationship. This scene opens in the dimming light of the afternoon, with a white church dominating the background, and ends in the dark interior of a car, with the big city bursting with life all around the lovers, who are entirely focused on one another. The church is the Greater Church of the Ascension on Bolshaya Nikitskaya Street, which is famous for its association with Pushkin, Russia's revered poet and courageous political dissenter, who wedded there. Its presence hints at the fraught relationship between politics, art and love. Another significant building in this scene, the Cinema of Repertory Films, a movie theatre dedicated to replaying old movies, serves as a reminder of the cyclic nature of politics and art and seems to ask: just where does the current relationship fit into the vast history of film romance? ⬦ *Rimma Garn*

Photo © Birgit Beumers

"

Directed by Eldar Ryazanov
Scene description: The first rendezvous of Filimonov and the nurse Lida
Timecode for scene: 0:42:00 – 0:44:25

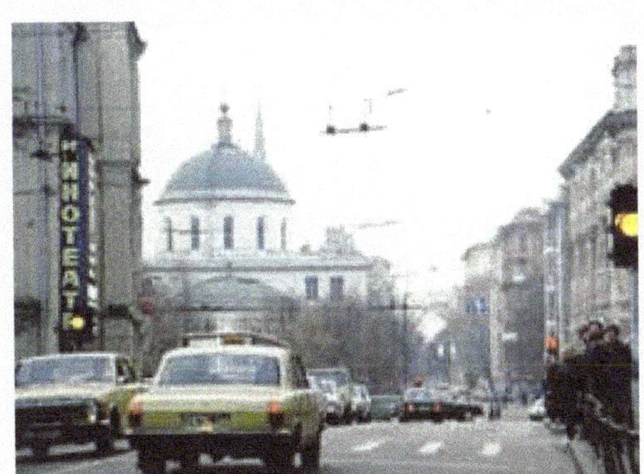

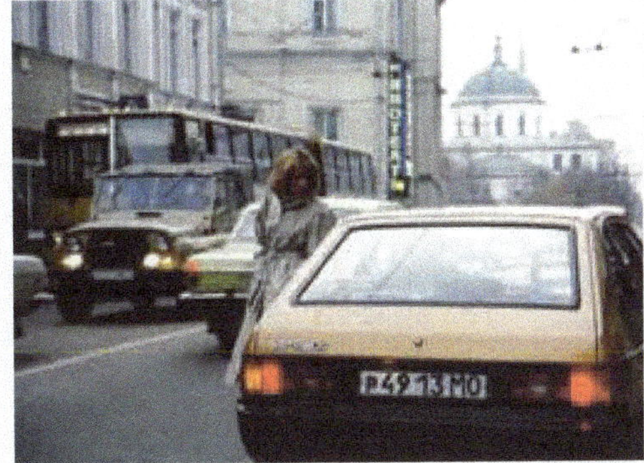

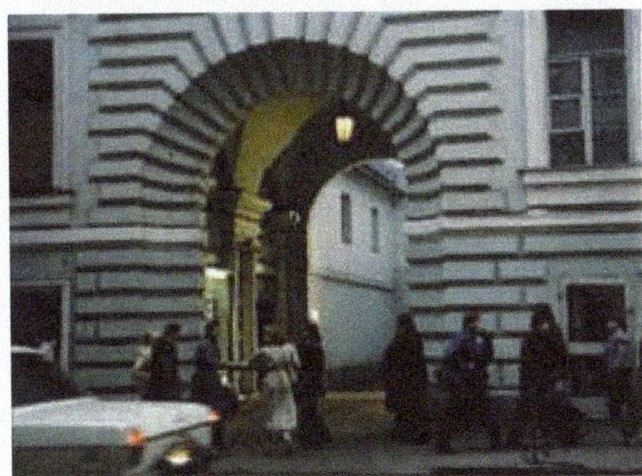

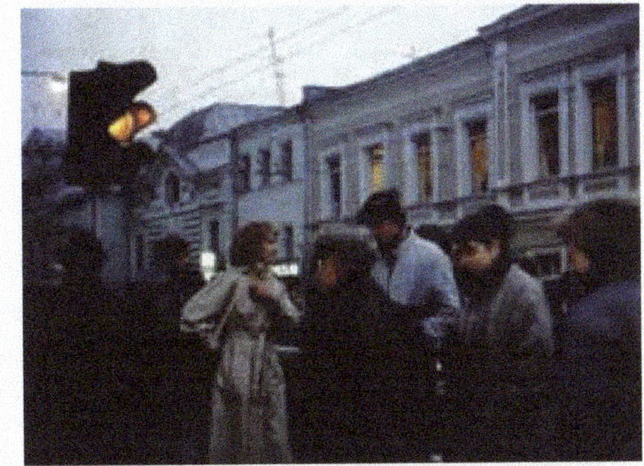

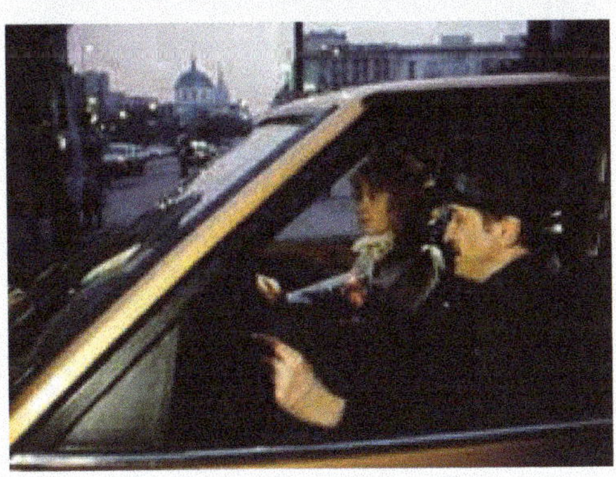

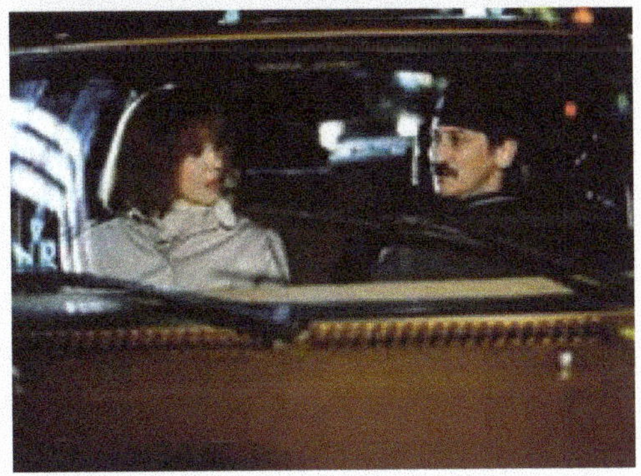

COLD SUMMER OF '53/ KHOLODNOE LETO 53-EGO (1987)

Intersection of Yauzsky Boulevard and Podkolokolny Lane

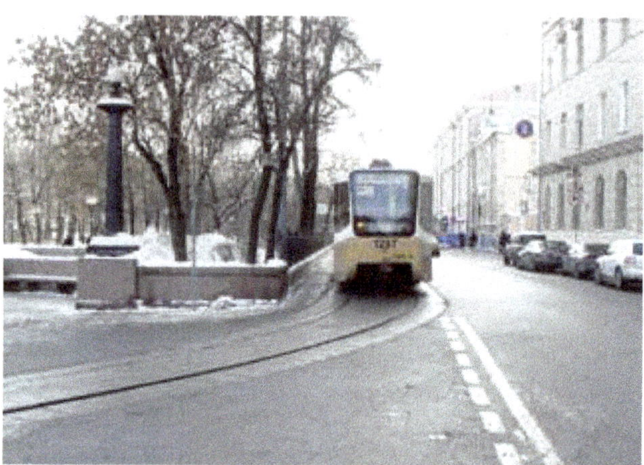

ALEXANDER PROSHKIN'S *Cold Summer of '53* is set in a Soviet Russia on the cusp of change. Stalin is dead and an amnesty of Gulag prisoners soon finds a band of released common criminals terrorizing a small village in the far north. Two political prisoners serving their time there protect the passive villagers against the criminals. 'High noon' in the village resolves the situation both predictably and satisfyingly. In the final few minutes of the film, the protagonist Sergei 'Luzga' (Valeri Priëmykhov), returns to a Moscow beautifully captured in flux. Sergei wants to tell his friend's family of his death two years earlier. The Moscow *kommunalka* (communal apartment) evokes a Soviet sphere both hopeful, as patriotic music blares and a woman in a bright flowery dress answers the door, and threatening, as a nosy neighbour briefly listens at the door and the family greets Sergei with mistrust. Sergei exits the building and enters a bustling, animated Moscow full of contradictory markers. Celebratory communist banners are being hoisted onto the tall grey slabs of buildings, a Stalinist skyscraper looms in the background, and Sergei jostles with well-dressed passers-by and new cars on the road. A uniformed official glances at this nondescript, yet eminently recognizable denizen of the Gulag, carrying a battered suitcase and making his way into a Moscow park. Amid the fallen autumnal leaves, he stops to give a light to an old man, another returnee with the obligatory suitcase. It is the only moment of real human interaction in the Moscow of these final scenes, a city perhaps remaking itself, but with no space for these two men from a different time and place. ◆*Frederick Corney*

Scene description: Sergei returns to Moscow to visit his dead friend's family
and encounters another Gulag returnee in the park
Timecode for scene: 1:29:11 – 1:35:22

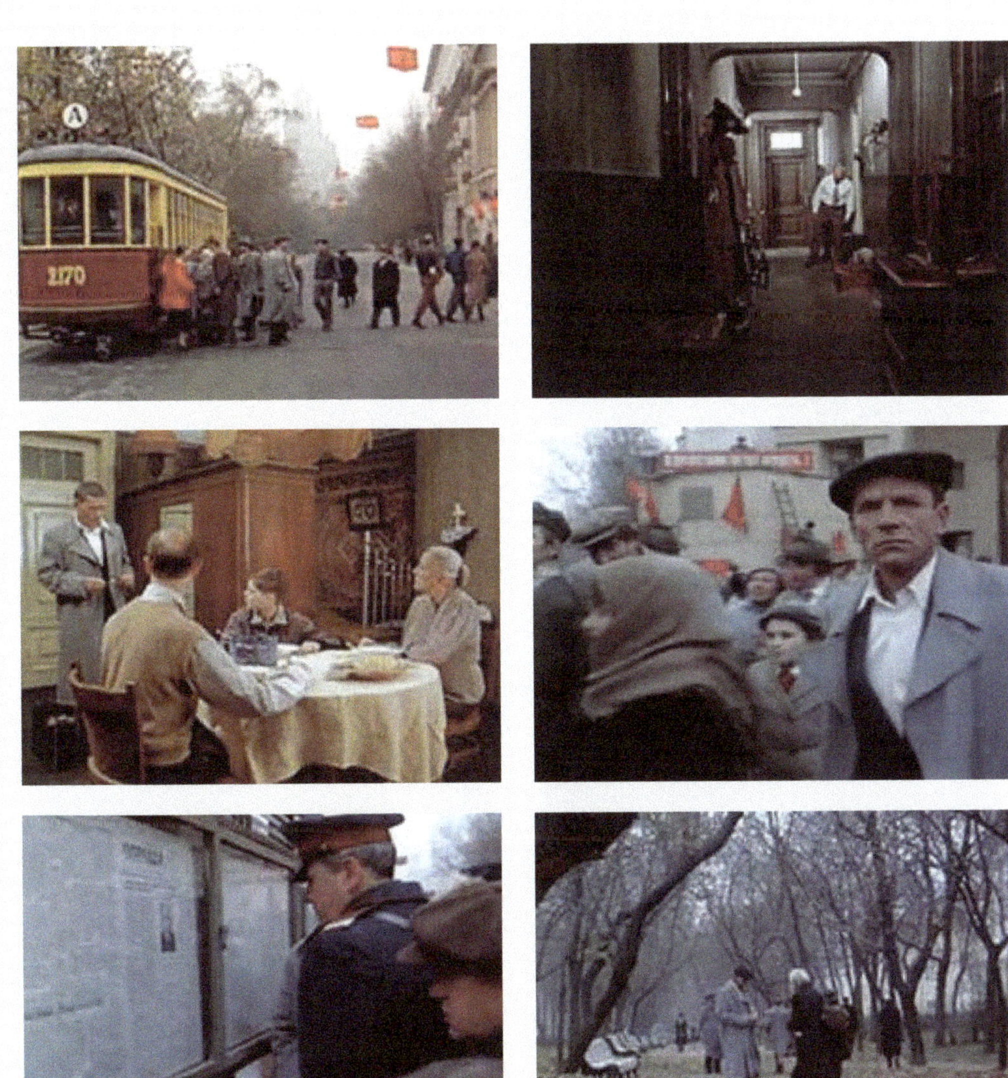

DEAR ELENA SERGEEVNA/
DOROGAIA ELENA SERGEEVNA (1988)

Vernadsky Avenue Student House of Moscow State University

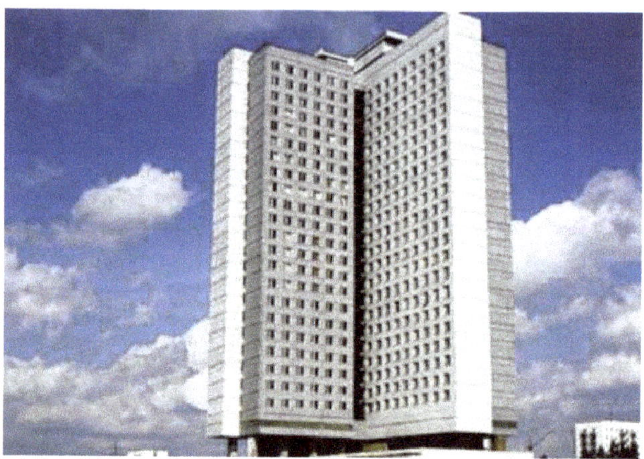

ELDAR RYAZANOV'S *Dear Elena Sergeevna* is considered a key perestroika-era film focused on the crisis of values and intergenerational conflict. Four fashionably dressed and self-confident secondary school students, just days from graduating, visit their mathematics teacher (Marina Neëlova), a lonely middle-aged woman, on the pretext of wishing her happy birthday, but with the intention of altering their exams to improve their chances of entering prestigious universities. A tense stand-off ensues, with the teacher appealing to ethical rules and the students arguing they no longer apply in present-day society. The film challenges viewers by demonstrating that its young characters are capable of casual cruelty in what amounts to psychological torture of their schoolteacher. A fine psychological study, it presents all the characters as complex, conflicted and self-contradictory. The teacher, too, emerges as a broken-down person who sacrificed her personal happiness at the altar of ideological dogma, now about to be swept away by the survival-of-the-fittest logic of the coming era. The film's three-minute opening episode introduces the four characters, basking in their youth and vigour and feeling invincible; they are the 'young lions' ready to claim their right to reign over the world. Their foil is the DSV building, an impressive late-modernist structure rising above a plaza and a small lake, both buzzing with activity; it becomes the epitome of 'new Moscow' – yet now it is not the city of utopian promise but a schizophrenic, frenetic metropolis. A concentrated visual representation of perestroika-era Moscow, the scene sets the tone for the rest of the film. ☙ *Vitaly Chernetsky*

Photo © Vitaly Chernetsky

Scene description: Four youngsters on the way to a fateful visit to their secondary school maths teacher
Timecode for scene: 0:00:00 – 0:03:08

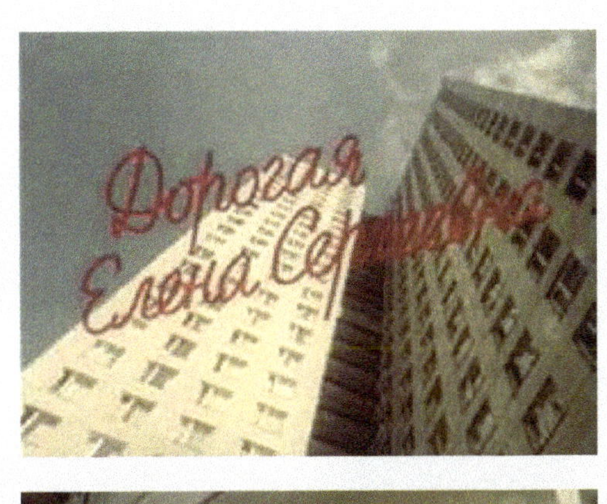

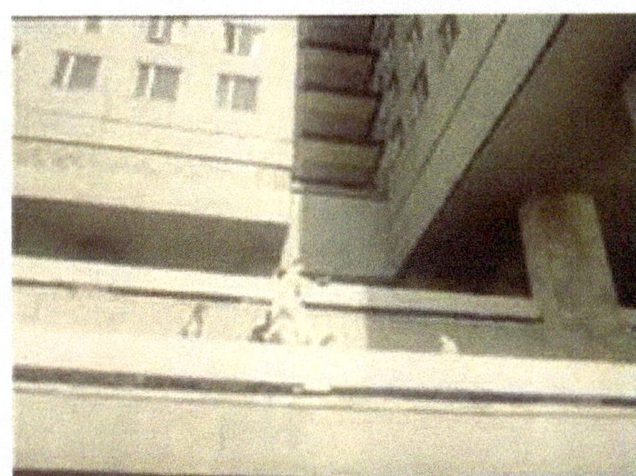

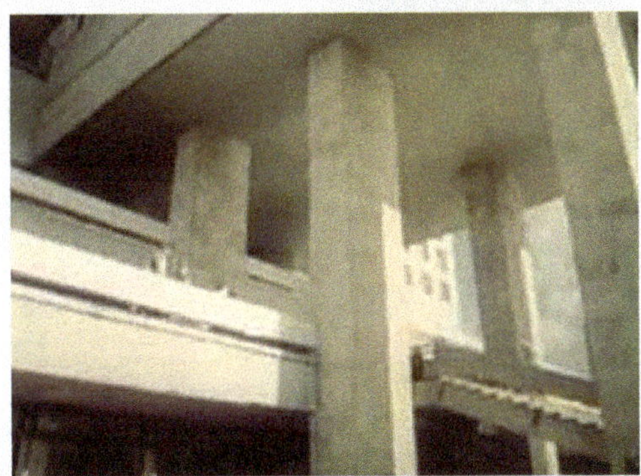

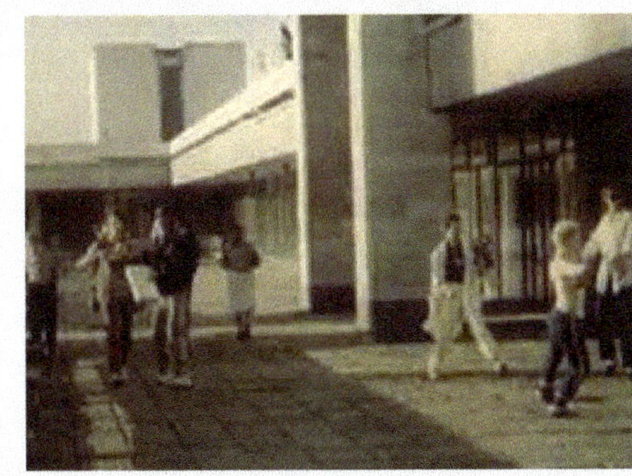

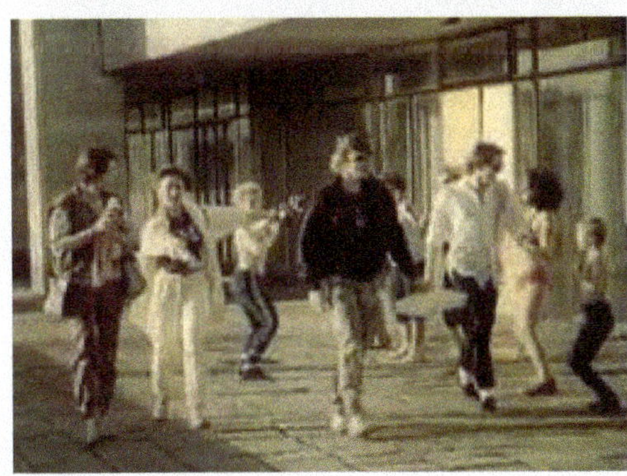

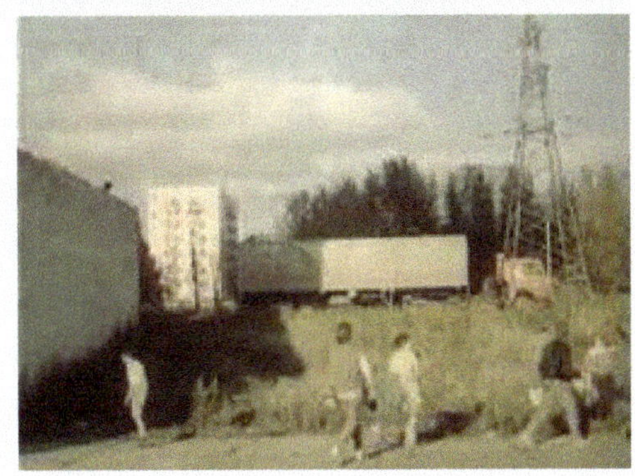

TAXI BLUES (1990)

Kauchuk Factory Club, Plyushchikha Street

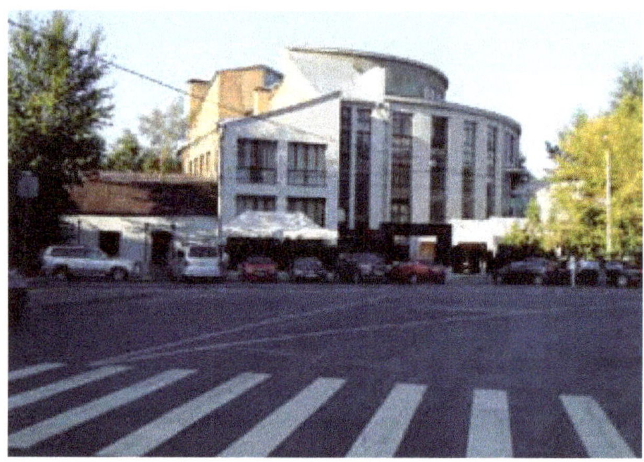

FILMED A YEAR BEFORE the collapse of the Soviet Union, Pavel Lungin's debut *Taxi Blues* captures the excitement of perestroika-era Moscow. The film centres on the unlikely relationship between cab driver Shlykov (Pëtr Zaichenko), the embodiment of Soviet values, and jazz saxophonist Lësha (Pëtr Mamonov), who enters Shlykov's world when he skips out on his cab fare. The authoritarian Shlykov forces Lësha to work off his debt through a series of menial tasks, even as the debt increases as a result of Lësha's erratic behaviour. Shlykov initially tracks the musician to the 'Kauchuk' Factory Club, a Soviet-era 'house of culture' erected as a worker club for rubber factory employees. One of several such clubs designed by Konstantin Melnikov, the Constructivist building was intended to unite proletarian and artistic cultures. Lungin references this utopian vision, as Shlykov enters the bohemian space in pursuit of Lësha. Though it occurs early in the film, Shlykov's confrontation with Lësha is the second of many bathroom scenes, as Lungin's characters consistently withdraw from a chaotic public sphere to negotiate their personal relations and private economies in the unobserved corners of Soviet life. Shlykov confiscates Lësha's saxophone as compensation for the owed fare, then proceeds to lecture and assault the saxophonist, pushing him into a toilet stall. Shlykov twice claims 'I've taught, and I'll teach again,' casting Lësha as his unwilling pupil in language redolent of Soviet rhetoric. Effectively commencing Lësha's 'bondage', Shlykov's attack is a fitting postscript to Soviet culture, and the unresolved tension between worker and artist. **⇢Tom Roberts**

Photo © Tom Roberts

Scene description: Shlykov confronts Lësha, confiscating his means of subsistence
Timecode for scene: 0:13:05 – 0:16:14

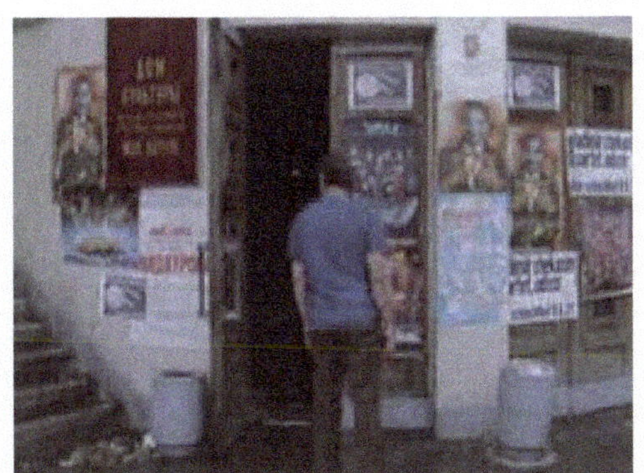
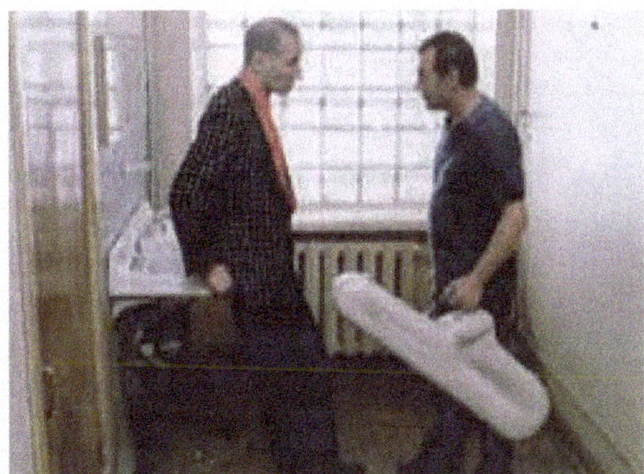
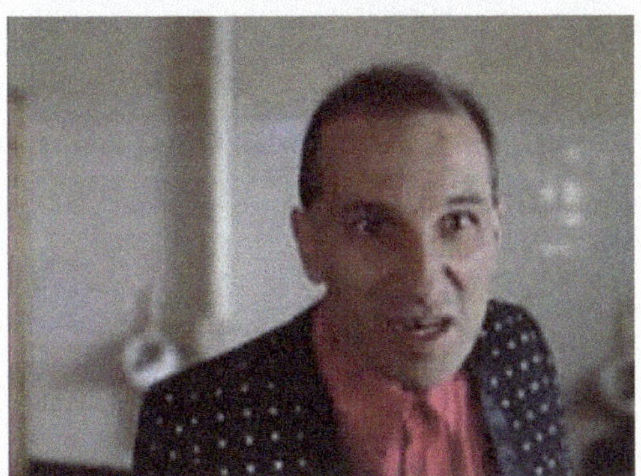
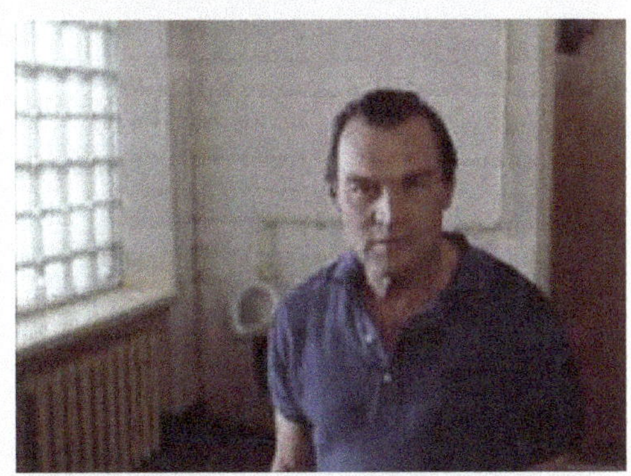
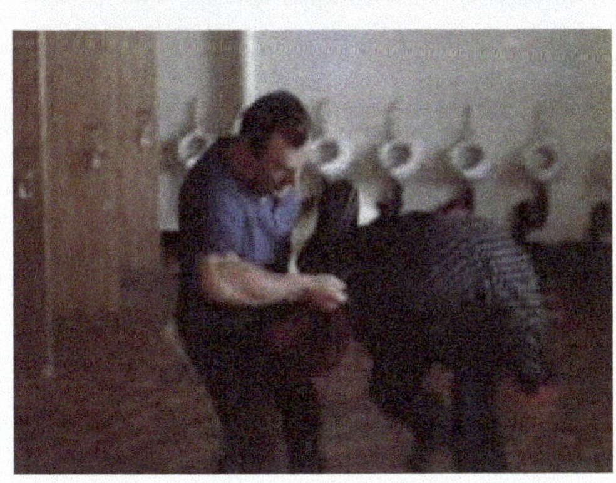
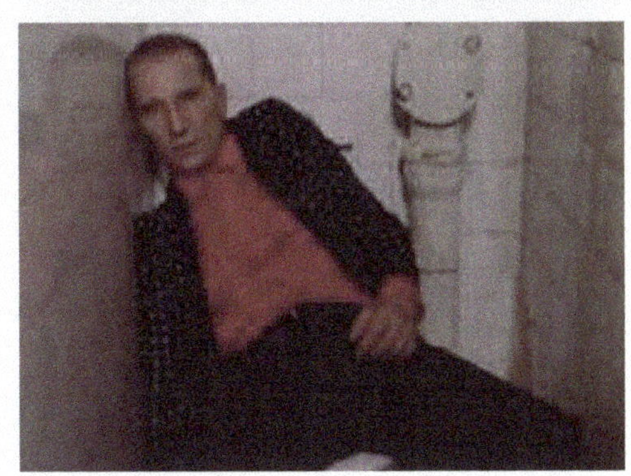

Images © 1990 Lenfilm, ASK (USSR); MK-2 Production (France)

LUNA PARK (1992)

Embankment in front of the Hotel Ukraina

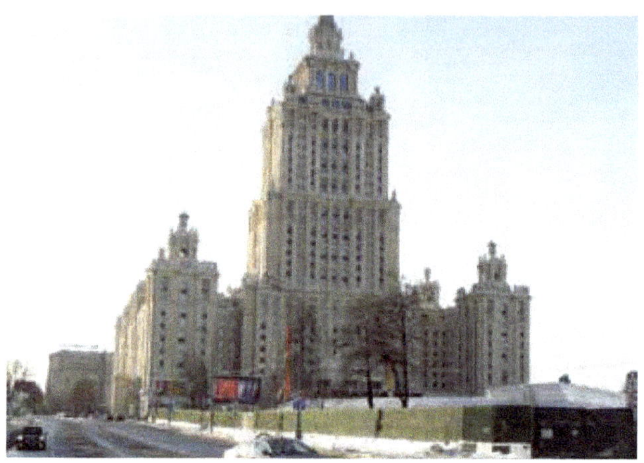

MOSCOW, 1992. The embankment before the Stalin-era Hotel Ukraina. A muscular, angry and confused new Russian generation emerges. Draped in the new Russian Federation flag, Andrei, the shaven-head leader of the skinheads, summons: 'Who are we?' His band of shirtless warriors brandishing old fashioned axe-handles and chains responds: 'We are the Cleaners!' – 'What are we cleaning?' – 'Russia!' A band of dirty bikers and punks storm up to the battlefield on their black machines. Andrei confronts them, demanding 'Drink Coca-Cola!' while crushing a can in his hands. The bikers cannot stomach this provocation and attack the skinheads in a ruthless wave of man and machinery. The skinheads, like the Russian folkloric heroes of yore, are ever resourceful as they grab a metal picket fence and trudge in a joyful phalanx at the bikers. A brutal battle ensues, invoking Eisenstein's *Alexander Nevsky* (1938), and the good men of Novgorod against the grotesque Teutonic Knights. The staging is dynamic, with powerful but outlandish effects of burning motorbikes falling off roofs. Appropriately both gangs unite to destroy the hapless police who stupidly attempt to intervene. The fighting continues inside a burnt-out apartment with the bikers in quasi-Nazi helmets fighting the skinheads under the shadow of the Stalinist skyscraper, adding to the delicious confusion of working out who the real patriots in this scene are. The vicious symbolic mix of this scene powerfully captures the confusion, the brutality and the flimsy pack associations of the early years of the new Russia as it searched for its true identity. •**Greg Dolgopolov**

Photo © Birgit Beumers

Scene description: A brutal confrontation between the skinheads and the bikers
Timecode for scene: 0:00:10 – 0:03:00

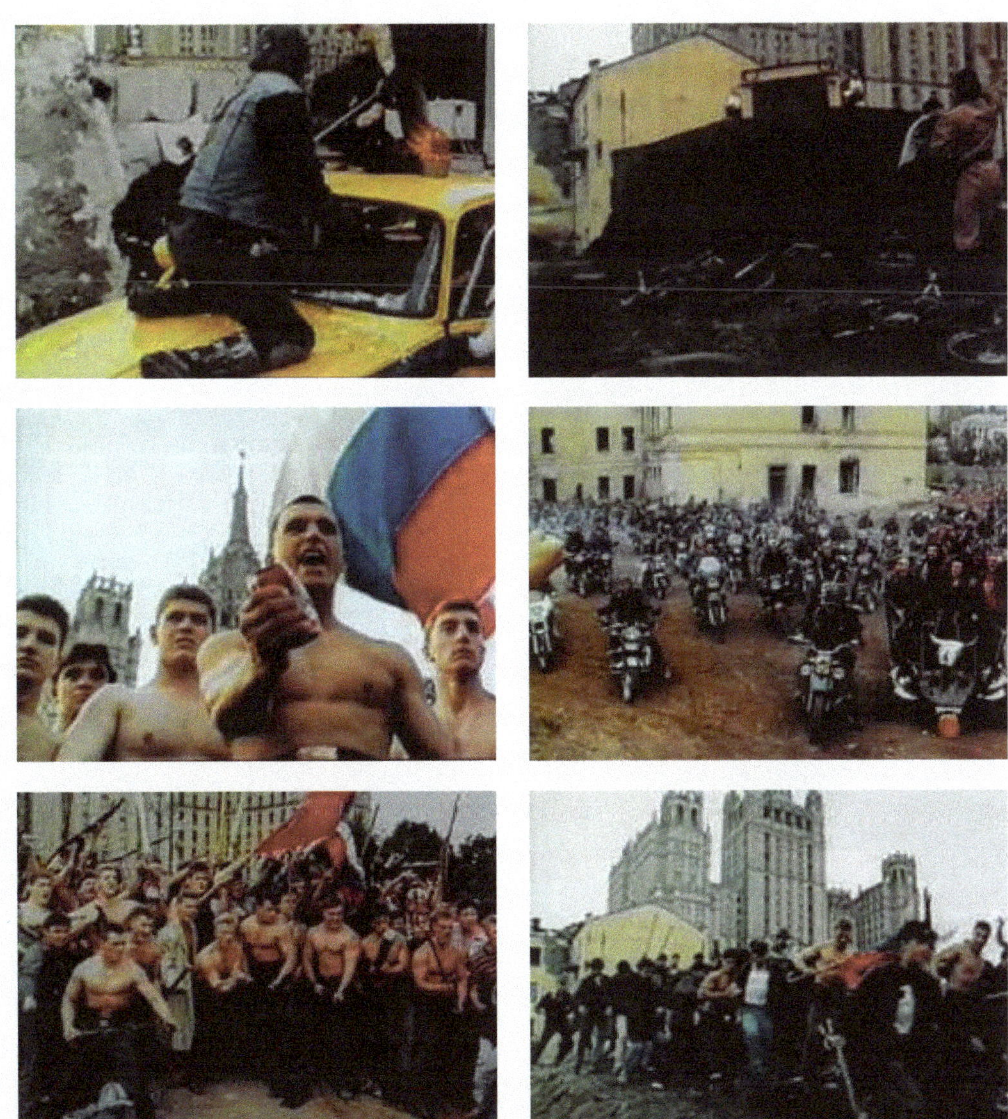

Images © 1992 Bliuz Film (Russia); CiBy 2000, IMA Productions (France)

HOUSING ESTATES

Cheremushki On Screen

Text by
SERGEY
DOBRYNIN

AT THE BEGINNING of *Ironiia sud'by*/*Irony of Fate* (1975), Eldar Ryazanov's New Year's Day perennial, the narrator muses with gentle mockery:

Those villages near Moscow – Troparevo, Chertanovo, Medvedkovo, and of course, Cheremushki – never suspected that they were gaining immortality just as they were being wiped off the face of the earth. The village of Cheremushki gave its name to the well-known new Moscow neighbourhood in the capital's south-west. Now nearly every Soviet city has its own Cheremushki.

The name did indeed become generic, and thousands of such apartment-block neighbourhoods (*mikroraion*) dotted the entire country.

The mass movement from the communal

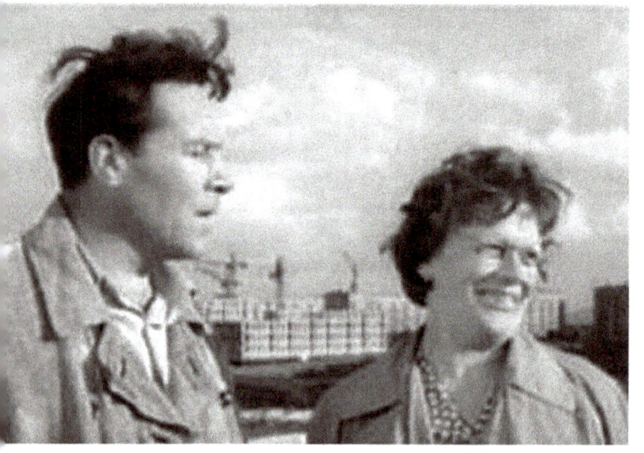

apartments, barracks and village-style log houses into separate apartments in housing projects is commonly associated with Khrushchev and his era. These five-storey blocks of flats came to be known as *khrushchoby* (from Khrushchev's name and the word *trushchoby*, meaning slums) or – a slightly less derisive word – *khrushchevki*. The first apartment building of the new variety was designed and built in Moscow by veteran architect Ivan Zholtovsky in 1954. It was a very elaborate structure, complete with porticos, colonnades, sculptures and a myriad other architectural detail. Khrushchev, however, was unimpressed. He said: 'Architects don't understand a thing. You don't need all this for living.' The architects' profligacy was condemned in the 1955 Party statement 'On the Eradication of Excesses in Construction'. The officially approved austere style was initially explained by the necessity to save as much as possible in mass construction. The 20th Party Congress (1956) set the goal of reducing construction costs by 20 per cent. Therefore, the early mass-produced buildings were no higher than five stories. That allowed the designers to do without elevators, which saved 8 per cent in building costs. Soon it turned out that the Soviet construction industry could only mass-produce prefabricated bare panels anyway. This homogenization and paring down to the basics was satirized in Vitali Peskov's animated prologue to *Irony of Fate*, and, a few years earlier, in yet another animation within a feature film, Sergei Gerasimov's *Liubit' cheloveka*/*The Love of Mankind* (1972).

In theory, a two-room apartment was supposed to accommodate three people (say, a couple with a child). In practice, however, it was typically

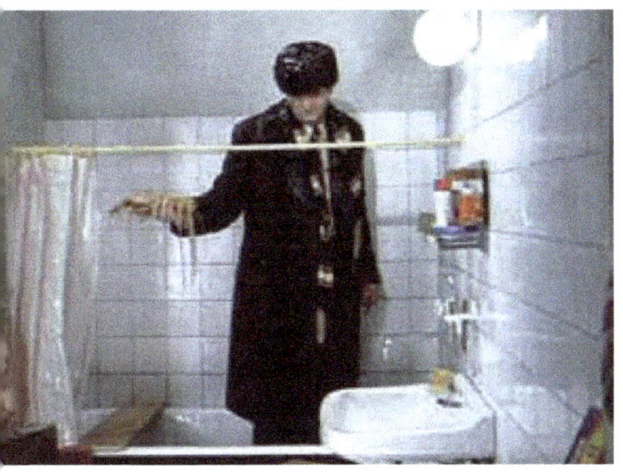

crowded with various relatives. Thus, the closet, itself a novelty, was nicknamed 'mother-in-law's room'. Given that space was very tightly regulated, down to how wide the doors had to be, it had to be negotiated carefully. According to the apocryphal story, the portly Khrushchev quipped: 'It's okay: if I got through, others will, too.' The narrow staircases made it impossible for a funeral procession to descend the stairs without carrying the coffin into other people's doors. However, after the horrors of the *kommunalka* (communal apartment), the *khrushchevka* was a sign of progress. If one adopts their broadest definition as any 'big-block' housing projects, then about 54 million apartments have been built that way since 1958. Their design has changed over time, the apartments have become bigger and the box-like buildings taller, typically nine, twelve or sixteen storeys high.

The original Moscow-Cherëmushki (Bird-Cherry Village), the prototype community for all Soviet cities, was begun in 1956. The film *Cherëmushki* (aka *Song over Moscow* and *Cherry Town*) appeared in 1962 and was directed by Gerbert Rappaport, based on an operetta by Dmitri Shostakovich (1957). One of its memorable moments comes when a young couple, Sasha and Masha, move into their own apartment. In the song number 'And All the Dreams Come True', they proclaim ecstatically: 'The kitchen is also ours, ours! / Our own windows, our own doors / I don't believe my own eyes!'

There is an overwhelming sense of joy here: the apartment issue has been solved – at least for the screen characters. However, this is not all a bed of roses. The corrupt superintendent, seeking favours from the construction manager, allows him to tear down the wall separating his apartment from the neighbours' on the unbeatable premise that four rooms are better than two. This being an operetta, the bad guys are soon unmasked, the wall mended and everyone lives happily ever after.

Konets staroi Berezovki/The End of Old Berezovka (aka *Apartment in Moscow*, Viktor Eisymont, 1960) offers a more realistic treatment of Moscow's housing expansion. It is the story of a young boy, his pregnant, unwed sister and a construction worker who befriends the kid and marries the girl, moving, of course, into a new apartment he has helped build. *The New York Times* summed it up as a 'friendly, uneventful and altogether mild tribute to some nice, hard-working people and to the rising building panorama in the background'. Unlike *Cherëmushki*, filmed in a studio set, *Berezovka* was shot on location in Moscow's South-West, on the First Builders' Street. It is an interesting setting, because one side of the street was finished in 1952–54 (the so-called 'Red Houses', featuring more colour and architectural detail), while the other side, built at the time of the filming in 1959–60, was unencumbered by any excesses. The Red Houses on Builders' Street also appear in *Veselye istorii/Merry Stories* (Veniamin Dorman, 1962). Incidentally, the street in *Irony of Fate* is called the Third Builders' Street. How typical.

Irony of Fate has its hapless, drunk Muscovite protagonist unwittingly flown to Leningrad, where, at the same address, he finds a housing complex just like his and an apartment just like his own. Tellingly, the interior does not raise his suspicions: Soviet furniture and interior decorations were characterized by as much uniformity as urban planning. The man is in for the surprise of his life when he discovers a woman living there. Overcoming the initial confusion, the two gradually fall in love. The boring homogeneity of the Soviet mass-scale housing projects serves as a starting point for *Irony of Fate*, but does not exhaust it. The film makes many wry, yet still relevant comments about Russian everyday life. The aerial panorama of the snowbound, labyrinthine apartment complex in the opening scene remains, however, one of its strongest visual tropes. 'Beautiful, isn't it?,' intones the narrator, and his irony is now unmistakable. ✣

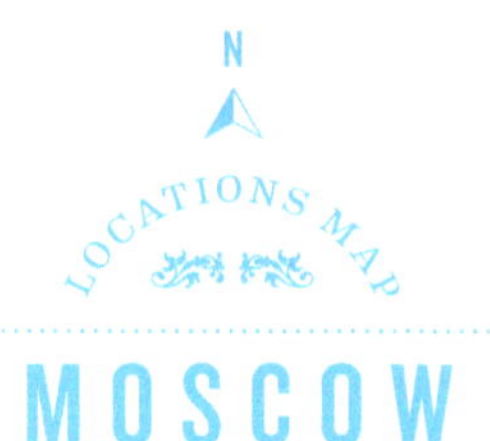

N
LOCATIONS MAP
MOSCOW
maps are only to be taken as approximates
33
Sokolniki
Khoroshevo
Maryina Roshcha
Tverskoy District
Basmann District
Presnensky District
37
Arbat
34
38
36
Tagansky District
Dorogomilovo
Zamoskvorechie
35
Khamovniki
Donskoy District
Ramenki
39

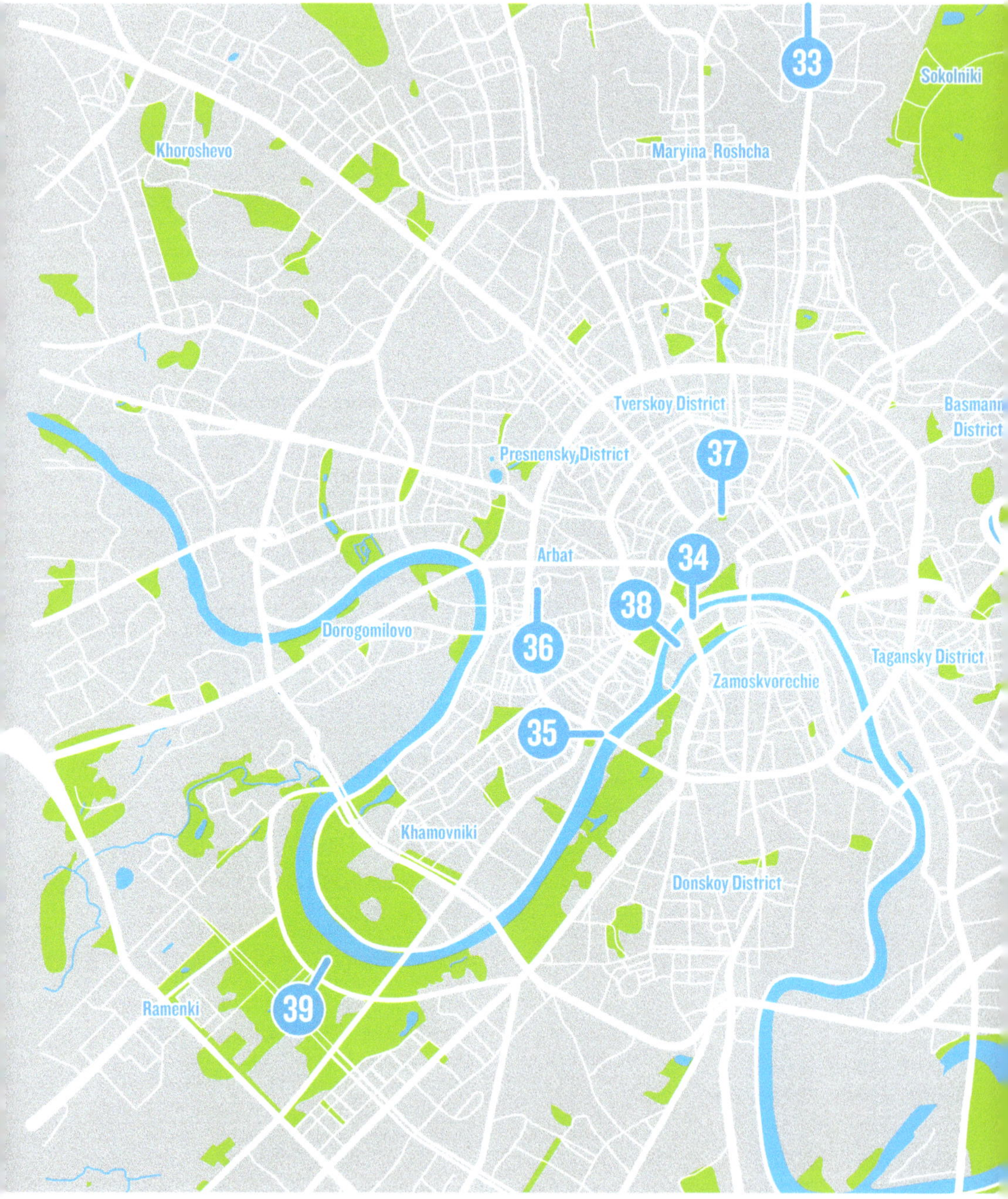

MOSCOW LOCATIONS
SCENES 33-39

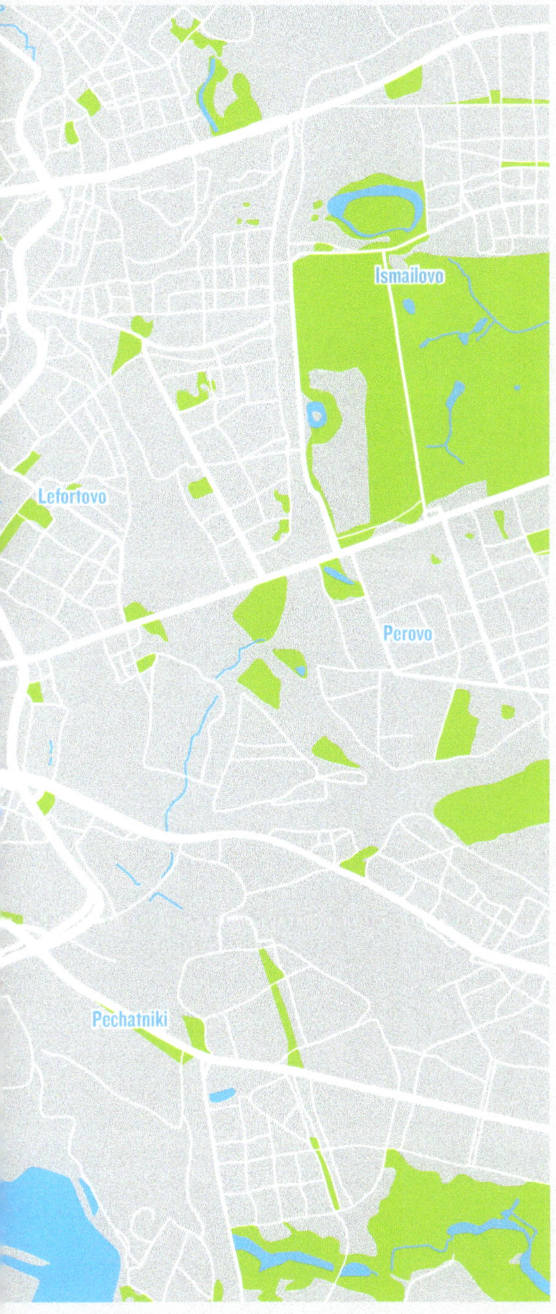

MOSCOW PARADE/PRORVA (1992)

*Fountain of the Friendship of the Peoples of the USSR,
All-Union Agricultural Exhibition (VDNKh)*

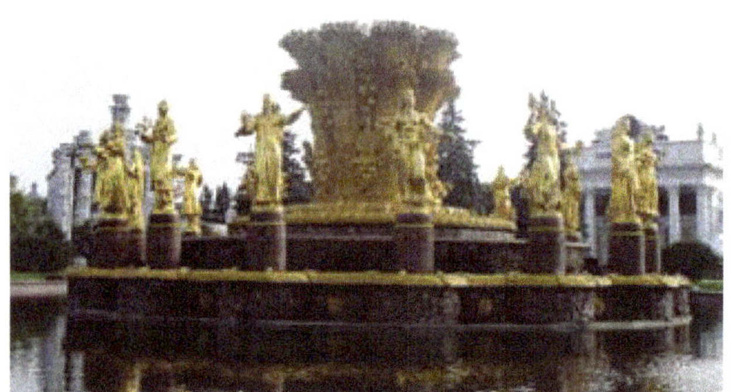

MOSCOW PARADE was a pioneering attempt to reassess Stalinism from
a purely aesthetic point of view: the director Ivan Dykhovichny and his
cameraman Vadim Yusov created a composite space of Moscow in the 1930s
that is more inspired by mythology and imagination than by historical reality.
The film tells the story of Anna (Ute Lemper), the wife of a high-ranking,
sexually impotent NKVD official. After being raped by a slimy singer –
another NKVD agent – Anna falls in love with Gosha, a luggage carrier
(Yevgeni Sidikhin) who works at the Kiev Railway Station. The attractive and
proud former aristocrat is also adored by other men, including an idealistic
young poet (Dmitri Dykhovichny). The latter believes in the eternal mission
of art; he even received a letter from French writer André Gide, whom
he met two years prior. A cowardly, two-faced critic and informer (Sergei
Makovetsky) meets with the poet near the fountain of the Friendship of the
Peoples of the USSR at the grandiose All-Union Agricultural Exhibition
(VDNKh). He offers 'friendly advice' on how to make up for his misdeeds
– the poet should avoid open statements and write something conformist.
Should he refuse to comply, he will be denounced at a public meeting. The
poet ignores the critic and is later humiliated at a show trial, after which he
commits suicide. Gosha abandons Anna and is arrested, while her husband
– together with other officials – is executed as punishment for causing an
embarrassment at a Red Square parade. **•Peter Rollberg**

Photo © wikimedia commons (Alex Zelenko)

Scene description: An opportunistic critic tries to manipulate a genuine poet
Timecode for scene: 0:12:11 – 0:13:51

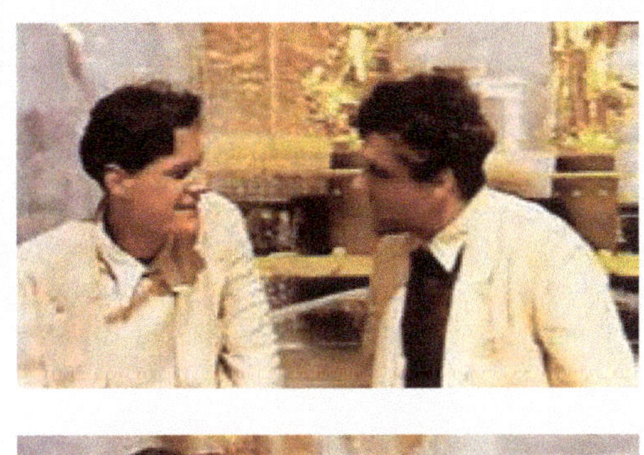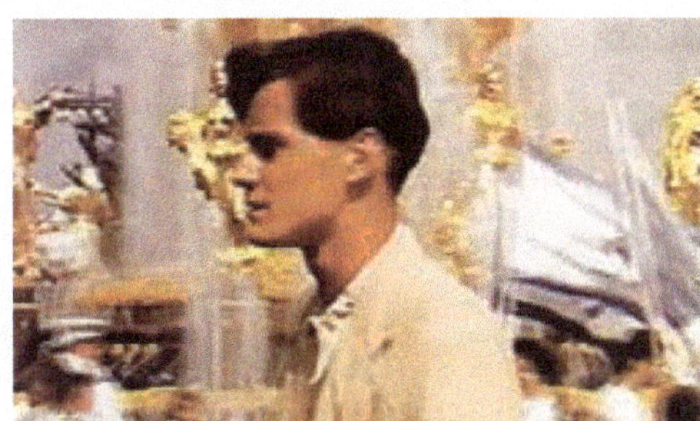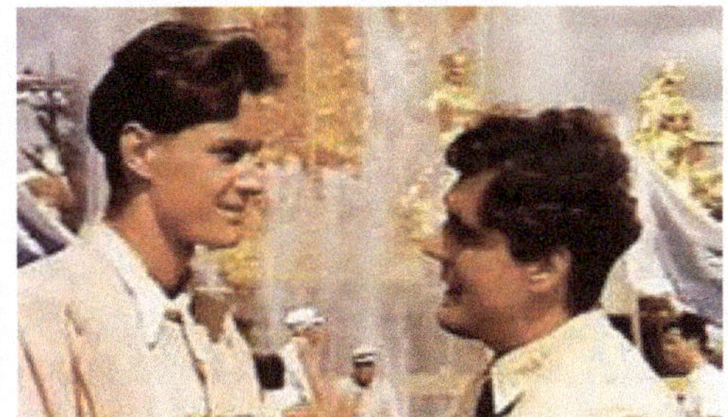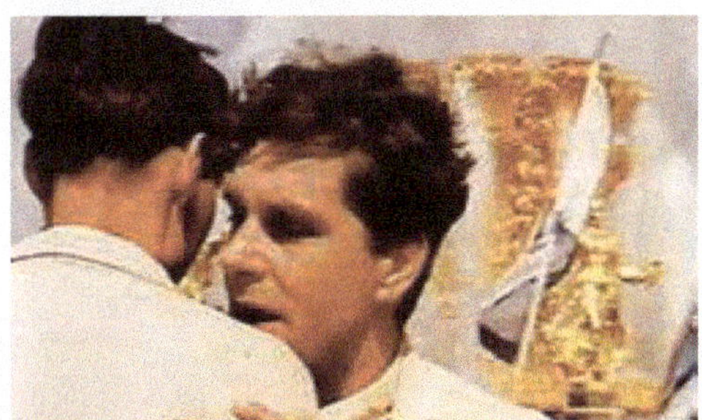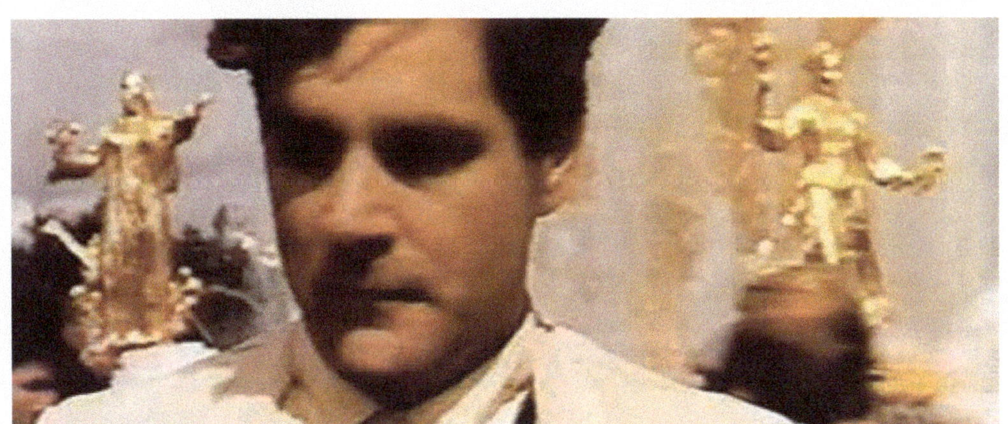

Images © 1992 Mosfilm (Russia), Canal + (France)

Bersenevskaya Embankment 20

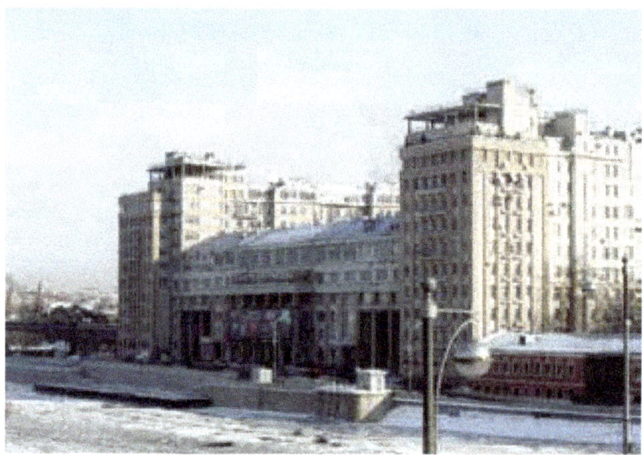

NIKITA MIKHALKOV'S Oscar-winning *Burnt by the Sun*, released in a period of national re-evaluation, revealed painful truths about the Stalinist Purges. It is the story of the arrest of commander Sergei Kotov (Mikhalkov), a Revolutionary hero who spends the summer on a dacha near Moscow. Kotov's heroic status and fairy-tale belief in the Revolution's ability to transform Soviet Russia are powerless to protect him from arbitrary Stalinist schemes, under which Kotov's old love rival and returned émigré Mitya (Oleg Menshikov) is turned into an – albeit reluctant – NKVD executioner. In this opening scene, the Kremlin's towers loom over a gloomy Moscow as the camera pans toward the House on the Embankment, the residence for the Soviet party elite and a building that saw a third of its residents disappear in the Purges. Mitya arrives at his well-appointed apartment, meeting his secreted, heavily-accented childhood tutor, Philippe. Receiving a phone call, Mitya realizes he must arrest Kotov. He plays Russian roulette, leaving the responsibility for Kotov's death to fate. Surviving the game, he leaves for the dacha, where he will soon arrest Kotov. Mikhalkov's film is a cycle of inevitable betrayal. At the film's conclusion, Stalin's image will rise over a lush landscape and Mitya, having played out his role as the agent of fate, will return to the house and slit his wrists in the bath. The Kremlin again rises over the dying man's apartment: Stalin's power, embodied in monumental form, now expands from city to countryside, arbitrarily destroying friends, foes, victims and perpetrators alike. **⬩Ian Garner**

Directed by Nikita Mikhalkov
Scene description: *Mitya submits to fate, playing a game of Russian roulette*
Timecode for scene: *0:00:50 – 0:04:33*

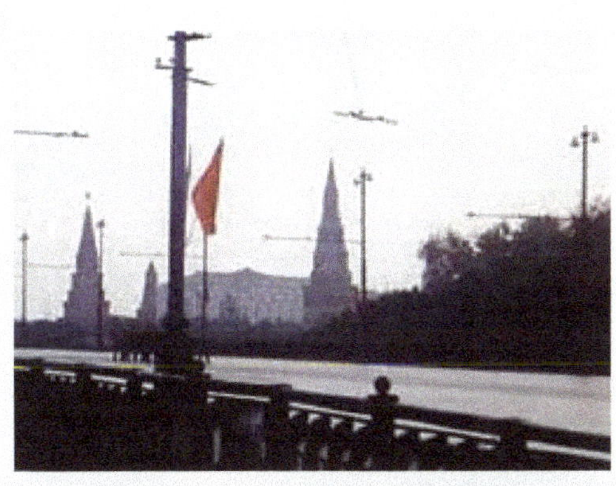

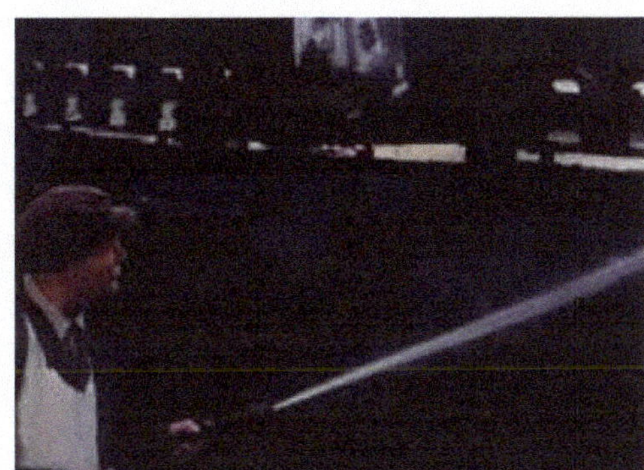

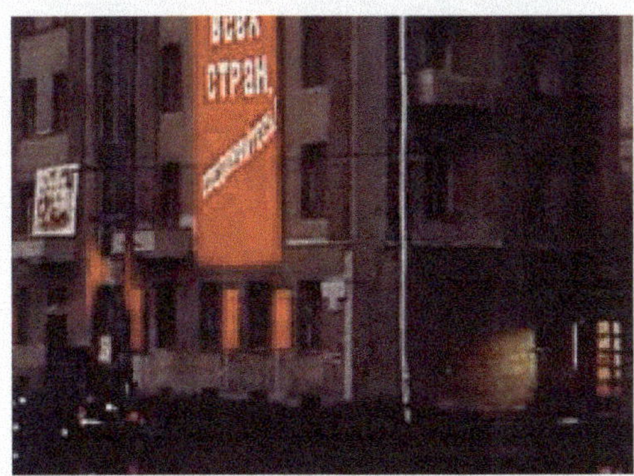

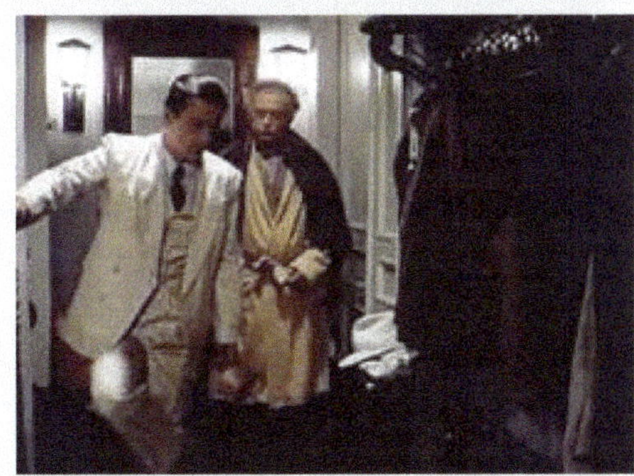

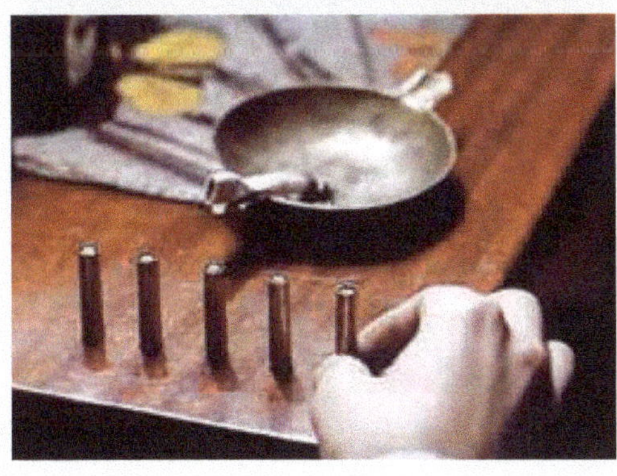

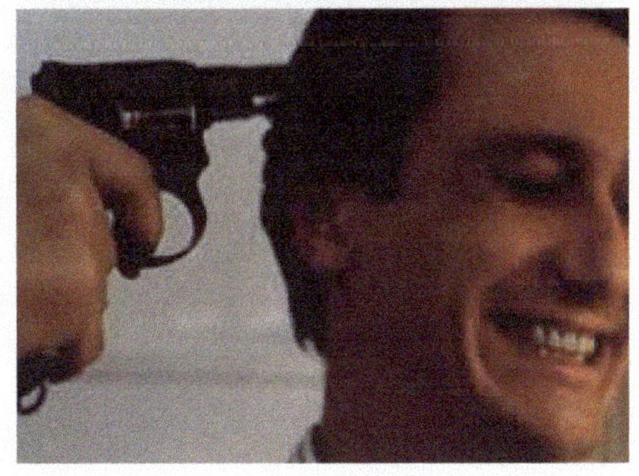

 Krymsky Bridge

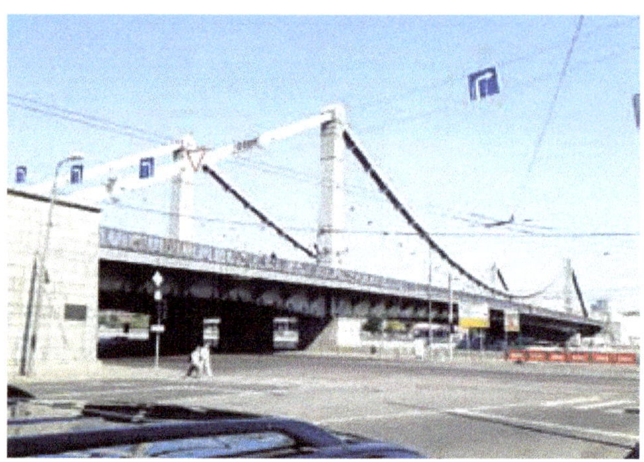

ADAPTED FROM RUSSIAN ACTRESS and writer Renata Litvinova's novella *To Have and Belong* (published 2007), *Land of the Deaf* subverts the mafia plotline so prevalent in 1990s Russian cinema. When Rita (Chulpan Khamatova) is held hostage by a nightclub owner, as collateral for the debt of boyfriend Alësha (Nikita Tyunin), she escapes with the assistance of deaf stripper Yaya (Dina Korzun), whose unusual, self-designated name translates as 'I-I' – the doubled assertion of the self. Yaya shelters Rita in the studio loft of a sculptor, where the two women grow close amidst the silent, inanimate creations of the absent artist. Todorovsky's film is a document of interior spaces and personal intimacy: even as Rita and Yaya scheme to earn money through various underworld connections, they gradually withdraw from the men of the public sphere, characterized by vanity and violence. Rita abandons her former life, and even learns sign language, as the heroines plot escape to the fictitious island of the film's title. In this scene, as the two cross the Krymsky (or Crimean) Bridge in central Moscow, they are beginning to sign to one another, reflecting on common experiences of feminine friendship. A pivotal moment in their shared life and developing relationship, the crossing enacts a symbolic transition to the 'land of the deaf' as an imaginative and emotional site, here spatialized on the banks of the Moskva River. Notably, the journey carries Rita and Yaya away from the Kremlin, glimpsed fleetingly in the background, as the male discourse of power recedes. **⟿ Tom Roberts**

Photo © Tom Roberts

Directed by Valeri Todorovsky
Scene description: Crossing the bridge by night,
Rita and Yaya discuss their past lives, and developing bond
Timecode for scene: 0:58:34 – 1:00:36

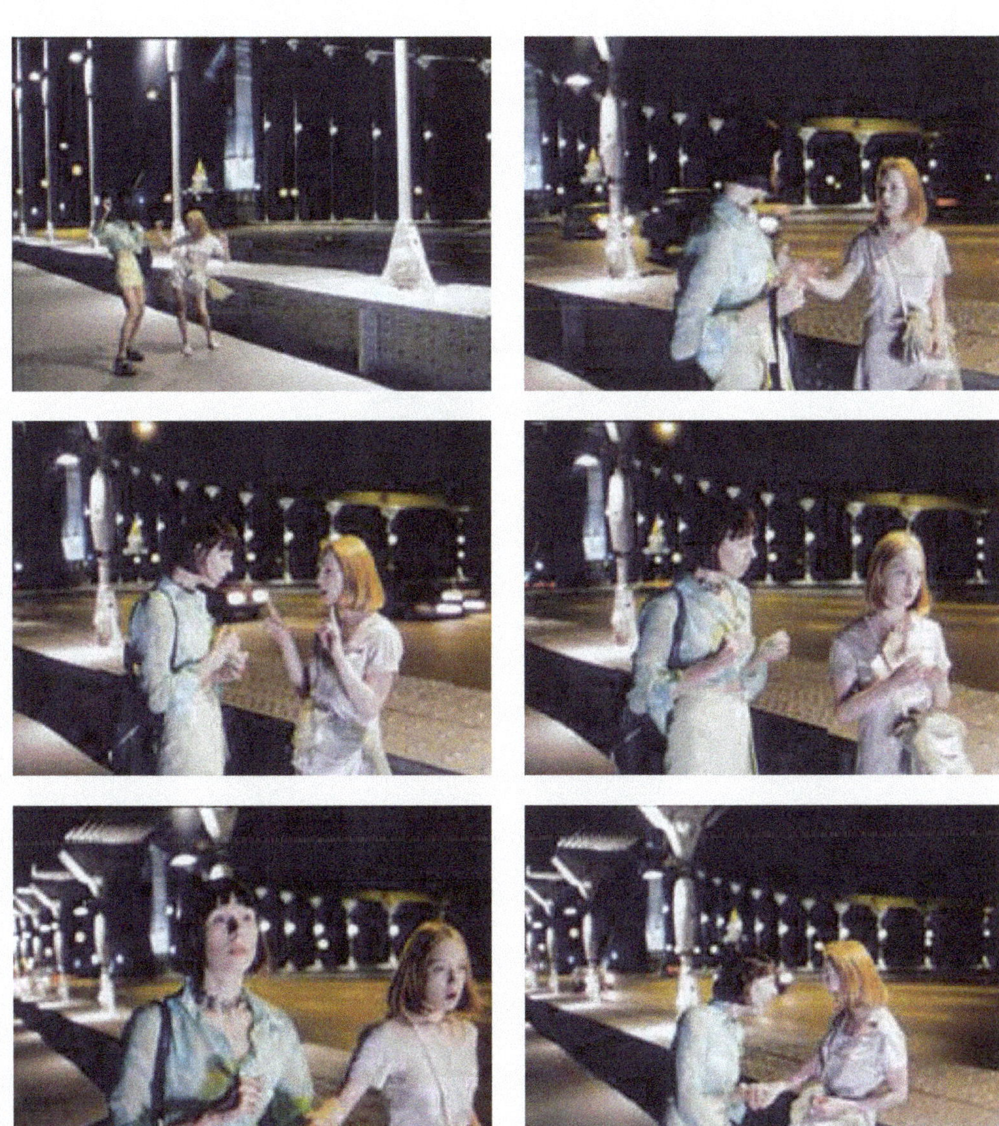

Images © 1998 Gorky Film Studio

OUTSKIRTS/OKRAINA (1998)

Ministry of Foreign Affairs, Smolenskaya Square

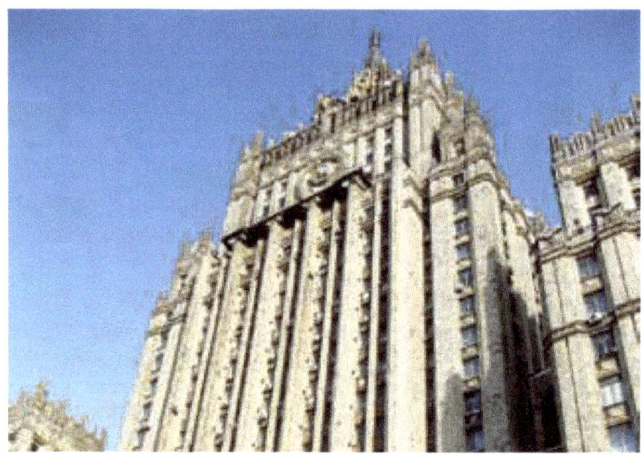

PËTR LUTSIK'S *Outskirts* is the only film directed by this extremely talented scriptwriter who, like his co-author Alexei Samoryadov, died tragically young. *Outskirts* was one of the few films of the late 1990s to celebrate the traditions of Soviet cinema, wedding it to the traditions of the Russian *bylina*, or epic legend. A film in which farmers set out on a quest to avenge the expropriation of their land, they travel from the periphery to the centre, meting out sadistic punishments to each supposed enemy, but each time finding that the main culprit is elsewhere. Finally they discover the true evildoer in the guise of an oil baron, who has his office in one of the Stalin-era wedding-cake high-rises in Moscow. The building is compared to the Egyptian pyramids, but in spite of their peasant unease at the court of such a pharaoh, they carry out their bloody revenge in spite of his scorn. The canisters of oil arranged in the baron's office turn out to be the destructive agent of an entire city, Moscow, built on deception and swindle. Shots of the Ministry of Foreign Affairs are shown as the fire slowly consumes the building, and eventually the whole city, as the peasant rebels make their getaway on motorbikes. It is only after having razed the city to the ground that the collective farmers can return to their fields and their tractors. **Giuliano Vivaldi**

Directed by Pëtr Lutsik
Scene description: *Visit of the peasant insurgents to the Moscow oil baron and destruction of Moscow*
Timecode for scene: *1:19:35 – 1:30:48*

BROTHER 2/BRAT 2 (2000)

Red Square, State Historical Museum

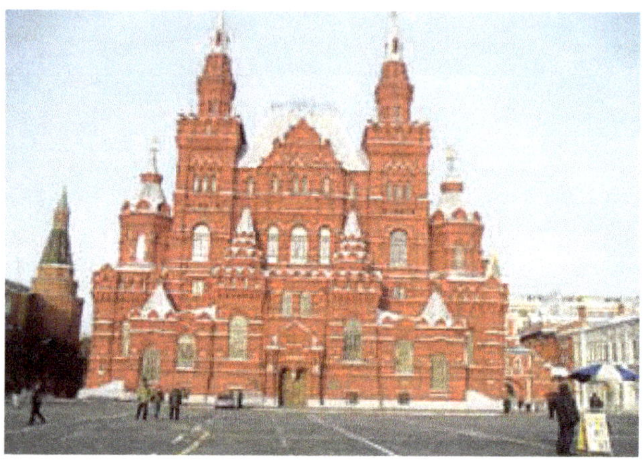

THE SEQUEL TO Balabanov's cult classic *Brother* (1996), this instalment finds Danila (Sergei Bodrov Jr) in Moscow, now possessing more self-confidence and having reunited with his Chechen War buddies, Kostya (Alexander Dyachenko) and Ilya (Kirill Pirogov), set to appear on a talk show dedicated to soldiers' experiences after returning home. Kostya runs afoul of an American businessman, who owns the Chicago Blackhawks hockey team, for which his twin brother plays. After Danila discovers Kostya dead in his apartment, he connects with Ilya at the State Historical Museum, where the latter works as a guard and archivist. It is here that Danila's brother Viktor (Viktor Sukhorukov) also joins the group. The iconic museum, on the edge of Red Square, was built in the 1870s in the Russian Revival style. While its holdings include everything from prehistoric artefacts discovered on Russian territory to exhibits on contemporary life, the small room that Ilya inhabits is filled with commonplace objects from the Soviet period: banners, flags and historic weaponry. For these soldiers of a failed post-Soviet war, such a nostalgic space conjures memories of past glory. Viktor asks whether an old machine gun is real, prompting him to identify it as 'like Chapaev's', a reference to the famous 1934 film *Chapaev* about the Russian Civil War. They later use this comically overbearing historical object in a shoot-out with Kostya's killers, foreshadowing the victory of the brothers over global capitalism.
➻*Joshua First*

Photo © Birgit Beumers

Directed by Alexei Balabanov

Scene description: Brothers Danila and Viktor meet in the State Historical Museum, where they plot revenge against a friend's killers in America
Timecode for scene: 0:29:18 – 0:31:10

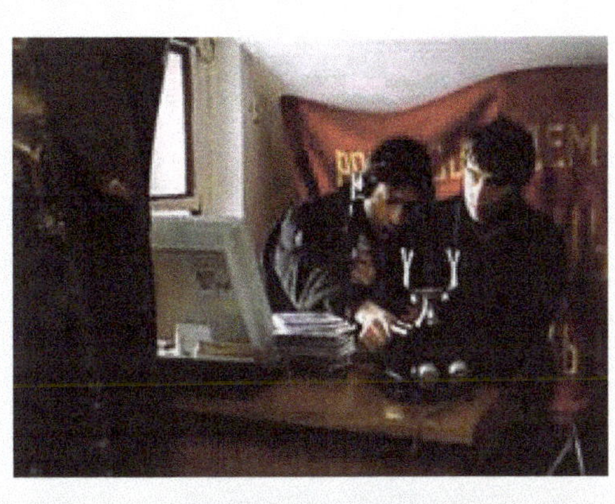
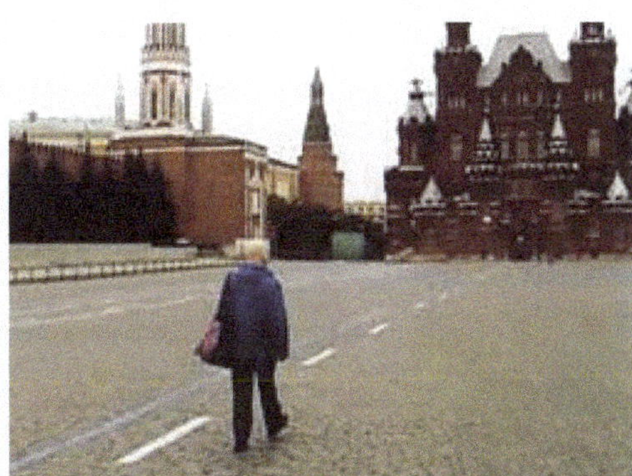
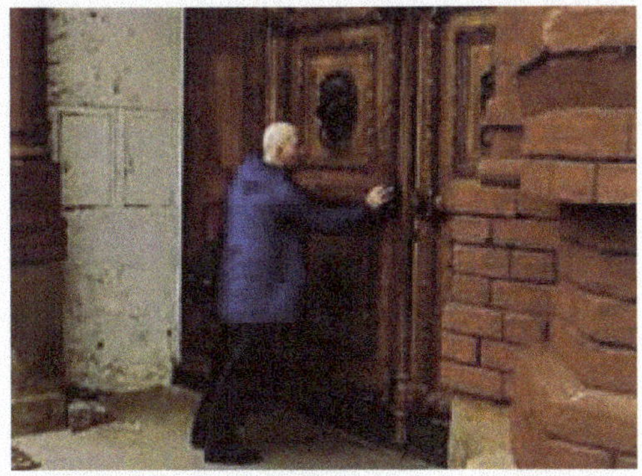
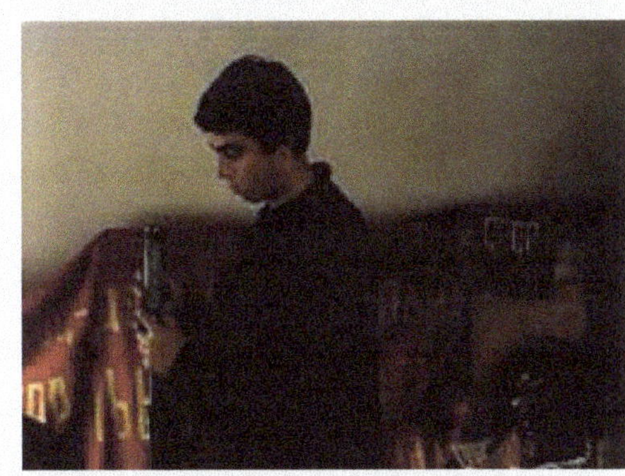
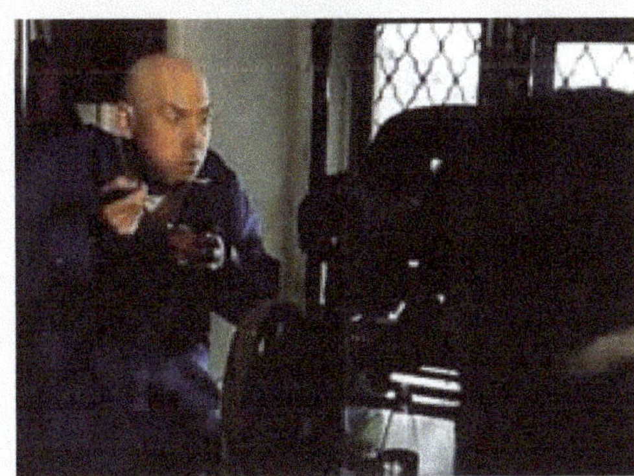
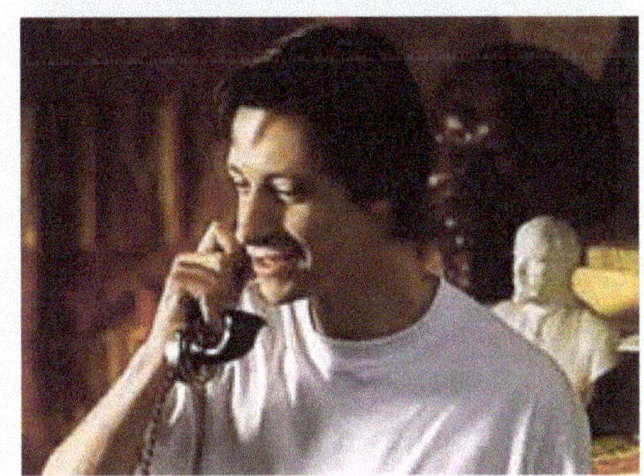

OLD HAGS/STARYE KLIACHI (2000)

Bersenevskaya Embankment, 'House on the Embankment'

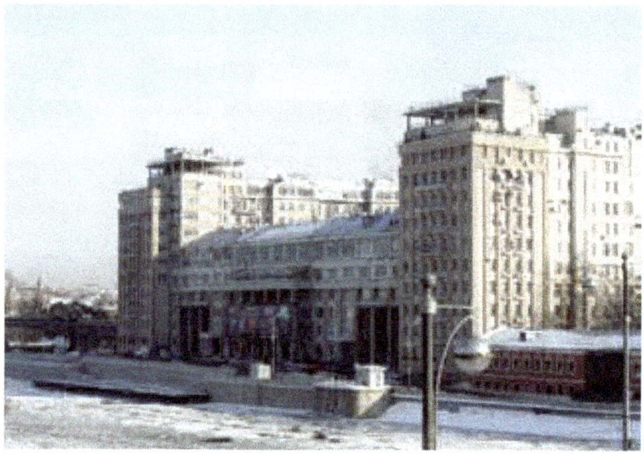

RYAZANOV'S MOSCOW is populated with amoral capitalists, impoverished pensioners and orphaned hooligans, while traditional institutions like the military remain without allocated funds from a now-absent state. The film's four female protagonists – old friends who performed together in amateur musical theatre during the Soviet period – are forced into the lowest rung of the hierarchy of Moscow's bandit capitalism. Three of them sell food and newspapers on the street, while the fourth, a former scientist, washes cars. All of them work within view of the Kremlin, not far from Moscow's most famous block of flats, the House on the Embankment, where one of the friends, Lyuba (Liya Akhedzhakova), has lived her whole life. While only a former school teacher, her family acquired a flat in this prestigious building because her father was a general. Built in 1931 for members of the Soviet government, the inhabitants of this example of early Stalinist architecture would include military leaders, veterans of the Revolution and important cultural figures. During the 1990s, Moscow's newly wealthy and multi-national corporations bought out many of the former residents, transforming the building into modern flats, offices and retail space. In *Old Hags*, a big-time caviar dealer, Khomenko (Nikolai Fomenko), cheats Lyuba out of her flat there by offering a fake cheque for $100,000, and a promise to transfer her to a 'quiet place in central Moscow', which turns out to be a small home in a cemetery. ➜ *Joshua First*

Photo © Birgit Beumers

Directed by Eldar Ryazanov
Scene description: Businessman Khomenko cheats Lyuba
out of her desirable flat in the House on the Embankment
Timecode for scene: 0:11:50 – 0:20:47

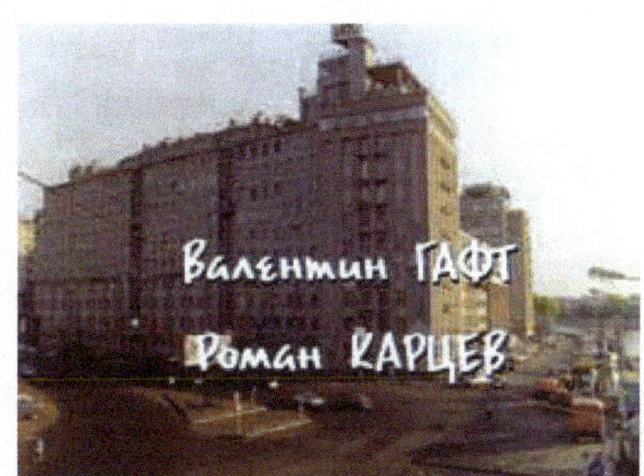

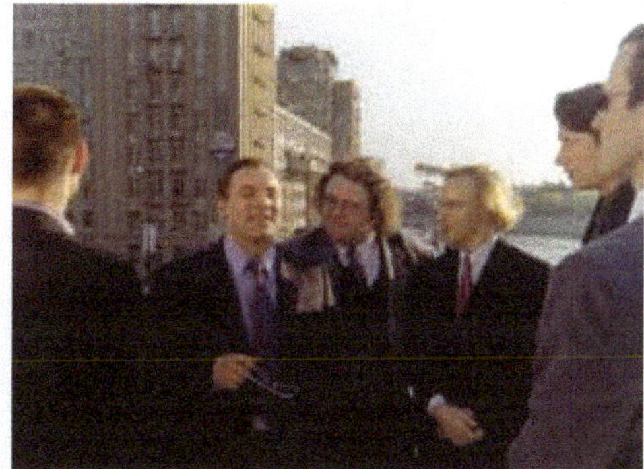

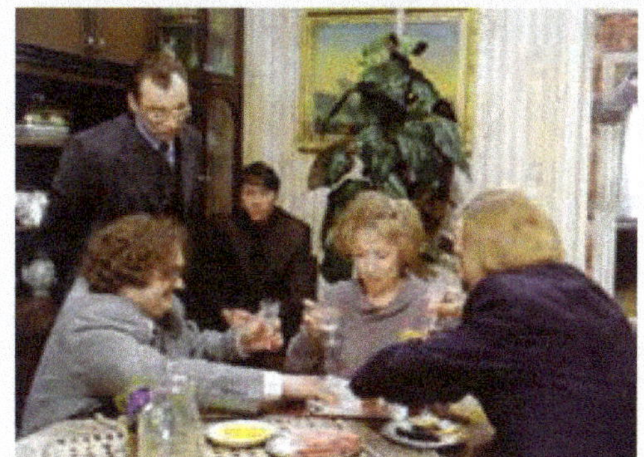

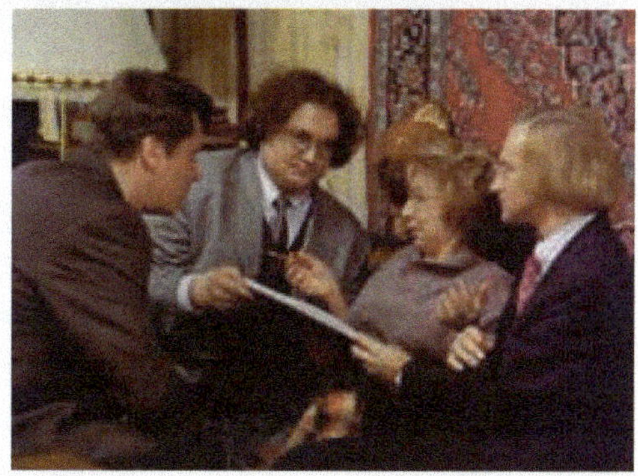

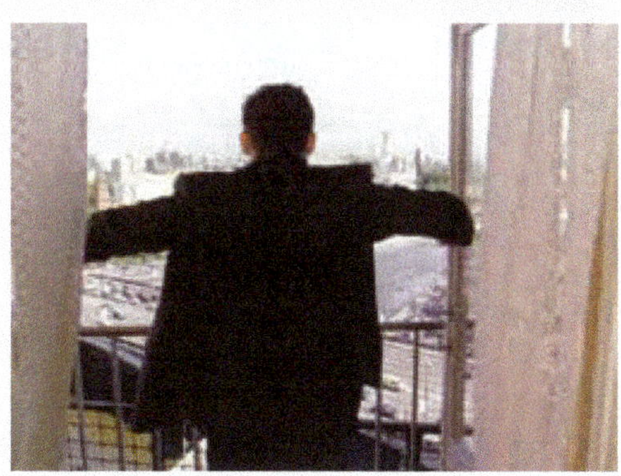

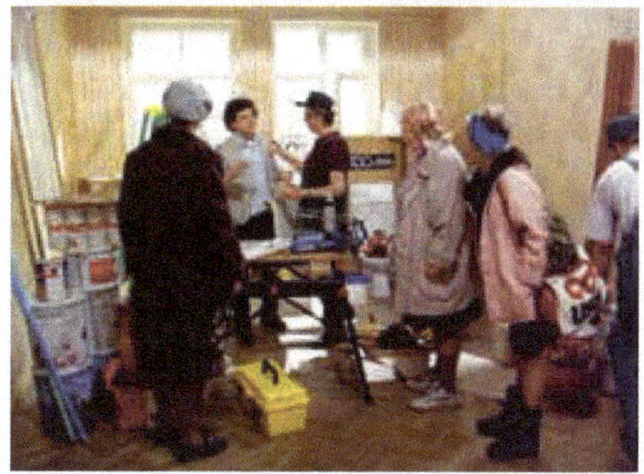

Images © 2000 Kinomost

MOSCOW/MOSKVA (2000)

Olympic Ski Jump, Sparrow Hills

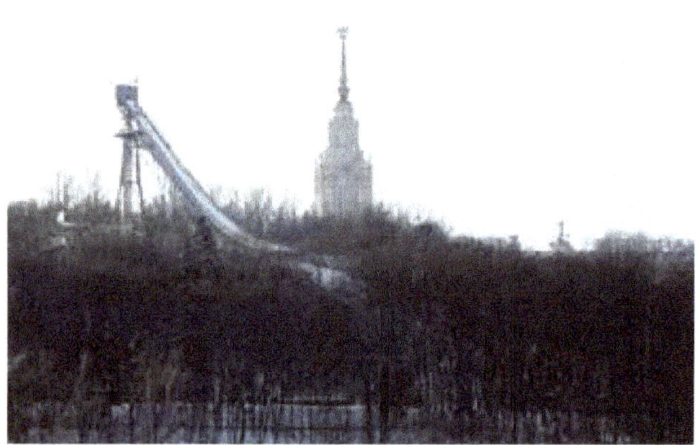

THE MOSCOW OF Alexander Zeldovich's film is a rather deserted and lifeless postmodern city, where the emptying-out of consciousness and history plays an important role. The space is inhabited by postmodern versions of Chekhov's 'three sisters', named Olga, Masha and Irina, who have made it to Moscow, but find themselves part of this estranged city fraught with violence and brutality. Both Chekhov's pre-Revolutionary Moscow and the Soviet capital as symbolized by the monument to the unknown soldier are replaced by the lifeless glamour of voguish cafes, a deliberately superficial tour through the city, and a performance of *Swan Lake* at the Bolshoi Theatre cut short by a Mafia hit. Moscow is a void: two characters have sex through a hole in a map from which Moscow has been cut out. The Olympic ski jump on Sparrow Hills down towards the Moskva River is a central location in the film: first, the protagonists gather on the platform for a dinner; later it will be the scene for the suicide of psychiatrist Mark (Viktor Gvozditsky). His downward flight towards his death, as he carries a bottle of whisky and a suitcase of English-language detective and spy-thriller books which are scattered on the ground after his fall, grotesquely mirrors the cosmic flight of Ilya Kabakov's installation *The man who flew into space from his apartment* (1984), showing a resident of a communal flat amidst the written notes of his neighbours.
➝ **Giuliano Vivaldi**

Photo © Birgit Beumers

Scene description: Mark's suicide on the ski jump
Timecode for scene: 1:51:40 – 1:52:46

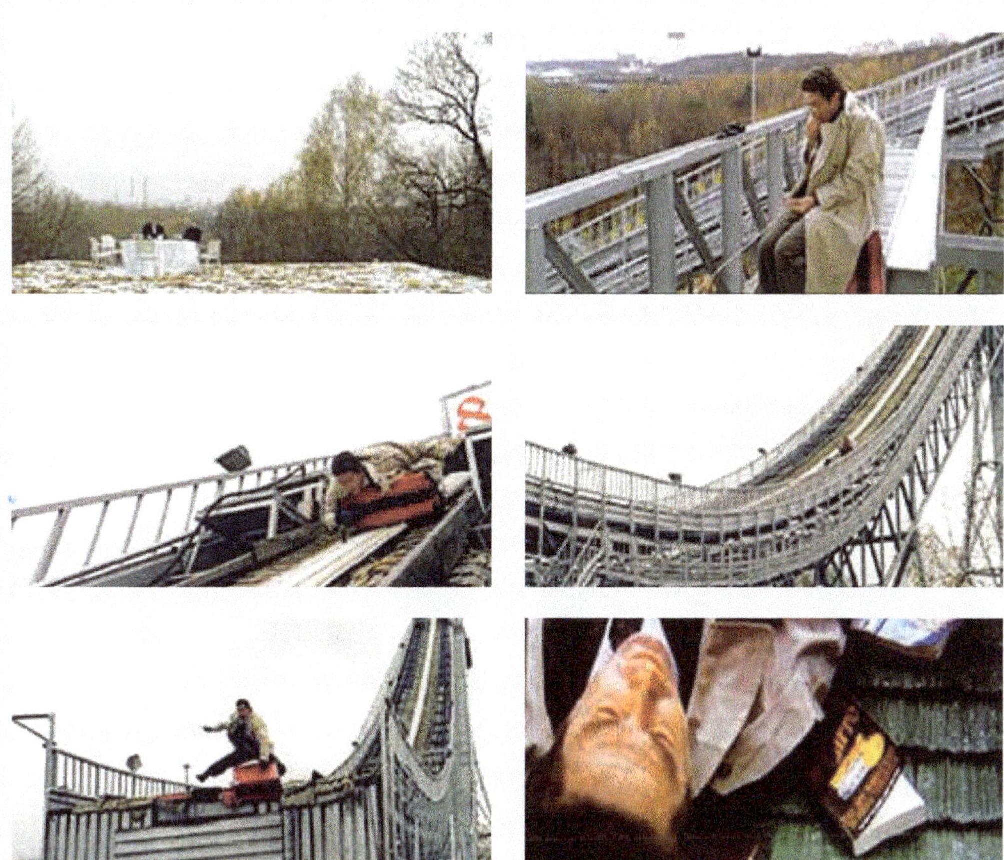

MARGINAL OR CENTRAL

Prostitution in Moscow

Text by
EMILY
SCHUCKMAN
MATTHEWS

SINCE NIKOLAI KARAMZIN'S eighteenth-century sentimental heroine, 'Poor Liza', went to Moscow to peddle her flowers only to be deflowered and driven to suicide by the nobleman Erast, Russia's capital city has been portrayed as a site of sexual allure, opportunity and danger for young women. This literary narrative is paralleled in early and post-Soviet cinematic representations of the city, which feature it as a site of promise, prosperity, poverty – and prostitution.

Oleg Frelikh's *Prostitutka/The Prostitute* (1927) is a prime example of early Soviet propaganda film, warning women of the dangers of entering the sex trade and presenting government solutions to societal circumstances which force them into it. Part fictional narrative, part public health lecture, the film blends the stories of three women (Lyuba, Manka and Nadezhda) driven to prostitution in Moscow with intertitle cards featuring statistics about women's poverty, education and the health consequences of promiscuous sex. Lyuba is eventually 'rescued' into a sewing collective, while Nadezhda is granted a government job as a tram

worker. Manka is left suffering from syphilis in a hospital. Most scenes are filmed on the outskirts of Moscow, largely in tenement-style homes or on snow-covered boulevards, spaces inhabited largely by people on the margins of both the city and society. The film offers these outliers hope that through government jobs, education and healthcare they will be brought into the communal fold of Soviet ideals.

Prostitution largely disappeared from Russian screens until the advent of perestroika, when the sex worker emerged as the ubiquitous symbol of newly-found freedoms in the country – a status which she retains to this day. Reflecting both reality and fantasy, women for sale become standard background characters in scenes filmed in bars, restaurants, saunas, clubs or on the crowded urban streets. Late and post-Soviet films featuring Muscovite prostitutes as more central characters vacillate between naturalistic depictions of the difficulties faced by these women in the city's large sex industry and glamorous portrayals of the capital's elites and the women who serve them. Though these two approaches offer very different depictions of Moscow, they both portray it as a sexually potent and economically thriving city, which is largely dominated by powerful and wealthy men.

Valeri Todorovsky's *Strana glukhikh/The Land of the Deaf* (1998), which chronicles the story of two women who calculatedly engage in prostitution, is iconic of the gritty dramas of the late Soviet period. This film incorporates many pertinent social issues, such as women's economic position, the underworld of the Russian mafia, sexual identity and disability. Many scenes offer important snapshots of a changing Moscow: a strip club, a floating casino, bustling markets and cafes, decrepit housing and imposing Stalinist buildings on the horizon. The women can only access the

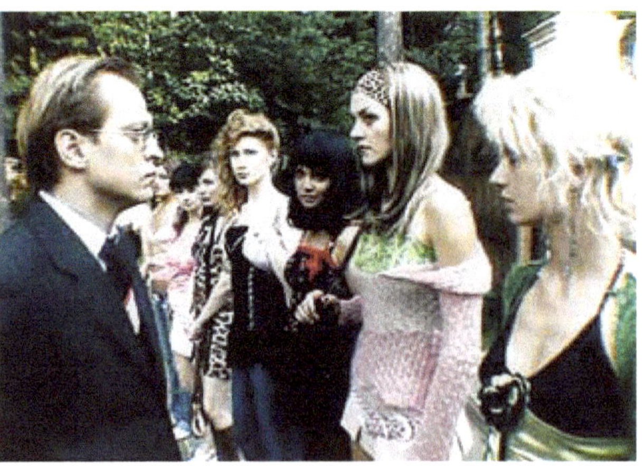

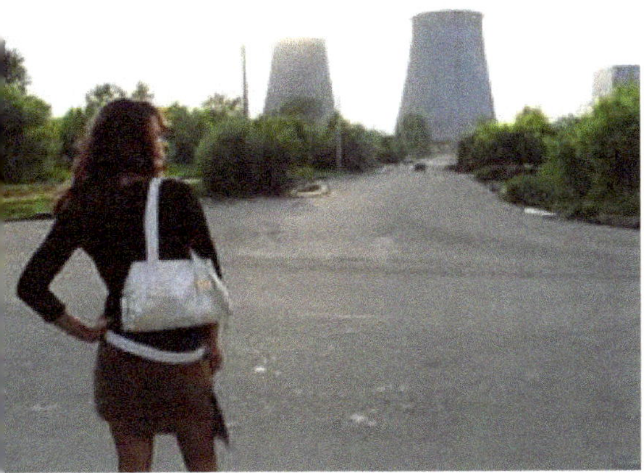

money they need to achieve their goals (one to pay her boyfriend's gambling debt, the other to escape to a utopian land of her imagination) by prostituting themselves to men who hold both the capital and power in the city. Like the women of *The Prostitute*, these women live in the dark corners of the city, but unlike for Lyuba, Manka and Nadezhda, there is no government or community-based solution to their problems. They are on their own. Despite their outsider status, the women are ultimately triumphant over their male exploiters, who kill each other in a shoot-out at the end of the film – leaving behind only white chalk outlines of their bodies as the women walk away unharmed.

A similar message about the city's power structure and even gloomier depiction of Moscow is offered in Yuri Moroz's film *Tochka/The Spot* (2006). The narrative features the stories of the three prostitutes Anya, Kira and Nina in Moscow, who all journey to the city to find new opportunities. The film's naturalistic approach captures the many facets of the city, from its darkest corners to its most glittering shopping malls. Perhaps one of the most revealing locations is the women's home, positioned on the edge of the city, metaphorically locating them on the edge of the dynamism of Moscow's city centre. The women penetrate the centre only when they stand at the 'spot' to sell their bodies to men who drive up in BMWs and whisk them away to their mansions or yachts. Anya and Nina ultimately become stakeholders in Moscow's booming economy, not through government aid or education, but by stealing money from Kira and setting up their own 'spot' where they are now the procuresses rather than the procured.

Andrei Konchalovsky's *Glianets/Gloss* (2007) captures the lives and lifestyles of Moscow's elite. The film's heroine journeys from the depressing provinces to shiny Moscow, seeking employment as a model for one of the country's top-selling women's magazines. Though she initially fails, the provincial beauty works her way through the ranks from seamstress to personal assistant for a man who runs a high-end escort business, to finally attaining the privileged position of being a woman for hire in the agency. Transformed into a Grace Kelly lookalike, she charms her wealthy client, eventually marrying him, thus entering Moscow's elite social circles and finally appearing on the cover of the very magazine which originally rejected her. The film features scenes in the ultra-contemporary office building which houses the magazine, couture fashion shows, a designer-decorated photo studio/brothel, posh restaurants and gilded mansions. One of the film's goals is to critique and condemn the shallow materialism and brutal capitalism that these 'glossy' spaces represent, but the viewer is ultimately drawn in by the film's voyeuristic look at beautiful, sexy people inhabiting gorgeous surroundings and can only wish to be a part of this world.

Contemporary Moscow is cast as a city of consumption, with its inhabitants devouring everything from the latest fashions and western fads to sex and the women who sell it. The city itself consumes those who cannot keep up with its frenetic pace, relying on the constant flow of people from the provinces and more far-flung regions to fuel its rapid development. Films that feature the city's prostitutes offer audiences a way to glimpse both the high and low of Moscow, from its crumbling Soviet housing structures and dark alleys to the mansions of the city's most successful people. These women also highlight the sexual allure that the city represents, a place where everything and everyone can be bought, sold and consumed. Both *The Spot* and *Gloss* aim to present cautionary tales, but the contrasts portrayed between the dead-end provinces and the lively and alluring city continue to assure that women and men will make the journey to the glittering capital to seek a better life. ✚

Films that feature the city's prostitutes offer audiences a way to glimpse both the high and low of Moscow, from its crumbling Soviet housing structures and dark alleys to the mansions of the city's most successful people.

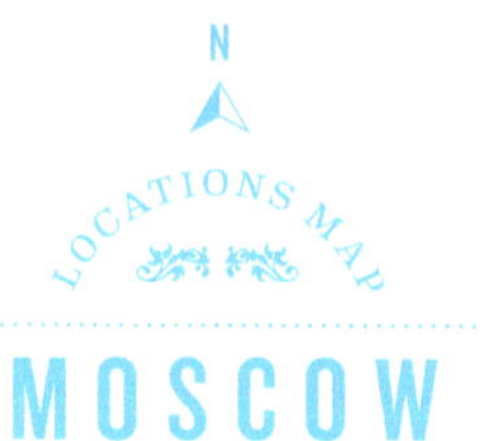

N
LOCATIONS MAP
MOSCOW

maps are only to be taken as approximates

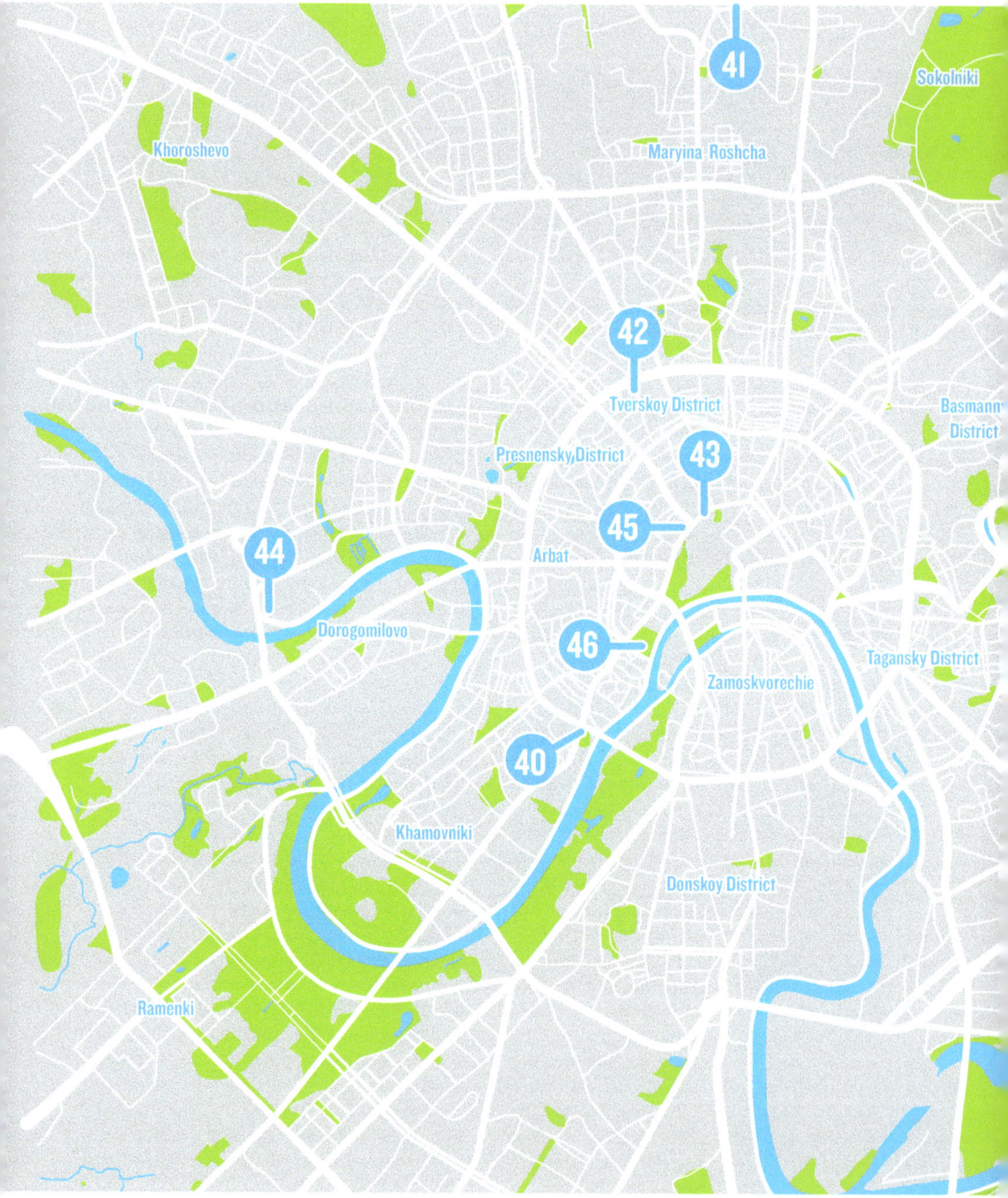

41
Sokolniki
Maryina Roshcha
42
Tverskoy District
Basmann District
Presnensky District
43
45
Arbat
44
Dorogomilovo
46
Tagansky District
Zamoskvorechie
40
Khamovniki
Donskoy District
Ramenki

MOSCOW LOCATIONS
SCENES 40-46

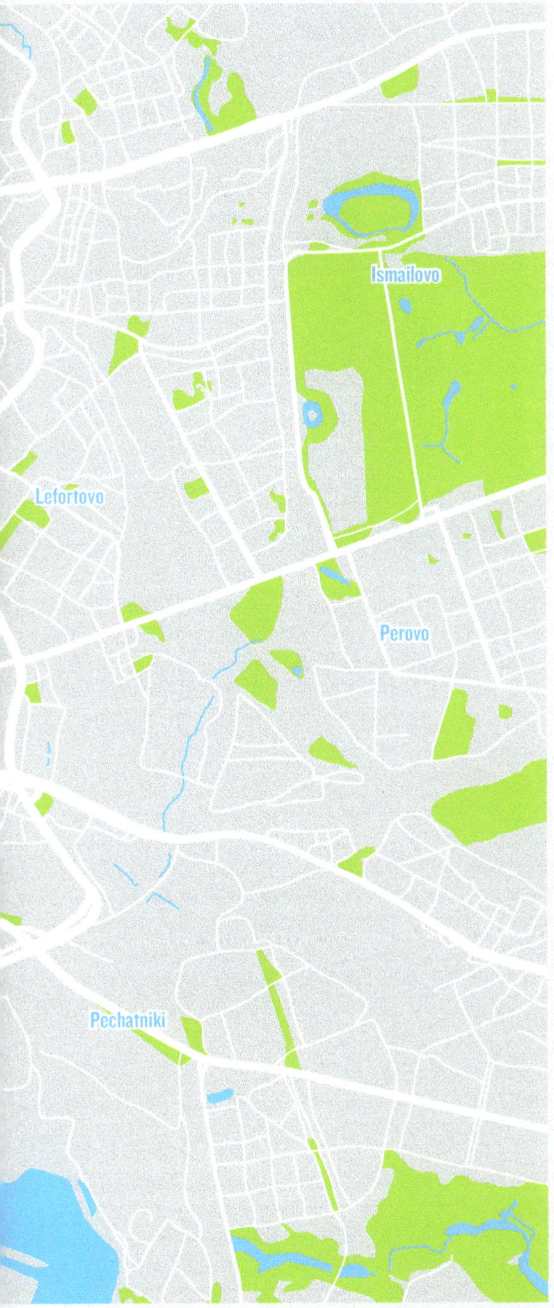

NIGHT WATCH/NOCHNOI DOZOR (2004)

Moscow metro

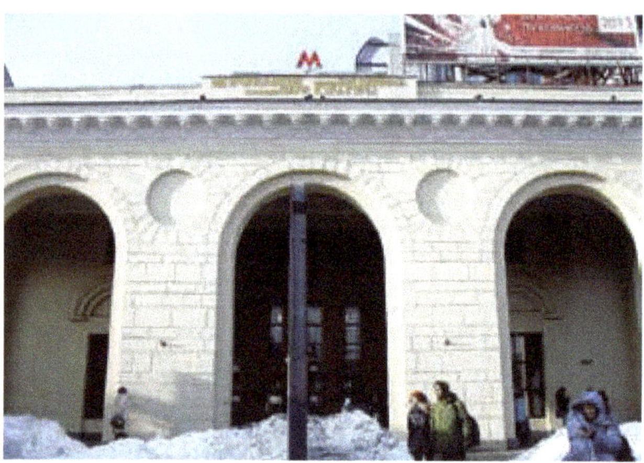

ONE EPISODE OF the fantasy thriller *Night Watch* takes place in the Moscow metro. Known as the world's third most-used rapid transit system, the metro is shown first through the external pavilion of the metro station Park Kultury at the intersection of the circle line and the radial (Sokolniki) line, and then at the stations VDNKh and Sviblovo of the orange radial (Kaluzhsko-Rizhskaya) line. The protagonist Anton Gorodetsky (Konstantin Khabensky) receives an assignment to find a potential victim, who is lost somewhere in the metro system. We see the victim enter Park Kultury station and take one of two potential routes: the brown circle line or the red radial line to change to the orange line, with Sviblovo being his final destination. The characters are taking the metro during the rush hour so that the viewer sees the typical Moscow crowd storming the carriages, and the police checkpoints at the exits picking suspicious-looking people and stopping them for a document check. Marketed as a Moscow film, *Night Watch* shows the metro as an everyday means of transport, not as a highly mythologized underground space popularized in Dmitri Glukhovsky's novel *Metro 2033* (2005). Unlike above-the-ground footage that features tourists' points of view on Moscow, the film's underground scenes avoid geographic specificity: the metro station names are barely shown, while their most remarkable architectural elements are missing altogether. *Night Watch* shows the metro from Gorodetsky's point of view, privileging fast-paced editing and exaggerated perspectives over topographic exactitude. ⇢ *Sasha Razor*

Scene description: Anton Gorodetsky travels on the metro to follow
a potential victim of a vampire attack in his battle against evil
Timecode for scene: 0:18:01 – 0:22:50

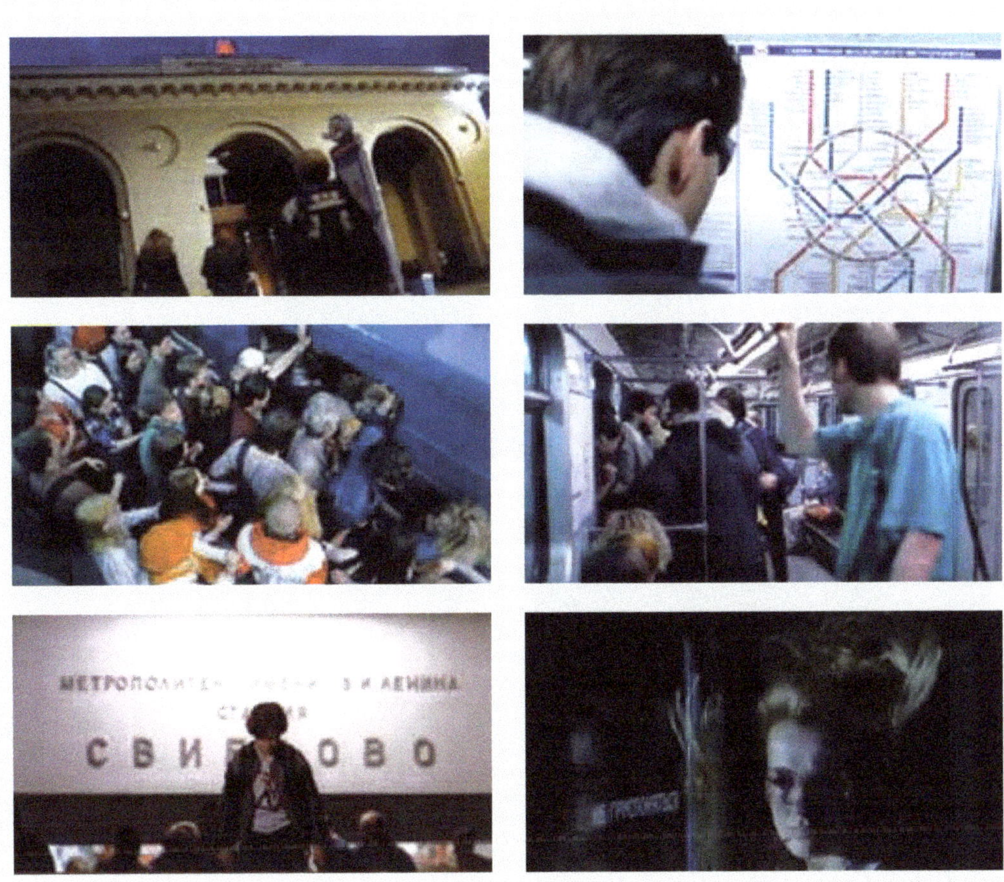

Images © 2004 Bazelevs, Channel One Russia, TABBAK

DAY WATCH/DNEVNOI DOZOR (2006)

Residential area around the Kosmos Hotel,
Ostankino Television Tower, VDNKh

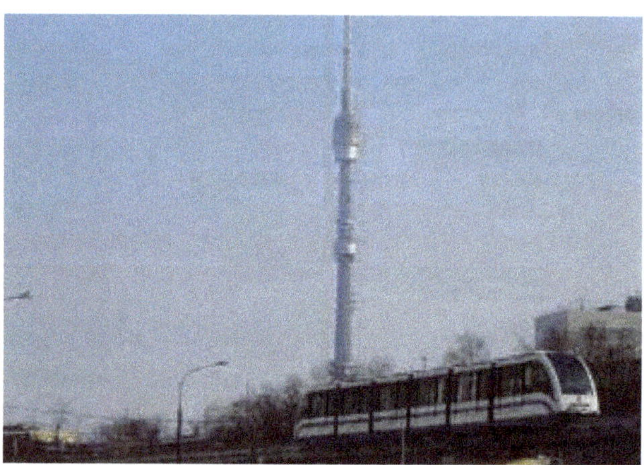

THE SEQUEL TO Bekmambetov's 2004 hit *Nochnoi dozor/Night Watch* and based
on the second half of the same novel by Sergei Lukyanenko (1998), *Day Watch*
depicts the struggle between supernatural beings contending on battlefield
Earth: the Light Others who guard the night, against the Dark Others patrolling
the day. Caught between these two forces by familial dysfunction, the post-
Soviet everyman Anton Gorodetsky (Konstantin Khabensky) must resolve
a domestic dispute between his abandoned son Yegor (Dmitri Martynov),
a powerful Great Other for the dark side, and his lover Svetlana (Maria
Poroshina), Yegor's nemesis on the side of light. This conflict erupts into the
wholesale destruction of a wintertime Moscow, seen through stark imagery
of familiar landmarks exploding in showers of debris: the Ostankino tower
collapses; the Kosmos Hotel is ripped apart; the Moscow-850 Ferris wheel rolls
unmoored down the street; countless apartment blocks crumble around and
onto panicked citizens. The scene partakes of a grandiosely expansive, hyper-
kinetic, CGI-driven style familiar from US disaster and science fiction films
of the late twentieth century, especially *Independence Day* (Roland Emmerich,
1996). *Day Watch*'s resolution has Anton grimly striding through a grey post-
apocalyptic Moscow-scape (which resembles Grozny after the first Chechen
War), on his way to change history with the magical Chalk of Fate. This will
undo the destruction and catapult our hero back to a fresh, innocent 1992. The
scene thus functions as a *deus-ex-machina* dream of return, to a time when the
trauma of the post-Soviet 1990s never happened. ➛*José Alaniz*

Photo © Nikolai Izvolov

Scene description: Yegor destroys Moscow
Timecode for scene: 1:57:38 – 2:11:00

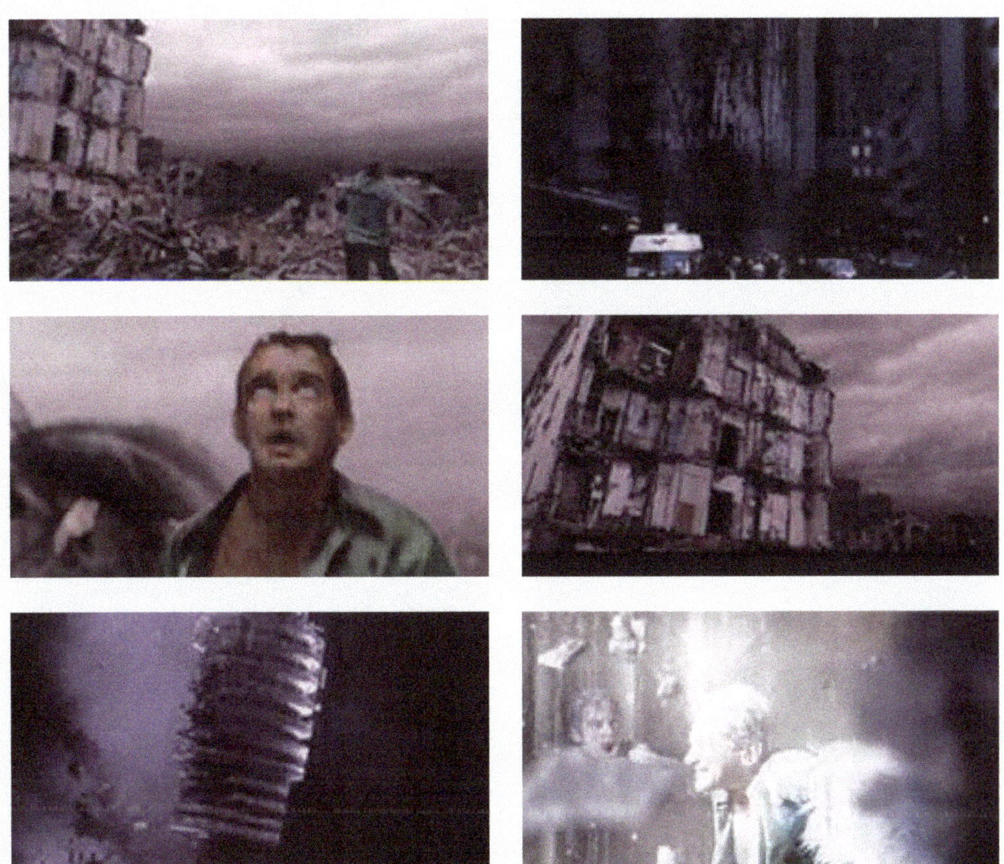

THE SPOT/TOCHKA (2006)

Staropimenovsky Lane

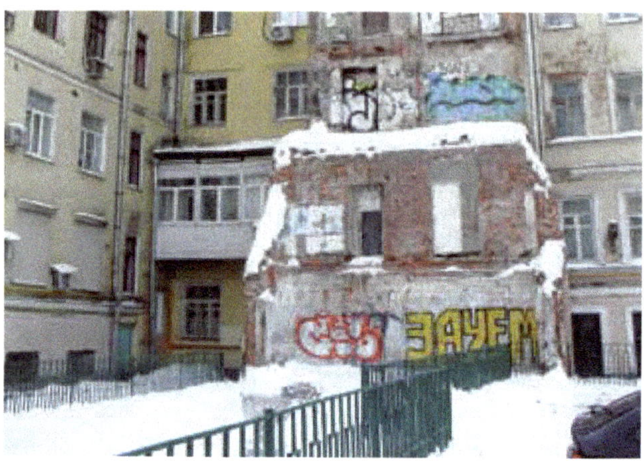

YURI MOROZ'S FILM *The Spot* portrays in stark realism the lives of three prostitutes in Moscow. Anya (Anna Ukolova), Kira (Viktoria Isakova) and Nina (Darya Moroz) work at the same 'spot' (*tochka*) – a word which designates the 'spot' where prostitutes are procured. Moroz enhances the naturalistic narrative by filming on location at a real spot on a Staropimenovsky lane and including actual prostitutes as extras. In this scene, the actresses and their real-life counterparts line up for a client inspection. The man selects Anya, Kira and Nina for a party that will ultimately end with them being threatened by attack dogs. The women of *The Spot* are both a fully integrated part of Moscow's landscape, yet exist largely in the shadows of the glittering city. The capital looms large as a place of opportunity and exploitation for the women, representing the clichéd end point of their journeys from the provinces to the big city. Nevertheless, the three-dimensionality of the women's characters and the sensitivity with which Moroz approaches their narratives infuses the film with complexity and provides a fresh critique on women's vulnerable status in Moscow and Russia at large. The grittiness of the spot, a dark, dirty and graffiti-covered site where the women line up for inspection and selection, often illuminated only by the headlights of their clients BMWs, stands in stark contrast to the spaces their clients inhabit: gated mansions, houseboats and cosy apartments. Moroz's juxtaposition of these environments successfully captures a tale of two Moscows.
➽ **Emily Schuckman Matthews**

Photo © Birgit Beumers

Directed by Yuri Moroz
Scene description: Clients pick up prostitutes
Timecode for scene: 0:01:12 – 0:01:58; 0:15:15 – 0:17:45

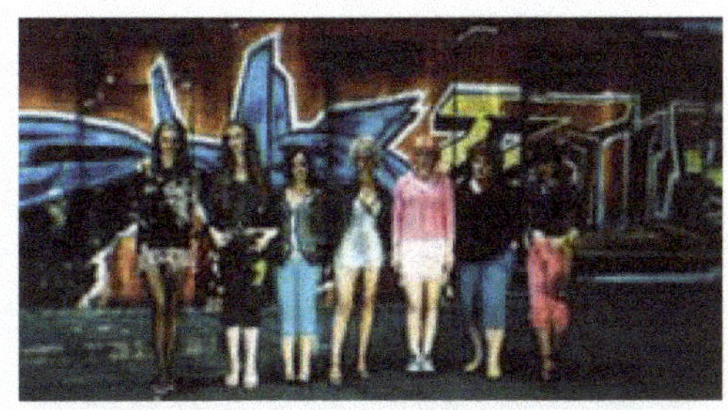
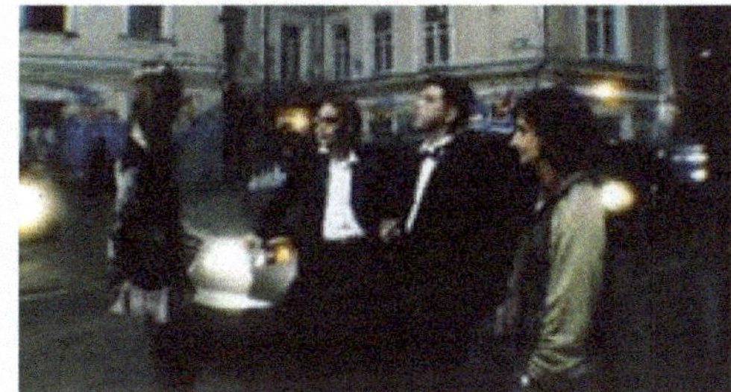
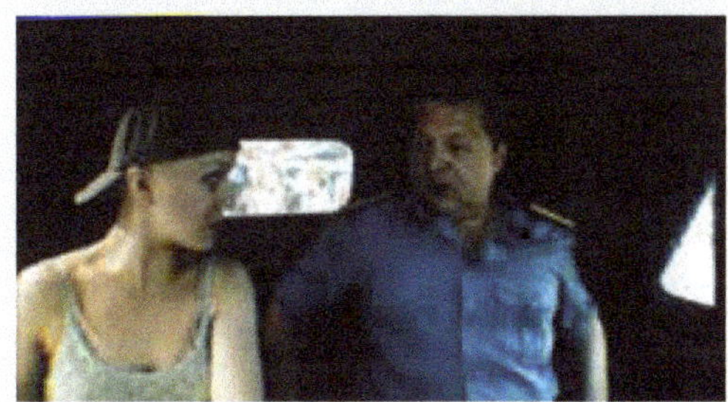
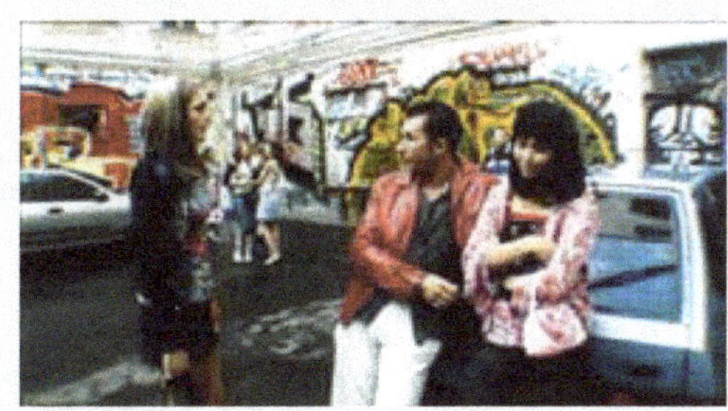
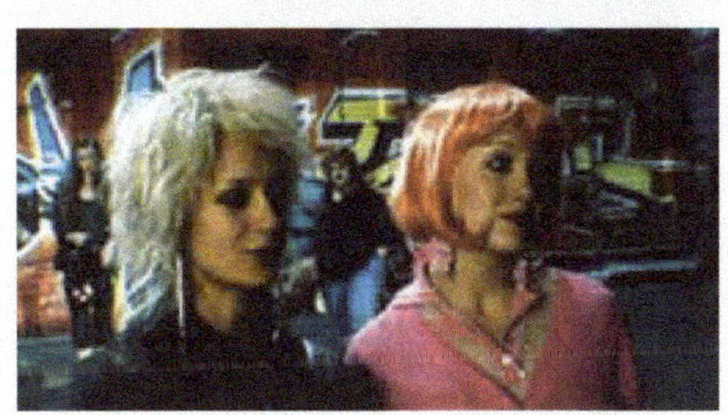
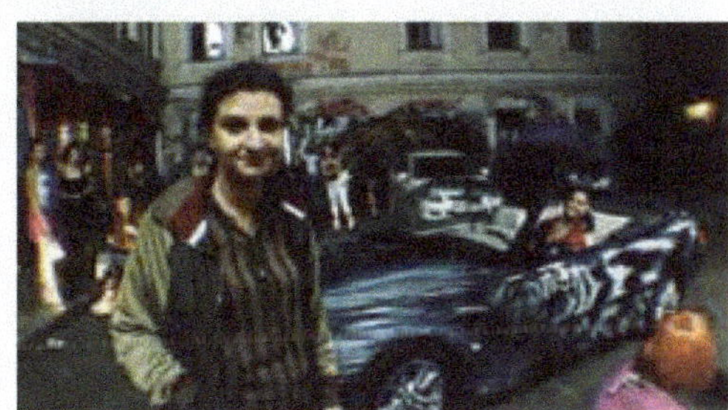

MERMAID/RUSALKA (2007)

Tverskaya and Bolshaya Dmitrovka Streets

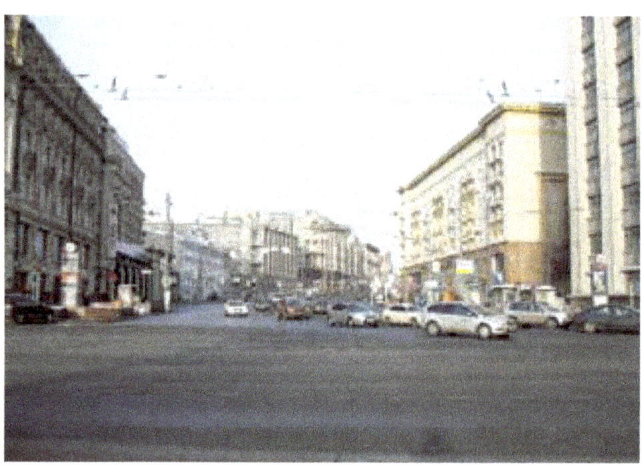

IN ANNA MELIKYAN'S *Mermaid*, the protagonist, Alisa (Maria Shalaeva), ends up in the wrong place at the wrong time on more than one occasion. After a hurricane destroys her seaside house, she moves with her mother and grandmother to Moscow. Alisa gets a job working for a mobile phone company, walking around the city dressed as a phone for advertisement purposes. In this scene, Alisa prepares to celebrate her eighteenth birthday, her first birthday in Moscow. She strolls down Tverskaya Street and through the surrounding area in her cellphone costume, observing passers-by. As she stares wistfully through the window at a ballet studio, remembering her unfulfilled childhood dream of becoming a ballerina, suddenly the glass breaks and Alisa finds herself in the middle of a riot. The story of the riot is told as if it were a newscast, with Alisa-the-cellphone seen wandering through the chaos of hooligans destroying cars and anything else in their path. The event Alisa experiences is the riot that broke out after Russia lost to Japan 0–1 in the 2002 World Cup finals. A massive riot broke out near an outdoor screening of the game in Manège Square and as many as 8,000 rioters swarmed the city, killing two people. Alisa is detained by the police and her cellphone costume is ruined, leading to a serious confrontation with her boss. **⁕Erin Alpert**

Directed by Anna Melikyan
Scene description: A soccer riot interrupts Alisa's daydreaming
Timecode for scene: 0:41:39 – 0:44:27

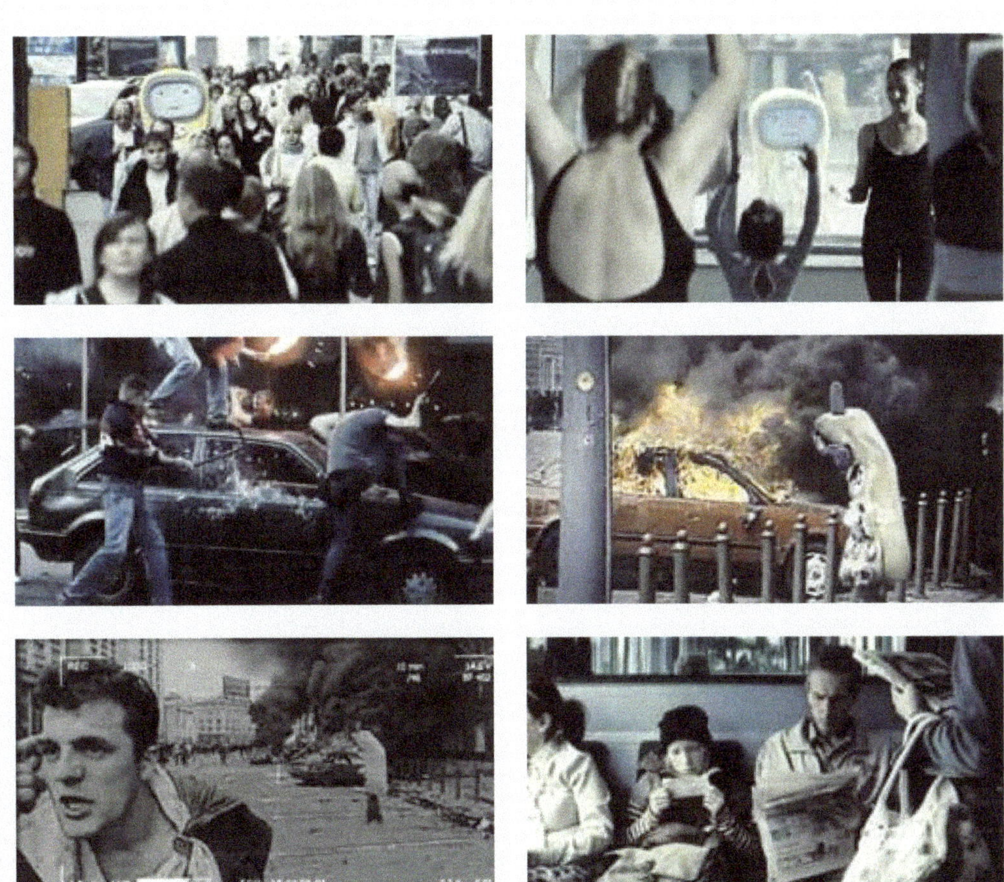

CRUELTY/ZHESTOKOST' (2007)

Naberezhnaya Tower, Moscow International Business Centre ('Moskva-Siti')

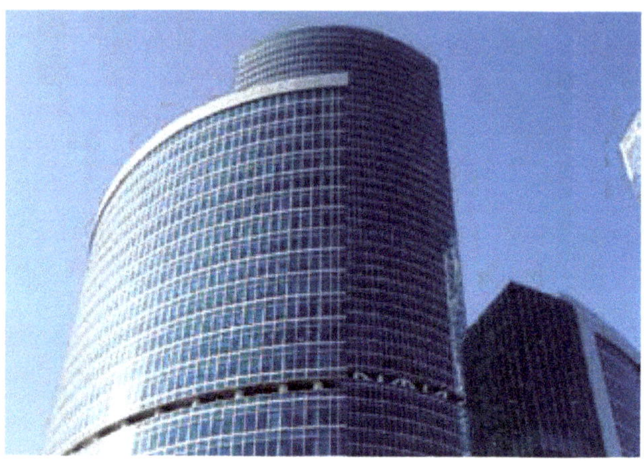

MARINA LYUBAKOVA'S *Cruelty* traces its themes of exploitation and betrayal across the periphery of a fragmentary, hyper-capitalist Moscow. When teenager Vika (Anna Begunova) photographs married neighbour Boris (Yevgeni Serov) conducting a romantic affair with fellow neighbour Zoya (Renata Litvinova), she attempts unsuccessfully to blackmail the businessman. Met instead with a violent reprisal, Vika subsequently befriends Zoya, since abandoned by Boris. The pair's complex relationship unfolds as they take revenge on the philanderer, in a series of destructive acts that drive Zoya to the margins of Russian society. Their project begins at the Naberezhnaya Tower, where Boris works; the building was still under construction at the time of the film's production. After the two women infiltrate the building, Vika slips upstairs to the targeted man's office in the guise of a courier, as Zoya waits in the parking garage; finding his desk unattended, she leaves a package containing a paint bomb and steals his car keys. Returning to the garage, Vika cajoles Zoya into stealing the car, and the two speed away. Meanwhile, a female co-worker finds the package and triggers the device, becoming an accidental casualty of Vika's plot. *Cruelty* is among the first films to utilize the 'Moskva-Siti' complex, succinctly evoking the culture of 'new' Moscow. While the episode initiates the shared journey of Vika and Zoya, it also foreshadows its conclusion: though the woman who activates the paint bomb bears only a passing resemblance to Litvinova's Zoya, the correspondence is sufficient to suggest that this project may yet explode in the heroine's face. **•◦Tom Roberts**

Photo © Tom Roberts

Scene description: Vika and Zoya initiate their revenge on Boris, claiming an unintended victim
Timecode for scene: 0:31:17 – 0:35:24

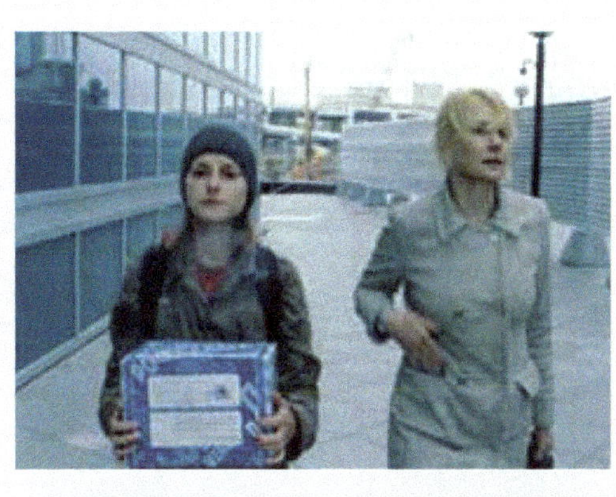
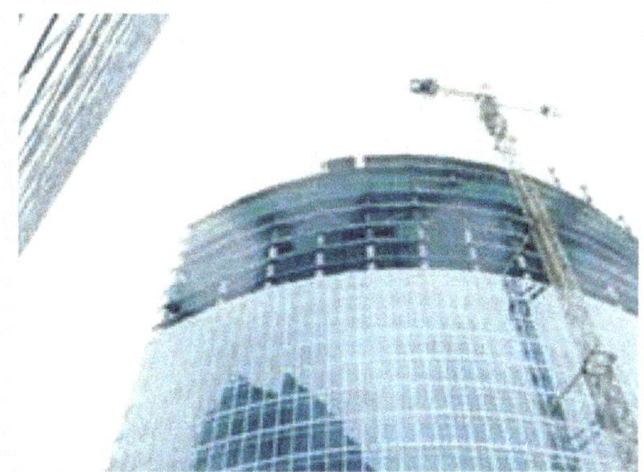
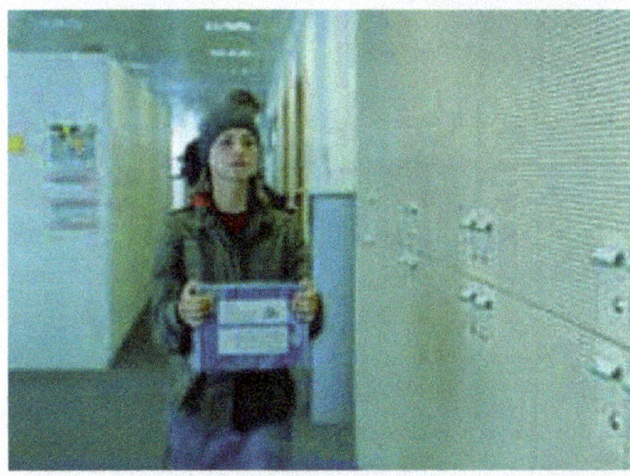
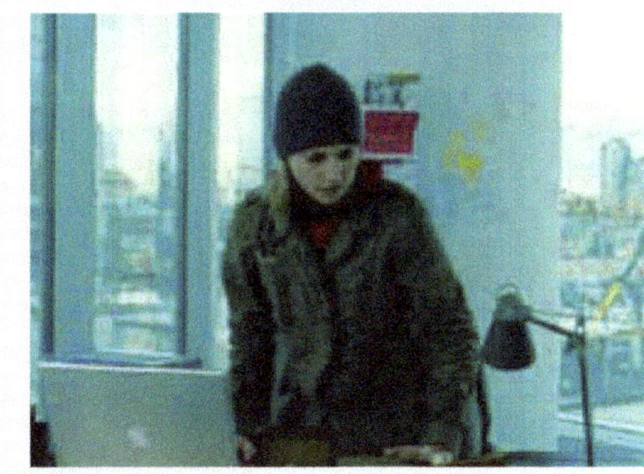
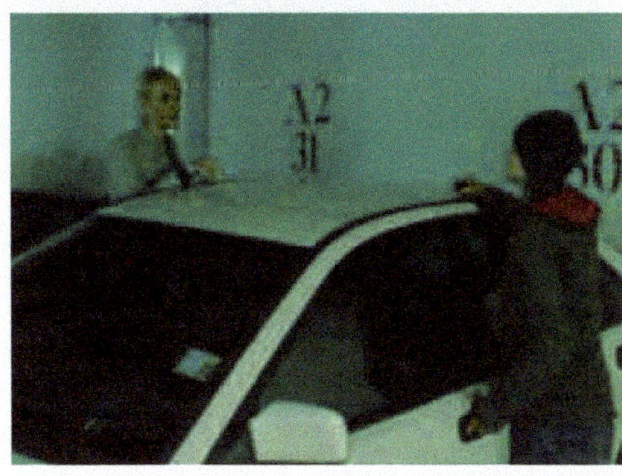
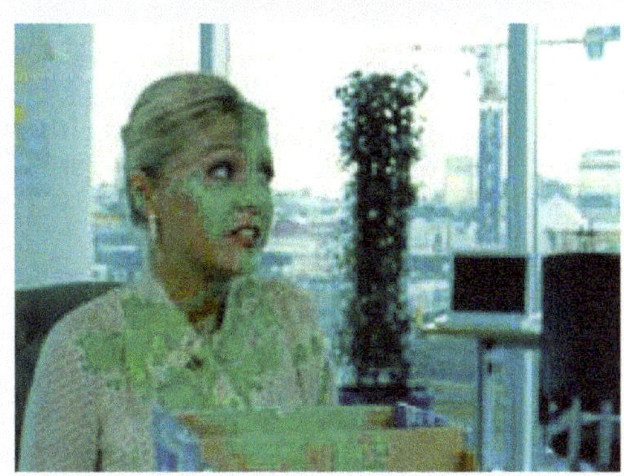

HIPSTERS/STILIAGI (2008)

Tverskaya Street

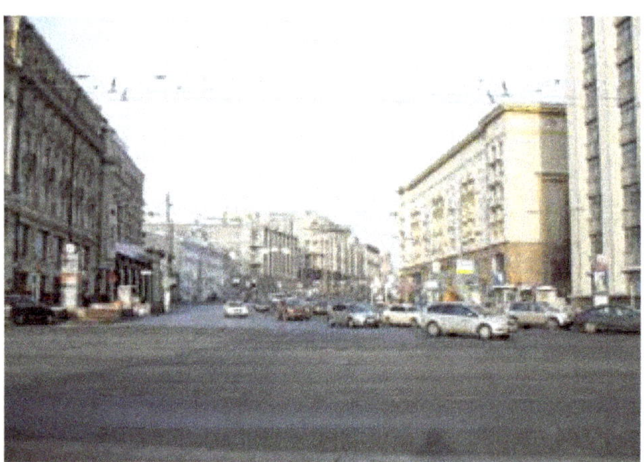

THE END OF Valeri Todorovsky's musical *Hipsters* features an extraordinary scene, one where the past blurs into the present to offer a timely political commentary. The film is set in the post-war era, when a number of young Muscovites have adopted names, styles and attitudes associated with the West in general and America in particular. These 'style hounds', or hipsters (*stilyagi*), would go on to inspire other youth subcultures in the USSR. Todorovsky's film captures the emergence of the hipsters, who wear garish clothing, adopt outrageous hairstyles and call themselves 'American' names such as Fred or Bob. Throughout the film Todorovsky makes thinly-veiled comparisons between the conformity of Stalin's time and the conformity of the Putin era. The finale, however, collapses these historical eras and features Fred (Maxim Matveev), the son of a Soviet diplomat, returning from America to meet two fellow hipsters, Mels (Anton Shagin) and Polza (Oxana Akinshina). Fred now wears real American clothing and tells Mels that their imagining of the West was all wrong: there are no comparable hipsters there. Mels tells Fred to get lost and walks out on Moscow's main artery, Gorky Street. He breaks out into song. As he walks down the street, the viewer realizes it is present-day Tverskaya Street (the original name for the thoroughfare restored in 1990). Mels is joined by a collection of youth subcultures: punks, hip hop artists, skateboarders, gamers, and so on. The past has collapsed into the present. *Hipsters*'s use of Tverskaya therefore captures the ways that Stalinist nonconformists can inspire present-day ones, turning Tverskaya Street into a giant celebration of difference. •→*Stephen M. Norris*

Photo © Birgit Beumers

Scene description: *Fred tells Mels that the America they imagined does not exist*
Timecode for scene: 2:00:00 – 2:02:00

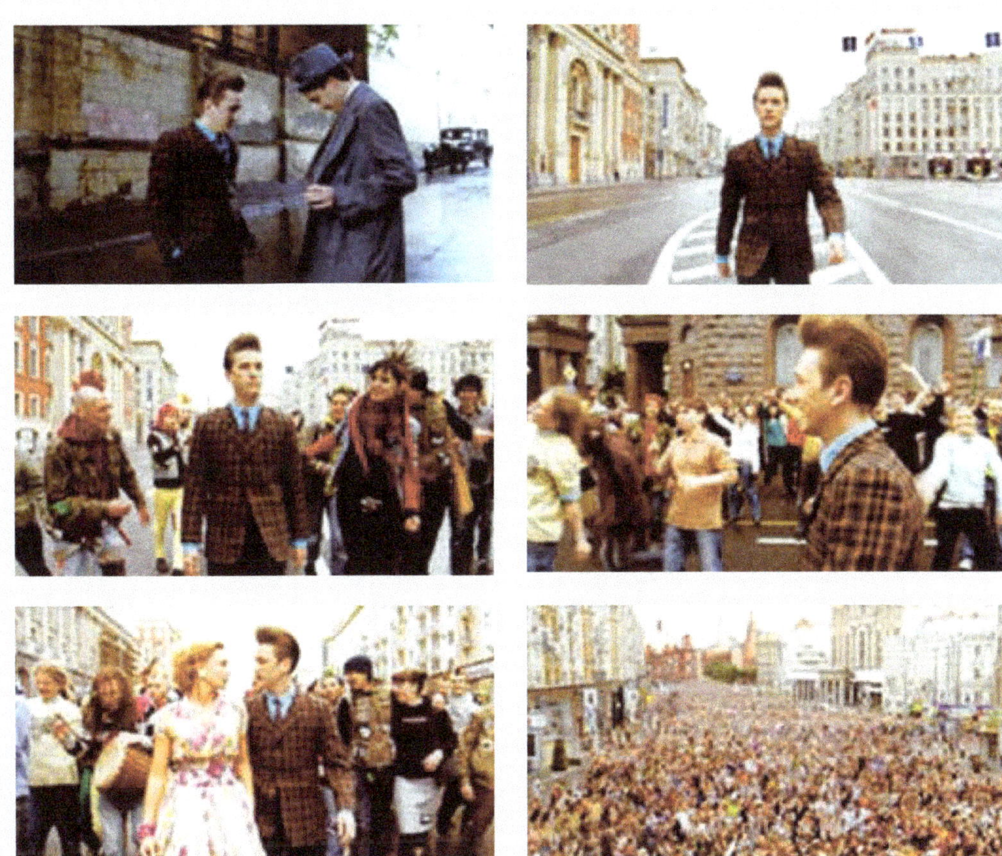

THE SPY/SHPION (2012)

 CGI of the Palace of Soviets

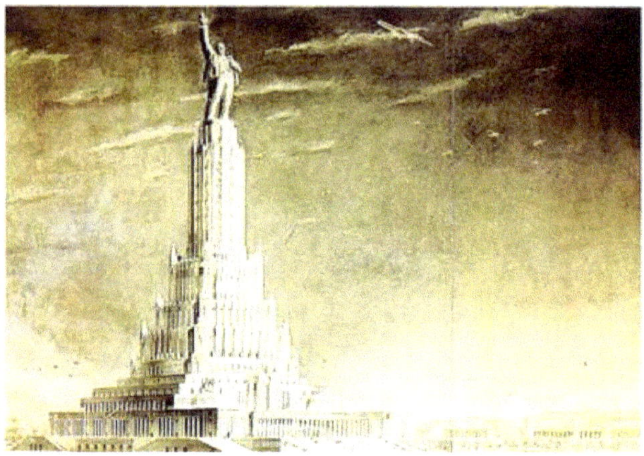

ALEXEI ANDRIANOV'S FILM, adapted from a Boris Akunin *Spy Novel* (*Shpionskii roman*, 2005), focuses on the tense build-up to the 1941 Nazi invasion of the USSR. A puzzle-full of twists and turns, *The Spy* attempts to explain how the Wehrmacht seemingly took Stalin by surprise on 22 June of that year. The film provides an answer by focusing on the dealings and double-dealings of Nazi and Soviet agents in the weeks leading up to invasion. Yet the star of the film, as many critics claimed, was not the plot or the actors, but the bold reimagining of Moscow on-screen. *The Spy*'s Moscow was not the actual city of 1941, but the city Stalin planned to have. This Moscow shows the results of an imaginary push to fulfil the 1936 plan to remake the capital city into a truly 'Soviet' and truly 'socialist' paradise. Capped by the massive Palace of Soviets – planned as the centrepiece to Stalin's new showcase city, with foundations laid in 1937, but never finished because of the war – Stalin's Moscow now exists on-screen and the Leader gazes from its heights on the remade avenues and boulevards that lead to it. The definitive answer to the puzzle of June 1941 comes through a series of encounters in the massive building, nearly 500 meters tall. Yet is this answer a plausible explanation to the real conundrum of the Nazi invasion or an answer for an alternate Stalinist universe where the Leader's plans got fulfilled? Viewers will have to debate the answers, but in doing so they too can gaze on a Moscow that was not meant to be. **↔Stephen M. Norris**

Scene description: Stalin's view of Moscow from the Palace;
Beria and an NKVD agent arrive to talk about the spy
Timecode for scene: 1:09:05 – 1:10:03

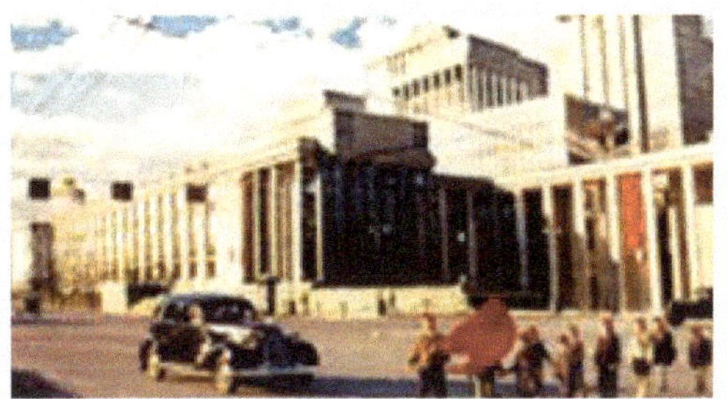
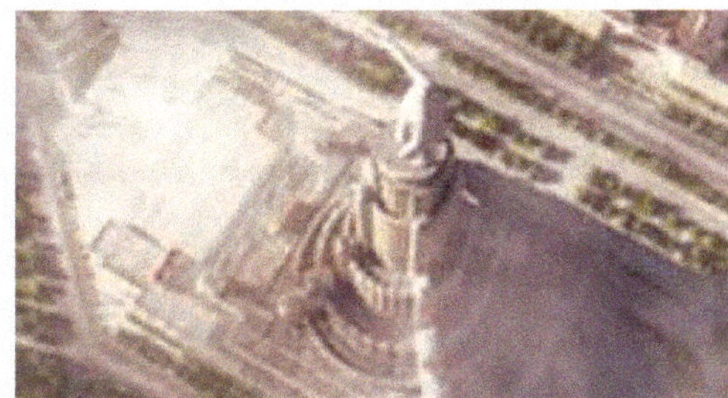
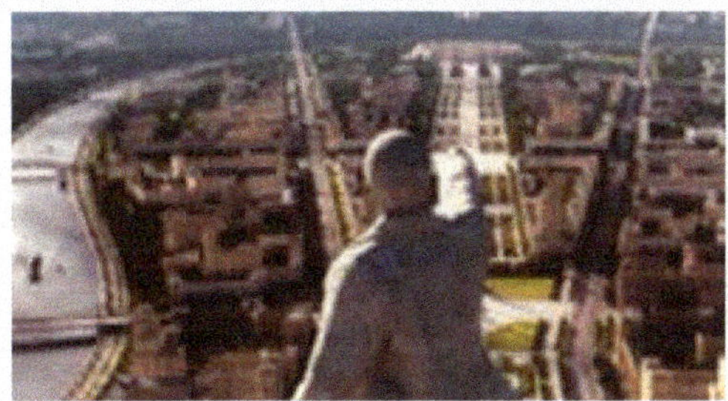
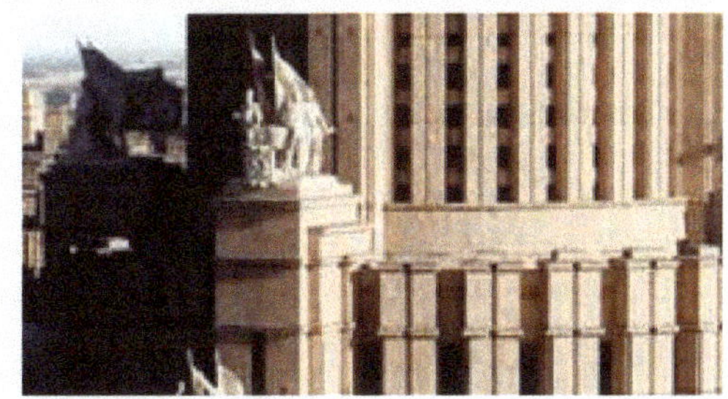
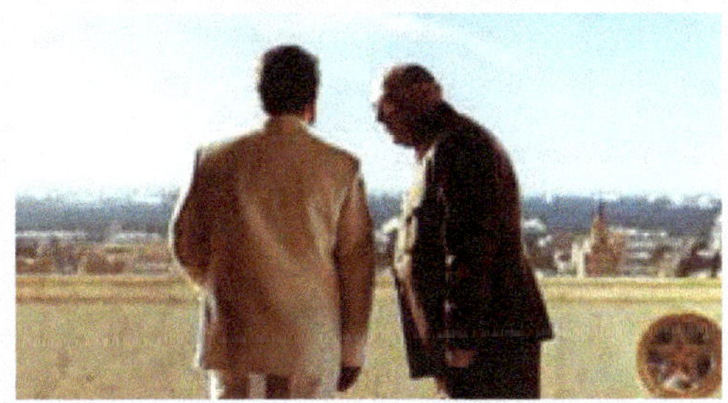
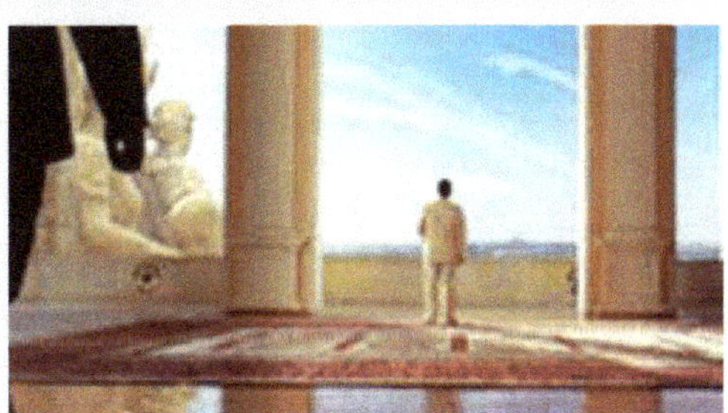

GO FURTHER

Recommended reading, useful websites and film availability

BOOKS

A History of Russian Cinema
by Birgit Beumers
(Berg, 2009)

**Common Places: Mythologies of
Everyday Life in Russia**
by Svetlana Boym
(Harvard University Press, 1994)

Russian Cinema
by David Gillespie
(Longman, 2003)

**Visions of a New Land:
Soviet Film from the Revolution
to the Second World War**
by Emma Widdis
(Yale University Press, 2003)

**The Illustrated History of
Soviet Cinema**
by Neya Zorkaya
(Hippocrene Books, 1991)

**Moskva v kino:
100 udivitel'nykh mest i faktov iz
liubimykh fil'mov/Moscow in
cinema: 100 amazing places and facts
from favourite films**
by Oleg O. Rassokhin
(Eksmo, 2009)

BOOKS (CONTINUED)

Moskva v kino/Moscow on Screen
ed. by Pavel Snopkov, with Aleksandr
Shkliaruk and Liubov' Arkus
(Kontakt-Kul'tura, 2009)

**Domashniaia sinemateka:
otechestvennoe kino 1918–1996/
Domestic cinemathèque: Russian
cinema 1918–1996**
by Miroslava Segida and Sergei
Zemlianukhin
(Dubl' D, 1996)

ONLINE

Kinopoisk
http://www.kinopoisk.ru/

Kino-Teatr
http://www.kino-teatr.ru/

Mosfilm
http://www.mosfilm.ru/main.php

'Progulkino' (created 13 June 2011)
http://progulkino.livejournal.com/

'Mos-Day' / 'Moskovskii den'
*http://mosday.ru/forum/viewtopic.
php?t=1725*

CONTRIBUTORS

Editor and contributing writer biographies

EDITOR

BIRGIT BEUMERS is Professor of Film Studies at Aberystwyth University.

CONTRIBUTORS

JOSÉ ALANIZ is Associate Professor of Comparative Literature at the University of Washington, Seattle.

ERIN ALPERT is a doctoral student at the University of Pittsburgh.

NADJA BERKOVICH is a PhD candidate in Slavic at the University of Illinois at Urbana-Champaign.

VINCENT BOHLINGER is Associate Professor of Film at Rhode Island College.

RAD BORISLAVOV is ACLS New Faculty Fellow at Columbia University.

VITALY CHERNETSKY is Associate Professor at the University of Kansas.

FREDERICK CORNEY is Associate Professor of History at the College of William and Mary.

CHIP CRANE holds a PhD from the University of Pittsburgh, where he also lectures.

SERGEY DOBRYNIN holds a PhD from the CEU Budapest and lives in Toronto.

GREG DOLGOPOLOV is a lecturer in film at the University of New South Wales.

JOSHUA FIRST is Croft Assistant Professor of History and International Studies at the University of Mississippi.

RIMMA GARN is Assistant Professor at the University of Utah.

IAN GARNER is a doctoral student at the University of Toronto.

TIM HARTE is Associate Professor of Russian at Bryn Mawr College.

JAMIE MILLER specializes in the Soviet film industry of the 1920s and 1930s and lives in Scotland.

JEREMY MORRIS is Senior Lecturer in Russian at the University of Birmingham.

STEPHEN M. NORRIS is Professor of History at Miami University, Ohio.

SASHA RAZOR is a doctoral student at UCLA.

JOHN A. RILEY holds a PhD in film from Birkbeck College, London; he currently lives in South Korea.

SASHA RINDISBACHER majors in Political Science at Lewis and Clark College in Portland.

TOM ROBERTS is Visiting Assistant Professor of Russian at the University of Illinois at Chicago.

PETER ROLLBERG is Professor of Russian and Film at the George Washington University.

LARISSA RUDOVA is Professor of German and Russian at Pomona College.

EMILY SCHUCKMAN MATTHEWS is Assistant Professor at San Diego State University.

SASHA SENDEROVICH is an Assistant Professor at the University of Colorado at Boulder.

GIULIANO VIVALDI blogs on Russian cinema and Latin American literature.

➔

FILMOGRAPHY

All films mentioned or featured in this book

Aelita (1924)	6,9,12
A Forgotten Tune for the Flute/	
Zabytaia melodiia dlia fleity (1987)	77,80
A Girl with Character/Devushka s kharakterom (1939)	25,34
Alexander Nevsky (1938)	88
Battleship Potemkin/Bronenosets Potyomkin (1925)	57
Bed and Sofa/Tret'ia Meshchanskaia (1927)	9,16
Belorussian Station/Belorusskii vokzal (1970)	59,62
Brother/Brat (1992)	102
Brother 2/Brat 2 (2000)	93,102
Burnt by the Sun/Utomlennye solntsem (1994)	93,96
Chapaev(1934)	102
Cigarette Girl from Mosselprom,The/	
Papirosnitsa ot Mossel'proma (1924)	9,14
Circus/Tsirk (1936)	25,28
Cold Summer of '53/Kholodnoe leto 53-ego (1987)	77,82
Cranes are Flying,The/Letiat zhuravli (1957)	43,44
Cruelty/Zhestokost' (2007)	111,120
Darkest Hour, The (2011)	2,6,7
Day Watch/Dnevnoi dozor (2006)	7,111,114
Dear Elena Sergeevna/	
Dorogaia Elena Sergeevna (1988)	77,84
End of Old Berezovka,The (aka Apartment in Moscow)/Konets	
staroi Berezovki (1960)	91
Extraordinary Adventures of Mr West in the Land of the	
Bolsheviks, The/	
Neobychainye prikliucheniia Mistera Vesta v strane	
bol'shevikov (1924)	6,9,10
Five Evenings/Pyat vecherov (1978)	74
Girl with a Hatbox,The/Devushka s korobkoi (1927)	9,18
Gloss/Glyanets (2007)	109
Grunia Kornakova (1936)	43
Happy -Go-Lucky/Pechki-lavochki (1972)	59,64
Hipsters/Stiliagi (2008)	111,122
House I Live in, The/Dom,v kotorom ia zhivu (1957)	43,46
House on Trubnaya Square,The/Dom na Trubnoi (1928)	9,20
Ilyich's Gate(aka I am Twenty)/	
Zastava Il'icha(aka Mne dvadtsat' let) (1965)	43,52,74
Independence Day (1996)	114
Irony of Fate/Ironiya sudby (1975)	90,91
Ivan Vasilievich Changes Professions/	
Ivan Vasil'evich meniaet professiiu (1973)	59,66
Jolly Fellows/Veselye rebiata (1934)	25,26
July Rain/Iul'skii dozhd' (1966)	43,54,74,75
Land of the Deaf, The/Strana glukhikh (1998)	93,98,108
Love of Mankind, The/Liubit' cheloveka (1972)	90
Luna Park (1992)	77,88
Mermaid/Rusalka (2007)	111,118
Merry Stories/Veselye istorii (1962)	91
Messenger, The/Kur'er (1986)	77,78
Mimino (1977)	59,70,75
Mirror/Zerkalo (1974)	50
Moscow/Moskva (2000)	7,23,93,106
Moscow Does Not Believe in Tears/	
Moskva slezam ne verit (1979)	59,72
Moscow Parade/Prorva (1992)	93,94
New Moscow/Novaia Moskva (1938)	7,22,25,32,40
Night Watch/Nochnoi dozor (2004)	1,7,111,112,114
Office Romance/Sluzhebnyi roman (1977)	59,68
Old Hags/Starye kliachi (2000)	93,104
Outskirts/Okraina (1998)	93,100
Prostitute,The/Prostitutka (1927)	108,109
Radiant Path,The/Svetlyi put' (1940)	25,36
Road to Life/Putyovka v zhizn (1931)	57
Scientific Section of Pilots/	
Nauchnaia sektsiia pilotov (1996)	23
Song over Moscow and Cherry Town/Cheryomushki (1962)	91
Space Journey/Kosmicheskii reis (1935)	41
Spot,The/Tochka (2006)	109,111,116
Spy,The/Shpion (2012)	7,41,111,124
Steamroller and the Violin,The/Katok I skripka (1960)	43,48
Taxi Blues (1990)	77,86
Three Poplars on Plyuschchikha Street/	
Tri topolia na Pliushchikhe (1967)	59,60
Three Songs about Lenin/Tri pesni o Lenine (1934)	38
To Love/Liubit' (1968)	74,75
Volga-Volga (1938)	25,30
Volunteers,The/Dobrovol'tsy (1958)	22
Vow,The/Kliatva (1946)	25,38
Walking the Streets of Moscow/	
Ia shagaiu po Moskve (1963)	22,43,50,57,74,75
Without Witnesses/Bez svidetelei (1982)	74